Collections of the
New Jersey Historical Society,
Volume 18

Citizen-Soldier

Published with Funds from
the New Jersey Committee for the Humanities,
the University of Houston,
Friends of the Society,
the Estate of Edward J. Grassmann,
and an Anonymous Gift
Dedicated to the Memory of
Delia Brinkerhoff Koster

CITIZEN SOLDIER

The Revolutionary War Journal of Joseph Bloomfield

Edited by
MARK E. LENDER
JAMES KIRBY MARTIN

NEWARK • 1982
New Jersey Historical Society

The publication of this book was made possible, in part, by a
grant from the New Jersey Committee for the Humanities,
through the National Endowment for the Humanities.

Library of Congress catalog card number 82-3618
ISBN 0-911020-05-5

Printed in the U.S.A.

Library of Congress Cataloging in Publication Data

Bloomfield, Joseph, 1753–1823.
    Citizen soldier.

    (Collections of the New Jersey Historical Society; v. 18)
    Bibliography: p. 160
    Includes index.
    1. Bloomfield, Joseph, 1753–1823.   2. United States—History—
Revolution, 1775–1783—Personal narratives.   3. United States.
Continental Army. New Jersey Regiment, Third—Biography.
4. United States—History—Revolution, 1775–1783—Regimental
histories.   5. Soldiers—New Jersey—Biography.
I. Lender, Mark E., 1947–   .   II. Martin, James Kirby, 1943–
III. Title.   IV. Series.
F131.N62 vol. 18 [E263.N5]   974.9s   82-3618
ISBN 0-911020-05-5   [973.3'449'0924]   AACR2

Contents

With love, for
Robert Joseph, Shannon Rebecca,
Darcy Elizabeth, Sarah Marie,
and Joelle Kathryn Garrett

Illustrations

ᛏoreword

Slowly but surely we are getting to know the enlisted men and the ju-
nior- and middle-grade officers of Washington's Continental Army. But
the process of finding and then publishing their diaries, journals, and
memoirs has been a slow one. Partly because so many eighteenth-century
Americans were illiterate, far fewer revolutionary war soldiers recorded
their encounters in arms than was the case in the Civil War, when it appeared as though every Union and Confederate participant kept a journal of daily occurrences in his knapsack or scrawled long, descriptive
letters to the folks back home. In fact, we know so much about the boys
in blue and gray that Bell I. Wiley was able to publish two exhaustive
accounts, *Billy Yank* and *Johnny Reb,* of everyday life in the armies of
the 1860s. Bruce Catton, drawing upon much the same sources, penned
a three-volume, Pulitzer prize-winning story of the Union's Army of the
Potomac, which is unsurpassed in showing what the conflict was like in
vivid human terms for those who fought and died.

In contrast, these studies are far superior in every way to C. K. Bolton's *The Private Soldier under Washington,* the only book of its kind,
which appeared nearly eighty years ago. Bolton, of course, had a mere
handful of contemporary narratives to draw upon as opposed to Wiley
and Catton. As late as 1977, Howard Peckham observed that scarcely
somewhat more than fifty diaries and memoirs of revolutionary war veterans had reached print since 1783.

Not surprisingly, then, the arrival of *Citizen-Soldier: The Revolutionary
War Journal of Joseph Bloomfield* is an event of no small importance,
particularly since the young New Jersey officer wrote perceptively and
participated in some of the most significant events of the struggle. One

of the real advantages to having accessible Major Bloomfield's journal is that we still have relatively little understanding of the role of officer leadership at the company and regimental levels of the Continental Army. In their own way, such officers may have played a part almost equal to the Washingtons, Greenes, and Waynes in holding together a tiny, ill-equipped, ill-clad, and poorly paid insurgent force.

Certainly a careful reading of this journal gives one a very high opinion of Bloomfield, who became the kind of leader he hoped to be when he wrote that his objective was to treat his officers and men with "Tenderness & humanity" and to secure their "Love & esteem." He explained the issues of the war to them, cared for the sick, and now and then helped with heavy labor—beneath the dignity of some officers. At the same time, he was an exacting disciplinarian, and rightly so if the army was to keep the respect of the American people. Looting, pillaging, and other such behavior would have turned Washington's republican army into a praetorian horde. If anything, garrison duty caused Bloomfield more problems than the field of combat. Boredom combined with miserable camp conditions resulted invariably in excessive drinking. Indeed, Bloomfield declared that "Drunkeness is undoubtedly the *primum Mobile* of all mischief & disorderly Conduct."

Thanks to the first-rate editing of historians Mark E. Lender and James Kirby Martin, Bloomfield's journal is fully and clearly annotated and accompanied by an illuminating introduction and biographical sketch. It helps to fill a gap in the literature of the unsung officers and men of the Continental Army.

Don Higginbotham
University of North Carolina,
Chapel Hill

ᴾreface

Editorial Note

When he marched off to war in 1776, Captain Joseph Bloomfield of the Third New Jersey Regiment took with him two notebooks with marbled covers, containing 256 blank pages. The young Continental officer intended to keep a daily record of his activities. Until he left the service as a distinguished and wounded veteran in late 1778, he filled his journal with a fascinating account of life in the revolutionary army. He also offered a revealing perspective on the impact of the armed struggle as it affected his native state. He then continued his journal entries, albeit sporadically, until February 1782, offering a brief glimpse of the civilian side of the war years as well.

It is not an overstatement to list the Bloomfield journal as among the most fascinating records left behind by a New Jerseyan active in the American Revolution. The journal, however, has not been widely known to scholars, and it is largely inaccessible to the general public. Those few individuals who were aware of the journal found it difficult to use. Sometime in the past, the two notebooks were given up by the Bloomfield family and were separated. One volume found its way into the collections of the New Jersey Historical Society; the other volume was acquired as part of the Lloyd W. Smith Collection, now housed in the library of the Morristown National Historical Park. Neither the Society nor the Historical Park knew of the existence of the other's portion of the journal.

Mark E. Lender used both halves of Bloomfield's journal while doing research for his doctoral dissertation, a study of New Jersey's Continentals, as a graduate student at Rutgers University. Lender informed appropriate officials of the Society and the Historical Park that they each owned half of the whole and discussed the importance of the journal with James Kirby Martin, then his thesis director at Rutgers. All parties agreed that such an important historical document deserved a much wider audience. With the permission of the two historical agencies, Lender and Martin obtained copies of the journal's two parts, for the purpose of combining, editing, and preparing them for publication. Permission from the respective agencies and generous grants from the New Jersey Committee for the Humanities made this work possible.

Revolutionary war journals and diaries vary greatly in quality, depending upon the subject matter and the author's range of interests. A number of unique factors lend particular importance to the Bloomfield journal. First, not only was Bloomfield himself a distinguished Continental officer, but he later became a major figure in New Jersey's political affairs (see the biographical sketch of Bloomfield following these prefatory remarks). Second, the journal is one of the most useful kept by any American soldier and certainly the most significant kept by any New Jersey Continental. Third, the Bloomfield journal corroborates and expands our knowledge of events and individuals mentioned in other revolutionary era sources, and it even permits us to make better sense of certain incidents, mentioned only briefly or left unexplained in other documents.

Too many revolutionary war journals and diaries have come down to us as mere compilations of marches, notes on the weather and terrain, or of appointments kept, with only passing notice of weightier matters. With Bloomfield it was different. Although a young and inexperienced officer at the outset, he was an educated man. The journal reflects his command of the English language and his keen understanding of events in which he played a part. He provided more than brief glimpses, and he often pursued his thoughts on noteworthy subjects. Instead of mere jottings, then, his record offers a lively narrative with insight into the momentous events swirling around him. And because he was conscientious, Bloomfield took care to fill in gaps for periods of time in which he was unable to keep a day-by-day record. At one point in 1779, for example, he provided a running commentary covering almost a year, before again returning to his basic pattern of daily entries.

The result is a full record. Indeed, some portions of the published Ebenezer Elmer journal, which appeared in various issues of the *Proceedings of the New Jersey Historical Society*, lean heavily on Bloomfield's journal, to which Elmer once had access as Bloomfield's subordinate. Portions of Bloomfield's journal, especially those relating to the activities of the New Jersey Brigade, even rank with sections of the noteworthy revolutionary era account by Connecticut's Joseph Plumb Martin (published in 1962 as *Private Yankee Doodle*). The Martin record was really a carefully compiled memoir, written years after the war, to accompany Martin's pension application (such applications for pensions, we should note, were made possible in part by Bloomfield's efforts as a Congressman). Bloomfield's journal, considering its contemporary and immediate nature, becomes all the more impressive.

A few examples easily illustrate how Bloomfield's journal illuminates its times. On one level, he captured the shifting moods of the army and populace as the fortunes of Patriot arms changed. In early 1776 Bloomfield assured himself that the men of his own company in the Third New Jersey had enlisted not from motives of personal gain, but "from Motives purely to Serve their Country." Here is a clear expression of the patriotic enthusiasm that swept the land early in the war. Later, however, the diaries show Bloomfield to be increasingly anxious. Some of his soldiers, he found, could be thieves, drunkards, and malingerers as easily as they could be dedicated Patriots. The initial patriotic fervor was beginning to wane. Later in 1776 we find the young captain both amazed and despondent at American defeats. He delayed his proposed marriage to Polly McIlvaine at one point because he was so uncertain about what the future might hold. He was shocked by the enemy's pillaging of his family's property in the Woodbridge area, and he lamented that his father had been "taken a Prisoner and his house & farm plundered of the best moveables to the Value of £500." Aging Moses Bloomfield, his son sadly recorded, had become disspirited and thus had taken the king's pardon after General William Howe's army had swept through the state in pursuit of Washington's forces. Plainly angry, Bloomfield hoped "in some future day to see . . . an impartial Historian" accurately tell the story of the crimes committed by "the petty Island of G.B. [Great Britain]" while its forces occupied the state.

Bloomfield meticulously recorded notes about the Indians that the Third New Jersey encountered in the Mohawk Valley of New York. He was fascinated by the tribes, mostly members of the powerful Iroquois Confederacy of the Six Nations. He wrote down all that he could remember about their customs, eating habits, relations with local white settlers, and Patriot efforts to win their support for or secure their neutrality in the war. Their languages also impressed him, and at one point he even made note of the Lord's Prayer as it sounded to him in the Mohawk tongue.

In addition, as a military commander he was always conscious of the dangers inherent in a breakdown of relations with the Iroquois, and he openly recorded the fears of his men in this regard. The "howling" of the Indians at night, he reported, especially upset the Continentals. Considered as a whole, Bloomfield's extensive notes on the Indians of New York are among the most impressive and perceptive handed down to us by any revolutionary war soldier.

The journal pointedly conveys the sweep of military operations involving the New Jersey Brigade between 1776 and 1779. In fact, operations and military affairs, not surprisingly, constitute a major part of Bloomfield's narrative. In mid-1776, for example, when his regiment was sent into the Mohawk Valley, Colonel Elias Dayton had secret orders to capture John Johnson, son of the recently deceased Sir William Johnson, in an attempt to break up Loyalist and hostile Indian activity. At the time, the Johnsons had more influence with the Iroquois than did anyone else, either British or American. Bloomfield's account of this mission against Sir William Johnson's son and his associates offers information unavailable elsewhere.

Bloomfield's combat reportage is often of a high caliber. At Brandywine Creek in September 1777, he recalled the unsuccessful effort to stop Charles Lord Cornwallis's flanking attack against the Continental Army's position. He graphically describes the action as he participated in it, as elements of the New Jersey Brigade "broke and Rallied and Rallied & broke" again and tried to stand as long as possible in desperate fighting. It was during this battle that Bloomfield was seriously wounded in the arm. Yet he still managed to rescue a wounded brother officer in the midst of a final redcoat bayonet charge.

The journals likewise record the tightening and rebuilding of the Continental Army after the 1777 campaign, and Bloomfield leaves little doubt that it emerged as a better force after the harrowing winter at Valley Forge. After noting the efforts of Baron Friedrich Wilhelm Augustus von Steuben to train the army in "the Prussian Exercise" [drill], he glowed with pride at the results of the confrontation with Sir Henry Clinton's forces at Monmouth in late June 1778. Fighting in the opening rounds of that battle, his regiment was ordered to help "form the second line whilst the Front line commanded by our illustrious Genl. [Washington] in person engaged the flower of the British army" and "drove the proud King's-Guards & haughty British-Grenadiers, & gained Immortal-honor." Bloomfield also roundly denounced Major General Charles Lee for his retreat earlier in the day, this at the time that the Washington-Lee controversy was just becoming a matter of public record.

His observations on the war also contain a sense of humor and irony. When convalescing from his wound, for example, Bloomfield witnessed the attempt of Silas Newcomb, a militia general and fellow New Jerseyan for whom he had little respect, to engage a British foraging detachment in South Jersey. The redcoats advanced, he wrote, and "fought the Militia under Genl. Newcomb." It seemed that "this old granny of a Genl. [was] pretending with 300 undisciplined Men to make a stand, but soon retreated helter skelter with his Men, who eminently distinguished themselves by the swiftness of their heels." Bloomfield, a regular army officer, wrote openly about the ineffectiveness of the militia.

In other situations, there was more pathos than irony. Before the war, Bloomfield had studied law under Cortlandt Skinner, attorney general of the province. By 1778, however, Skinner commanded the greencoated battalions of New Jersey's Loyalist forces. Yet on January 1 of that year, the former student found a way to visit his mentor. He explained: "Went on Staaten-Island with a flag [of truce] & had an opportunity to converse with my old master Genl. Skinner . . . and others [of] my Acquaintance in Arms agt. their Country, who I have reason to believe now wish they had taken a different part in the contest." As much as Bloomfield saw the anguish of his own family members when the war had forced them to flee their homes, he still understood what his exiled neighbors, now his enemies, were suffering. Observations such as these make Joseph Bloomfield's journal an important contribution to published sources on the revolutionary era

Rules of Transcription

The transcription of any eighteenth-century manuscript presents certain problems, and Bloomfield's journal is no exception. He made some retrospective entries in a very legible hand. But entries made on the march or in the aftermath of combat are often much more difficult to decipher. In general, the editors conformed to standard rules of historical editing in transcribing the journal, with the goal of capturing as much of the essence of this eighteenth-century record as possible. Bloomfield's original spelling was retained whenever possible. If a word was so unclear as to create misunderstanding, and the editors were confident of its meaning, the modern spelling was inserted in square brackets. The editors also let original abbreviations and contractions stand, spelling them out in square brackets only if otherwise unclear.

Illegible sections (resulting from tears in the manuscript or peculiarities in Bloomfield's literary style) were few in number, but they required special explanation and were noted in square brackets: for instance, [illegible] or [entry incomplete]. If a conjectural transcription was supplied, the unclear word or phrase is followed by a question mark in square brackets: for example, [off the battlefield?]. Bloomfield's original capitalization was retained, though it was often quite arbitrary. The only changes made in this regard were to capitalize silently the first letter of each sentence and of proper names and place names.

Some important changes proved necessary in punctuation. After the fashion of the day, Bloomfield frequently used dashes instead of periods and commas, often resulting in some points of grammatical confusion. The editors reverted to modern practice in such situations, as well as in a few other cases in which the original punctuation was unclear.

Bloomfield did not spell proper names or place names with any degree of consistency. Editorial practice was to insert the proper spelling in square brackets immediately after the first misspelling of a proper name, but only specifically for officers of the Third New Jersey and major historical figures: for example, William How [Howe]. It would have been impossible to do the same for all the private soldiers mentioned by Bloomfield, since his rendering of names was probably as accurate as any other source. With regard to place names, modern spellings were included in annotations and notes appearing throughout the text, particularly if clarification served to illuminate the passage in question.

All interlineations and marginal notes clearly intended by Bloomfield to be read on the line were inserted into the text without comment. The same practice has been followed in correcting obvious slips of the pen. All superscript letters and entry dashes were brought down to the line and redundant headings deleted. "Ye" was transcribed routinely as "the." Headings giving date and occasionally place were set in bold type to facilitate reading. Words underlined in Bloomfield's manuscript are here italicized. Signatures appear in large and small capital letters, and personnel rosters and other tabular displays were slightly rearranged, when necessary, to avoid confusion. It should be noted that all rules of transcription were followed in the appendixes.

Annotations are moderate in number and size. Important characters have been identified, along with most references of special New Jersey interest, and occasional notes clarify minor place names, obscure words, and foreign expressions. It was the editors' intention not to overwhelm the text with annotations but rather to let a fundamentally clear record stand on its own.

Acknowledgments

In the course of preparing Joseph Bloomfield's journal for publication, the editors were helped by many people and institutions, whose invaluable assistance must here be acknowledged.

The New Jersey Historical Society and the Morristown National Historical Park kindly permitted their two respective volumes of the journal to be edited; the Morristown National Historical Park also permitted its half of the journal to be published by the Society. All concerned at these two institutions gave the editors every possible consideration. At the Society the editors worked closely with Don C. Skemer, editor of publications, who prepared grant applications, made numerous suggestions to improve the manuscript, and saw the book into print; he was assisted by Robert B. Burnett, who provided many details on the identities of Bloomfield's contemporaries and helped with all phases of editorial work.

The New Jersey Committee for the Humanities, under the able leadership of Mrs. Miriam L. Murphy, generously supported the Bloomfield project with both editorial and publication grants. Paul A. Stellhorn, assistant director of the New Jersey Committee for the Humanities, was involved at every stage of the funding process and always offered sound advice. The University of Houston Publication Fund also provided a generous publication subvention, without which this book might have been impossible.

Joanne Ryan rendered critical assistance and advice in establishing rules for transcription and annotation of Bloomfield's manuscript journal and read the resulting transcription against the original manuscript. Rose Ullrich, Donna Smith, and Wendy Yin all lent a hand with secretarial help, and Robert T. Miller, at the University of Houston, worked closely with the editors on the transcription.

Finally, the editors wish to thank for their interest and often their patience, their families and close friends and have dedicated this volume to their children.

Joseph Bloomfield. Oil portrait by Charles Willson Peale. Major Bloomfield sat for this portrait in Philadelphia, April 1777. It shows him in the
full-dress uniform of a New Jersey Continental officer—gray with dark
blue facings, cuffs, and collar, a light blue sash, and silver epaulettes and
buttons. The New Jersey uniform was subsequently changed to blue with
red facings. Reprinted from Charles Coleman Sellers, *Charles Willson
Peale, with Patron and Populace: A Supplement to Portraits and Miniatures
by Charles Willson Peale . . . ,* Transactions of the American Philosophical
Society, n.s. 59, pt. 3 (Philadelphia, 1969), p. 120. Courtesy of the American Philosophical Society.

Gentleman-Republican

I hope I shall ever behave in such a Manner as to be wor-thy of the Post I fill, of the Confidence my Country has reposed in me & my Company by Inlisting under my Command. God Grant that the United efforts of the Col-onies may be crowned with success & that they may be made a free great and happy People.

(JOSEPH BLOOMFIELD'S JOURNAL, APRIL 1776)

Of the more than three hundred men commissioned as officers in the New Jersey Continental Line, few served their state with greater distinc-tion than Joseph Bloomfield. Perhaps fewer still rose as steadily to pub-lic acclaim and influence, and none placed greater importance on their participation in the American Revolution. What began as a youthful en-thusiasm for Whig politics first carried Bloomfield to modest fame in West Jersey as a radical Patriot, and then to danger and mature com-mand responsibility when the imperial controversy flared into open war. Yet for the junior officer, military experience proved more than a per-sonal expression of idealism and patriotism. It was also a crucial step in molding his future career. For Bloomfield's years of active duty were only the first steps down a long road of professional and public service —a road that carried him to the heights of political and social promi-nence in his native state.

The Young Whig

The rise of Joseph Bloomfield was no rags-to-riches saga. He grew up enjoying most of the advantages of colonial New Jersey society while enduring very few of its hardships. In fact, the Bloomfields were a prominent family. They traced their ancestry back to Thomas Bloomfield (a major in Oliver Cromwell's army and Joseph's great-great-grandfather), who immigrated to Massachusetts after the restoration of Charles II. In 1666 Thomas Bloomfield moved to East Jersey, where he and his associates purchased Woodbridge, a tract of land named after their ancestral town in East Suffolk, England. Here Joseph was born five generations later in 1753. His father was Moses Bloomfield (1729–91), a distinguished member of the colony's small professional community. He was a physician, and by the standards of the day, a good one. After completing his medical education in Edinburgh, Scotland, he built a highly successful Middlesex County practice, and in 1766 he was a leading figure in the founding of the New Jersey Medical Society. Civic recognition grew with his professional career. Moses Bloomfield became prominent in the affairs of the Woodbridge Presbyterian Church and in local government. His wife (Joseph Bloomfield's mother) was Sarah Ogden, daughter of one of the wealthiest and most socially prominent families in the province—she was the granddaughter of one of the original settlers of Elizabethtown (now Elizabeth).[1] The Bloomfields, then, while not representing the highest New Jersey social class, were certainly in a position to give young Joseph many advantages in life.

Little is known about his childhood, except that Joseph had the benefit of a relatively good formal education. While in his teens, his parents sent him across the province to Cumberland County, where he attended the Reverend Enoch Green's classical academy in Deerfield. The young student soon formed what became a life-long attachment to West Jersey and began friendships that in some cases carried through his revolutionary war service. He also decided on a career. After leaving Green's academy, Bloomfield returned to East Jersey to study law with Cortlandt Skinner in Perth Amboy. For any aspiring New Jersey lawyer, this was an enviable step. Skinner was the province's attorney general. Reading law with him carried not only the chance to learn under one of the most skilled legal practitioners in the region, but it also offered considerable prestige and the opportunity to make important professional contacts.[2] Bloomfield was admitted to the bar on November 12, 1774. Moving back to Cumberland County, he successfully launched his own practice in Bridgeton. By early 1776 he had already expanded his legal practice from Cumberland County to take cases in Gloucester, Salem, and Cape

May counties.[3] Bloomfield's fortunate birth had begun to pay handsome dividends, and his professional future seemed both satisfying and secure.

Events, however, quickly dashed any hopes Bloomfield may have had for a country lawyer's career. Even as he was accepting his first cases, the tide of rebellion was rolling over the land. While New Jersey was anything but a politically radical province, the fever of revolt was growing by 1775.[4] New Jerseyans began taking sides, and Bloomfield was one of the first to declare his sentiments: He was a committed and active Whig.

We can only guess at his reasons for siding with the Patriots. It was somewhat surprising, as there were bonds that might have kept him a loyal British subject. As a member of a well-to-do family, as well as a new lawyer building a successful practice, he potentially had much to lose in any social upheaval. Also, some of his most important professional acquaintances sided with the Crown. Andrew Bell, for instance, a friend and fellow law student under Attorney General Skinner, remained a firm subject of George III; Skinner himself became one of the most notorious of all New Jersey Loyalists.

Skinner, like many other colonists who later declared for the Crown, had actively defended American interests earlier in the imperial controversy. As late as October 1775, when the Whig-Loyalist fissure had become intense, Skinner predicted real trouble for the parent state unless it moderated its stand on colonial issues. In a letter to South Carolina Governor Thomas Boone, formerly governor of New Jersey, he displayed a clear understanding of the matter. Taxes, he wrote, as well as limits on trade with the British West Indies, would "force colonists into manufactures, and put independence into their heads. They are on the high road to it now." Though Skinner doubted the colonists could succeed, he thought England was "laying the foundation for great trouble and expense," by needlessly "alienating a people which she might make her greatest prop and security."[5] Yet the attorney general could not break with the Empire he had served so long, and while he clung to his office throughout 1775, he was powerless in the face of the rising patriotic tide. Thus, isolated and mistrusted, his animosity toward rebels smoldered, no doubt growing as he found that former friends, such as Bloomfield, had forsaken the Crown.

Yet Bloomfield never looked back in breaking with his mentor, and if he lost friends in siding with the Patriots, he kept many as well. Indeed, the loyalties of his friends and family were probably influential in shaping his own. His father, for example, was a vigorous Patriot, a fact of which Joseph Bloomfield was proud.[6] The doctor was a leading member of several Middlesex County Whig organizations, representing his neighbors in the New Jersey Provincial Congress in 1776; he later served with distinction as a military surgeon during the American Revolution. His brother Samuel also saw duty as a physician in the Continental Line.[7] Many of Joseph Bloomfield's closest associates were equally firm Patriots. Of these, perhaps the most zealous were a band of young Whigs in Cumberland County. While there was never any formal organization, this Cumberland group included the sons of some of the most prominent area families, notably (but not restricted to) the Elmers, Fithians, Ewings, Howells, Newcombs, and Hunts. Most of them, like Bloomfield, were in their early or mid-twenties, and most also served well when protest flared into open rebellion. Bloomfield no doubt had known many of them since his days at the Reverend Green's academy; certainly he had met others since opening his legal practice.[8] In any event, these radicals formed an essential part of Bloomfield's social circle as well as a tightly knit political network.

Some of their exploits ran ahead of popular opinion in New Jersey and placed Bloomfield in the vanguard of the provincial resistance movement. The most spectacular single incident was the Greenwich Tea Party. On the night of December 22, 1774, just over a year after the turmoil of the more famous Boston Tea Party, a band of Whigs in Indian dress broke into a warehouse in Greenwich, Cumberland County, seized a consignment of tea brought in by the brig *Greyhound*, and burned it. No one has ever fully identified the "Indians," but Bloomfield's associates were clearly involved. Indeed, the owners of the destroyed tea filed civil charges against several of his friends, including Richard Howell, Ephraim and Silas Newcomb, and others. Bloomfield became counsel for the defense, along with Jonathan Dickinson Sergeant and Elias Boudinot, both of whom also rose to prominence in the Patriot cause.[9] The case went before a grand jury in May 1775, where the influence of the local Whig network quickly told. Bloomfield, who carried the burden of defense, found his job quite simple. The sheriff of Cumberland County since 1772 had been Jonathan Elmer, a confirmed Whig himself and older brother of Ebenezer Elmer, a tea burner and Joseph Bloomfield's friend. Jonathan simply drew a Patriot jury, which for good measure included another Elmer brother, Daniel, as foreman. Not remarkably, the jury threw out the case. Later in the year, after the personal intervention of Royal Governor William Franklin, a Loyalist jury voted a presentment. But by then British authority in New Jersey was on the verge of collapse. Nothing came of the affair.[10] The Whigs had triumphed, helping to confirm the public mind in its defiant course. Bloomfield himself emerged from the incident as a confirmed, radical Patriot, and he was publicly known as such.

He was also a prime mover in another project of the Cumberland Whigs. Between mid-1775 and early 1776, Jonathan Elmer, Richard and Lewis Howell, and Bloomfield brought out the "Plain Dealer," a hand-copied newsletter posted in a local Bridgeton tavern for the political enlightenment of the citizenry.[11] Unfortunately, individual essays appear either anonymously or pseudonymously, so it is difficult to attribute any particular piece to Bloomfield. Yet the tone of the "Plain Dealer" was unmistakable; the young Cumberland group clearly was breathing the fire of republicanism. Their arguments focused repeatedly on the same central themes: Great Britain had no right to legislate taxes for America; a virtuous colonial citizenry had to stand up selflessly against tyranny, even to the point of dying for the common struggle; and society had to be regenerate, in contrast to the "luxury" and corruption infesting the parent state.[12] One author (perhaps Jonathan Elmer) waxed eloquent on the recruiting of Patriot troops in 1776:

> Words cannot express the Satisfaction I feell, on seeing such a number of respectable persons, voluntarily sacrificing their Ease and present Interest, for the sake of serving their country; & generously offering, at this critical juncture, to hazard their lives on the high places of the field, in order to defend those rights & privlledges, which our cruel and unnatural enemies, are endeavouring to wrest from us, with the points of their Bayonets.[13]

The "Plain Dealer" captured the mood of many Whigs as the contest with the Crown gained momentum. It certainly expressed Bloomfield's mood. He took to the rhetoric of public service and a virtuous citizenry with complete seriousness; in defending the tea burners and writing for the "Plain Dealer," he saw himself as performing an essential role in the defense of liberty.

Appeal to Arms

Peaceful protest, however, was not the only obligation of citizenship, and when the time came to take up arms, the Whig lawyer saw military duty in the same light. By late 1775 and early 1776, New Jerseyans had begun to fill the ranks of both the provincial militia and Continental Line. For Bloomfield, the days of pursuing the law and political agitation were about to give way to the soldier's life.

In early 1776, Patriot enthusiasm for the war was running high. Around Boston, General Washington's soldiers had their British opponents solidly penned in the city. Fort Ticonderoga, Crown Point, and several other posts in the New York interior had fallen to rebel arms. In Canada, where the American invasion had stopped just short of total success in 1775, the colonists hoped to press the attack again in the spring. Prospects seemed bright, and colonial manpower rallied willingly to the colors. In New Jersey, militia outfits strove to reach fighting form over late 1775 and into 1776; after a call from the Continental Congress in October 1775 for more regular troops, the province also set to work raising its first Continentals. (These initial battalions, or regiments—the terms were interchangable—were officially designated the First and Second New Jersey. They were later known collectively as the First Establishment.) The first elements of these new units went into garrison around New York City as early as mid-November, with additional companies joining them over the winter and early spring of 1776.[14] New Jersey was finally at war.

There had been little Continental recruiting in southwestern New Jersey during the drives to organize the First Establishment, which likely accounted for Bloomfield's not enlisting in one of the battalions. But clearly he wanted to serve, and he soon managed to take a hand in a "semi-military" operation. It was an ironic and, for Bloomfield, probably somewhat distasteful situation involving his former benefactor, Cortlandt Skinner. It was a test of both his personal and political loyalties, and it presaged how severe the partisan characteristics of the American Revolution would become in New Jersey.

In early January 1776, rebel authorities intercepted a packet of letters, including some virulently anti-Whig correspondence from Skinner to his brother, then an officer in the British army, and from Governor William Franklin to British officials. The Patriot response was forceful; on January 7, Colonel William Alexander sent militia detachments to check on both the governor and the attorney general. Franklin disdainfully told one party that he had no intentions of leaving the province, and the troops retired after posting a guard at his gate. But Skinner, fearing Patriot wrath, fled his Perth Amboy home to the safety of a British man-of-war. He later raised a corps of New Jersey Loyalists and led them as a brigadier general. The militia detachment arrived too late to catch him, but under Bloomfield's command (he was called captain on this occasion), they thoroughly searched his home. We have little idea of how Bloomfield came to command the search party, for at the time he held no official commission. But he evidently had consulted with Whig leader William Livingston before accepting Alexander's orders. Livingston may have felt that Bloomfield's prior relationship with Skinner somehow made him a logical choice for the job.[15] Bloomfield's sense of public duty obviously outweighed any qualms he may have had about leading troops against his old teacher. He had little time to think about misgivings anyway, for events would soon lead him to more direct participation in the Patriot military effort.

In fact, even as the First and Second New Jersey took the field, Congress and General Washington began a reassessment of the military situation, especially their estimates of Continental manpower. The more they looked at it, the more convinced they became of the need for additional battalions. Even as operations continued around Boston, Patriots had to plan for subsequent military operations. Canada in particular demanded attention. While Benedict Arnold doggedly held Quebec under siege over the winter of 1775–76, it was clear that he desperately needed substantial reinforcements for the coming spring campaign. So the Continental Congress once more sent out the call for men. On January 10, 1776, the New Jersey Provincial Congress found itself with a request for a third battalion of infantry.[16]

New Jersey took the new assignment in stride. Raising the first two battalions had gone so well that local Patriots foresaw no real problems in fielding the Third New Jersey. The New Jersey Provincial Congress substantially completed officer selection by early February, settling command of the new regiment on Colonel Elias Dayton of Elizabethtown. Dayton had an excellent military record. During the French and Indian War he had seen some tough action as a junior officer in the Jersey Blues, the provincial battalions that fought alongside of the British regulars.[17] He was a firm Whig, but at the same time he reflected a more conservative side of the rebellion than Bloomfield and his Cumberland County friends. The new colonel had accepted imperial ties for too many years to be in any hurry to lead New Jersey out of the Empire, and until independence was actually declared Dayton hoped for a reconciliation with the Crown.[18] After the final break, however, he never wavered, and his command abilities won high praise from his brother officers. Even Ebenezer Elmer, who served as an ensign in the Third New Jersey and was cut from a more radical political fabric than his colonel, was impressed. Dayton, he noted, was a "man of steady, easy, forgiving disposition, who uses both officers and soldiers with the greatest tenderness, by which he has gained the love of the soldiers in general."[19] Washington shared this view and took a personal liking to Dayton, seeing to it that he was promoted to brigadier at the end of the war.

The raising of the Third New Jersey finally brought Bloomfield to the colors. He received a captain's commission as a company commander on February 8, with seniority in rank that placed him fourth in command of the regiment. (Bloomfield was proud of his position as ranking captain, and he served behind Colonel Elias Dayton, Lieutenant Colonel Anthony Walton White, and Major Francis Barber.)[20] Battalion recruiting became very intense. Bloomfield's first assignment was to raise his own company, and although a military novice, he proved energetic and capable in rallying the men of Cumberland County. His efforts set something of a record for a recruiting drive, as he completed his entire company, some eighty men, in only eight days. His brother officers also did fairly well. Ebenezer Elmer, a newly commissioned ensign in Bloomfield's company, reported some units filling up within three weeks.[21] Thus the Third New Jersey took shape quickly, and by late March the various companies, which had been recruited in different locations around the province, were ready to link up as a full unit for the first time.

It was also in late March that Dayton ordered his subordinates to rendezvous their commands at Elizabethtown, before moving on to New York. From there they were to embark for Canada, where they would help shore up the faltering rebel effort against Quebec. Bloomfield's company prepared to move out on March 27. The night before that day there was a final ceremony to mark the occasion. A Whig speaker, probably Jonathan Elmer, addressed the men in a stirring republican oration. In front of a reportedly large crowd of local citizens, he charged the troops to be brave soldiers and exemplary sons of their province. The cause demanded, he maintained, a ready patriotism in the ranks and a strict attention to morality. He advised them "to live sober, temperate, & regular, & carefully guard against all those vices & irregularities, that are too common in Camps & Armies, particularly profane Swearing and the excessive use of spiritous liquor." A final plea asked that they conduct themselves in such a way as "to gain immortal honor" for themselves "& be a credit to the place" from which they came.[22]

What the rank and file thought of such oratory we have little idea. But Bloomfield, youthful Patriot that he was, was clearly moved and fully believed that his command would come up to the challenge. His men were, he confided in his journal, from the best Cumberland homes and, therefore, had nothing material to gain from service. They were in the ranks, he assured himself, "from Motives purely to Serve their Country."[23] Bloomfield in this case mirrored the idealism and faith in the virtue of the citizen-in-arms that characterized much of the early Patriot war effort. In the Third New Jersey, however, that faith had not yet stood the test of enemy fire.

The captain and his men then struck for Elizabethtown, and the trip was hardly uneventful. Shortly beyond Bridgeton, as Ebenezer Elmer recorded in his journal, the company "marched up to where Daniel Stretch," a local Tory, "abused us." Not willing to suffer in silence, the soldiery "gave him a new coat of tar and feathers, made him give three hearty cheers for Congress, and beg our pardon."[24] The rest of the trip apparently went smoothly, the lesson of Mr. Stretch perhaps discouraging further adverse comment from anyone of a Loyalist frame of mind. Bloomfield's unit arrived at its destination on April 4. Two weeks later, with the regiment assembled, they moved on to Perth Amboy (some men were apparently billeted on Staten Island as well), where they made final preparations to join the rebel army then gathering across the Hudson River in New York.

At this point Bloomfield's concerns took a brief but significant personal turn. He had received a short leave, during which he made a trip back to Cumberland County "to settle my *business*." He wanted to put his legal practice in order and lamented that leaving it for the army would cost him some £250 per year. He would willingly sacrifice it, he noted, out of "purely Patriotic Principles" while defending his country from "Tyranny & Oppression." But Bloomfield was "particularly " anxious "to settle" things with Miss Mary McIlvaine—he called her Polly—a daughter of a wealthy Pennsylvania businessman, William McIlvaine. Joseph Bloomfield and his future wife had met shortly before he enlisted, while at the wedding of a mutual friend. Bloomfield's journal indicates that he returned to his company a happy man, for he and Polly had become engaged.[25] He had settled his "*business*" indeed, which was fortunate, because he was about to begin some very serious soldiering.

War in the North

The two initial battalions or regiments of the First Establishment joined the Northern Army just in time to be swept up in one of the most catastrophic American defeats of the war. Most of the two battalions reached the Canadian lines by early spring, but they never had the opportunity to attack Quebec. British reinforcements reached the city in May, and the Patriots reeled under a brutal counterattack. To make matters worse, epidemics of smallpox, malaria, and dysentery wracked the retreating American columns. By the time the battered army finally reached a haven in early July at Fort Ticonderoga, hundreds of men had died, and the morale of those who remained in the ranks was at low ebb. Far from overrunning Quebec, then, the First Establishment was now part of a faltering effort to protect the northern flank of the rebellious states.[26]

The Third New Jersey, however, did not endure the pain of the Canadian debacle. In early May, it crossed from New Jersey to New York

City, where it formally mustered on the Continental Army roster. Bloomfield, who had rejoined his outfit, reported that "Generals Washington, Putman, Sullivan & Green[e]" reviewed the muster, and that they "esteemed & allowed" the Third New Jersey "to be the completest & best Regiment in the Continental Service."[27] The men then took ship up the Hudson on May 3, to Albany, where they reassembled five days later. They fully expected to be sent on to Quebec as part of Brigadier General John Sullivan's brigade, but last-minute orders intervened. The Third New Jersey would spend 1776 far from the battlefield of the North.

Rather, Patriot authorities determined to send the regiment into the Mohawk Valley, to the west of Albany. The region was crucial in the view of Whig commanders, and with good reason. The area was a prime link to Canada and had to be kept open as a communications route to operations in the North. At the same time, the loss of the valley would have allowed the British to penetrate from the West, most likely out of Fort Niagara on the New York–Canada frontier. Whig prospects in the Mohawk Valley, however, were anything but secure. There were effective Patriots living there to be sure, and the Tryon County Committee had proved able, at least through early 1776, to control the level of Loyalist activities. But the Mohawk Valley was also in the heart of the powerful Iroquois Confederacy of the Six Nations; the tribes, if they became hostile toward the rebels, clearly had the ability to tip the balance of regional power in favor of the Crown. Indeed, they were probably still strong enough to smash the Americans by themselves, if they decided upon unified action.[28] And by spring, there were signs that the Iroquois were leaning in that direction.

In fact, the Iroquois Confederacy of the Six Nations had some powerful white allies urging them to war. The chief instigators were the fiercely Loyalist relatives of Sir William Johnson, the recently deceased British superintendent of Indian affairs in the North. Sir William had had enormous influence with the Iroquois, gaining their trust as few white men ever had. He had held them loyal to the British cause during the French and Indian War, opened Indian lands to colonial settlement through careful negotiations, taken more than one Indian mistress, and had chosen to live near the Iroquois on a large family estate located on the Mohawk River (near modern Johnstown).[29] After his death in 1774, much of his prestige among the Indians passed to others: his son, Sir John, named superintendent in 1782; and to a lesser extent Guy Johnson, possibly Sir William's nephew, who was superintendent from 1774 to 1782. Also allied with Sir John and Guy were Daniel Claus, a close friend and son-in-law of Sir William, and a great number of local Tories (including a sizeable contingent of Scots Highlanders), many of whom were tenants on the vast Johnson family estate. Indeed, Guy Johnson and Daniel Claus had sailed for England in 1775, seeking the means to organize an effective Indian-Loyalist counter-offensive in the Mohawk region, while Sir John had worked for the same end at home.[30] For local Whigs, it appeared that the situation was all but hopeless, and they had persistently appealed for help.

The commander of the Northern Army, Major General Philip Schuyler of New York, did react to the Mohawk threat. Through General Sullivan (the Third New Jersey was in his brigade), he ordered Elias Dayton to lead a secret expedition up the Mohawk Valley to Johnstown, where he was to break up attempts to organize the Loyalist Highlanders and, if possible, to capture Sir John Johnson. Dayton was to lure Johnson in with word of a personal letter from Schuyler, and if he came "to make him *close* Prisoner."[31] The use of the Third New Jersey was probably no coincidence, as Dayton's experience in the region during the French and Indian War made him a logical choice for the job. So on May 17, Dayton moved up the Mohawk Valley with some 350 soldiers of the Third New Jersey.

On the whole, the uninitiated regiment behaved well in a potentially explosive situation. They never caught Sir John Johnson, who had already slipped away. And this was probably just as well with Dayton. He had thought well of Sir William and apparently disliked resorting to a subterfuge in order to capture his son. At any rate, the Third New Jersey quickly brought the Highlanders under control, generally cowed other local Tories, and maintained sufficient relations with the Indians to allow Philip Schuyler and other Patriot representatives to hold a conference at German Flats with some of the Iroquois. Dayton's Continentals also cooperated with local militia units in the construction of a number of fortifications, notably an extensive renovation of old Fort Stanwix, which Dayton renamed Fort Schuyler. When the outfit finally pulled out of the Mohawk Valley in late October and early November 1776, it deserved credit for keeping the area tranquil and leaving it in the hands of the Patriots.[32]

The months in the Mohawk Valley witnessed Bloomfield's first real test as a commander. Except for the routine of organizing his company and marching them to rendezvous points, he had never had any field responsibility. Even the most basic aspects of soldiering were novel experiences for him. The first evening on the road to Johnstown, for example, he confided to his journal that he was spending his first night in a tent.[33]

But as time went on Bloomfield overcame his inexperience. Throughout the spring and summer he effectively managed construction projects, directed guard and patrol details, and, putting his legal background to use, sat on court-martial proceedings. He also had his first taste of military danger. The cries of the Indians outside the camp at night occasionally terrified the New Jersey troops; at one point the firing of a few shots after dark alarmed the entire bivouac under Bloomfield's command. The captain hurriedly positioned his men while "Barefoot & my Cloaths in my Hands," and although his scouts reported that hunters had probably done the shooting, the young officer clearly was somewhat rattled. He entered the incident in his journal immediately afterward, still at a "later hour of the Night," as "an attack [may] be made & the writer hereof no more before Morning." The next day, or so Ebenezer Elmer reported, Bloomfield gave all his money to a friend, who promised "to secure it" if the captain were killed.[34]

Captain Bloomfield adapted quite well to military life. Dayton and other commanders recognized him as an able company-grade officer who carried out assignments effectively. More than once, the colonel delegated sensitive assignments to him. It was Bloomfield who guarded Johnson Hall against potential vandalism, who tactfully dealt with Sir John's wife when orders came to search the residence and to send Lady Johnson to Albany, and who served as personal escort and commander of the guard to Philip Schuyler when he came to the Mohawk Valley to negotiate with the Iroquois.

Bloomfield took no direct role in the negotiations held at German Flats in early August, but he followed events with keen interest. It was a crucial meeting. The Americans, seriously concerned about the security of the region and worried about a pro-British Indian uprising, did their best to get a pledge of neutrality from the Iroquois Confederacy of the Six Nations. There had already been some shooting, and Schuyler was desperate to restore peace. To the relief of the Continental Congress (and of the troops on the scene), the Patriot commissioners received the desired guarantees. Although many Iroquois ultimately did fight on the side of the king, the German Flats council bought valuable time for the Whigs, and many of the Oneidas and Tuscaroras did remain friendly to the Americans. In the meantime, Bloomfield took in everything as the talks progressed. Indian culture, in particular, fascinated him, and he made copious entries in his journal on their customs, religion, dwellings, drinking habits, language, and other aspects of tribal life. He had frequent personal contact with the Iroquois, some of whom even bestowed on him an Indian name, "Yo chee chiah raw raw gou," which translated loosely as "*Field*-in-Bloom" [35] Along with everything else, then, the young officer emerged from his time in the Mohawk Valley with his cultural horizons considerably broadened.

Without firing a shot, Bloomfield also gained quite a reputation for personal bravery. While escorting Lady Johnson to Albany, a Loyalist band surrounded him demanding that he turn over his horse; they charged that another Continental officer had stolen it from one of them, which Bloomfield later admitted was true. "I took my Pistols," he said, "& told them I would be the death of two of them . . . & sell my life as dear as possible before they should have the Horse." With help from another officer, Bloomfield forced the "Tory Animals" to retreat and, later, to his pleasure, found that he had "gained a great deal of Credit" · as a result. Certainly Dayton thought so, for in a forerunner of the modern army's officer efficiency report, the colonel noted that Bloomfield was a person who "merits preferment."[36]

While Bloomfield found some aspects of the service personally rewarding, life for the regiment became more difficult as time went on. While not in combat themselves, the prospect of conflict with local Tories or Indians kept the troops on edge. They were also aware that the Patriot war effort elsewhere had come on difficult days. As summer turned to fall, it was clear not only that Canada was lost but also that General Washington's forces were being routed around New York City. The situation had a negative impact on morale, and the Third New Jersey began to reflect the fact.

Trouble surfaced in various guises. Bloomfield, for example, who never wavered in his own dedication, found it increasingly galling that battalion discipline seemed to be flagging. Courts-martial dealt regularly with insubordination, fighting, dereliction of duty, and drunkenness. At one point, when a detail failed to apprehend a besotted soldier, Bloomfield personally arrested and almost killed him while beating him with the flat of his sword.[37] Desertion also increased, claiming not only enlisted men but one of the regiment's lieutenants as well. Later, a tribunal sacked another of the Third New Jersey's officers for helping a party break into Johnson Hall and loot the belongings of the Johnson family.

Even friendships felt the strain. A few officers resorted to duels to settle quarrels, while, in Bloomfield's ranks, as close a comrade as Lieutenant Ebenezer Elmer took to sniping at his company commander. The captain, Elmer complained in his diary, spent too much time playing up to senior officers.[38] The atmosphere was gloomy and, by fall, the optimism of the previous spring was clearly dissipating.

It was enough to find even Bloomfield depressed on occasion. In October 1776, as the Third New Jersey was nearing the end of its stay in the Mohawk Valley, he confided his feelings to his journal, stating with simple eloquence the loneliness of a young soldier far from those whom he held dear. On October 18 he wrote:

This day is my Birthday being 23 Years of Age, old enough to be better & Wiser than I am. This day Twelve months [ago] I was engaged in my Profession of the Law enjoying the calm sunshine of a peaceable quiet & easy life. Now I am 500 Miles from my Native place amongst strangers & exposed to all the hardships & fatigues of a Soldiers life, no ways Settled not knowing where I may be destined next week.[39]

Unfortunately, however, Bloomfield's next assignment brought him no closer to home.

Ticonderoga and New Jersey, 1776–77

On October 19, 1776, Colonel Elias Dayton received word of Benedict Arnold's naval defeat off Valcour Island, on Lake Champlain. This tactical defeat for the Continentals helped in time to convince the British to call off their drive south. At the time, however, most Patriots viewed the defeat as another disaster and a prelude to a massed assault on the rebel stronghold at Fort Ticonderoga. The American command thus made every effort to reinforce the fort. Dayton received orders to march the Third New Jersey there immediately. Leaving in detachments, this battalion began pulling out of the Mohawk Valley in late October.

In retrospect, the Third New Jersey had performed valuable, if unspectacular, service in the Mohawk Valley. They had bought the Patriot cause crucial time by maintaining peace in the area during 1776. It would be difficult, moreover, to overestimate their contributions to strengthening the defenses of Fort Stanwix. All of this became apparent the following year when war finally broke out in the Mohawk Valley in the most ambitious Royalist effort yet to smash the rebellion. While Sir William Howe's army marched toward Philadelphia, a two-pronged assault force cut into New York out of Canada. The main force came under Major General John Burgoyne, who attacked along the traditional Lake Champlain–Lake George route toward Albany. A second, smaller army advanced under Lieutenant Colonel Barry St. Leger. It moved eastward, down the Mohawk Valley, with the intention of forcing a junction with Burgoyne at Albany. But the scheme ultimately floundered. Burgoyne surrendered his entire army at Saratoga. St. Leger had already found Fort Stanwix all but impregnable. His forces besieged it, and he shattered a militia relief expedition in savage fighting at Oriskany, an engagement in which some of the New York officers Bloomfield had worked with in 1776 died. Indeed, the Fort Stanwix garrison even counterattacked at one point. When a Continental relief column under Benedict Arnold moved toward him, St. Leger conceded defeat and retreated.[40] The successful Continental defense proved to be an important Whig victory, so the pick-and-shovel-work of the Third New Jersey and the pacification of the Indians and Tories had paid important dividends.

But such action was in the future. In November 1776, Dayton's men reassembled at Fort Ticonderoga. The rendezvous, however, came just as the Patriot sense of urgency was passing. The British decision to turn back to Canada had finally become apparent, and, for the time being, the northern front was safe for the Patriots. Instead of battle, the Third New Jersey again went into garrison, with detachments on the lines around the fort and across Lake Champlain on top of Mount Independence. Once more the soldiery settled into the routine of local patrolling and guard duty; the regiment was not destined to see combat before enlistments ran out in early 1777.

Still, duty at Fort Ticonderoga was trying. For Bloomfield, the pattern was much the same as before. While his personal career continued to develop favorably, the regiment labored under seriously depleted morale. He was promoted to major on November 20, 1776. Major General Horatio Gates, recognizing Bloomfield's ample legal and administrative talents, personally appointed him deputy judge advocate for the Northern Army. It was all quite flattering, and Bloomfield was rightly pleased. Yet he had matured enough to put matters into perspective. It was no time to glow over personal triumphs. The British marched into New Jersey in November, overrunning the state as Howe drove Washington's army across the Delaware River by early December. The news filtering north was agonizing for the New Jersey regiment. With their homes and families facing invasion, assignment to garrison duty in upper New York became a heavy burden to bear. Promotion and position, if we can judge from the subdued tone of Bloomfield's journal at this time, seemed to mean little under the circumstances.[41] The mood, as one of the major's fellow officers wrote to Dayton, was one of resignation and despair: "Though our bodies are on Mt. Independence, you must certainly suppose our hearts are in New Jersey."[42]

None of this did anything to alleviate mounting tensions in the ranks. Arguments and fights, real or imagined, kept both officers and men on edge. Ebenezer Elmer, for example, was still nursing his grudge from the days in the Mohawk Valley. At one point, he believed Bloomfield was plotting to ruin his career. Bloomfield himself never gave any hint of trouble with his old Whig comrade, but the lieutenant became so quarrelsome that Francis Barber finally denounced him openly for "ill treating" both the major and himself.[43] Elmer's son later suggested that his father was perhaps a bit jealous of Bloomfield, who was not only a first-rate soldier—Elmer was more brave than gifted as a line commander, serving after 1777 as a surgeon—but several years younger as well.[44] The rift healed after the campaign, but the fact that it surfaced at all was sad testimony to the pressures bearing down on the soldiery.

As 1776 came to a close, the New Jerseyans thought only of going home. Attempts to persuade the troops to re-enlist generally fell on deaf ears—Washington especially hoped the men of the Third New Jersey would sign on again—and by mid-November the First Establishment began to disintegrate.[45] Despite the rage of General Sullivan, William Maxwell led the Second New Jersey, followed by the First New Jersey and a regiment of Pennsylvanians, through the gates of Fort Ticonderoga on November 15. They marched, as Bloomfield recorded the scene, "with Musick playing & Colours flying & with great Credit & honor." The Third New Jersey stayed on until March, when its time expired and it too struck south. It discharged on Morristown Green on March 22, and the First Establishment was gone.[46]

Major Bloomfield, however, arrived home before his men. With northern action unlikely, and the major himself ill over much of the fall and early winter, he took leave on December 20, 1776. After a stop in Philadelphia, where he delivered dispatches from Major General Philip Schuyler to a Congressional committee, he reached Woodbridge for an emotional homecoming on January 12, 1777.

What he saw there served to rekindle his patriotic fire as nothing else could. The Royal invasion of 1776 had hit the Bloomfields hard. British and Hessian troops had captured Moses Bloomfield and plundered his homestead, the old doctor "receiving the basest Treatment & the grossest insults from the Enemy." The elder Bloomfield, in despair after hearing false reports about Howe taking Philadelphia and dispersing Congress, finally accepted a general pardon from the British. Joseph Bloomfield's other relatives and neighbors fared little better. "Wherever the Enemy passed," he noted with disgust, they "were plundered & used in the same manner." Looking back on the matter several months later, Bloomfield was still outraged.[47] And he never entirely lost his sense that the enemy represented human baseness personified.

The treatment of his family angered and disturbed Joseph. Much of his leave from duty was anything but tranquil. He volunteered for two local combat patrols. On March 30 he finally got into a fight. He described the action as "very inconsiderable more than skirmishing." But he noted proudly that it was the first time he had seen "the Enemy in the Field" and that he had "Fired Eight rounds" himself. There was, however, time for some needed rest. He spent most of February recuperating from what was apparently a respiratory infection, and he had his portrait painted by Charles Willson Peale. On another "jaunt" to Philadelphia, he once more saw Mary (Polly) McIlvaine. Finally, after watching the Third New Jersey disperse at Morristown at the end of March, he paid off his old company out of his own pocket when the Continental treasury failed to provide funds. Bloomfield's first campaign was over, ending while he was still on leave. But in April another campaign was about to begin.

The Second Establishment, 1777–79

Bloomfield's second campaign was a considerably different affair than his first experience in 1776. So was the army in which he served. At General Washington's request Congress had voted an army of long-term enlistments (the shortest term was three years; the other choice was "for the war"), and the commander in chief had every intention of training it on the European model. New Jersey's contribution to the new regular force was four battalions (known collectively as the New Jersey Brigade), serving under Brigadier General William Maxwell. Major Bloomfield took up his duties in April 1777 in a reconstituted Third Regiment, with Colonel Dayton again in command. He immediately found the pace faster than garrison duty in the Mohawk Valley. Aside from training its many new recruits, the New Jersey Brigade participated in some small-unit actions around British positions near New Brunswick and across from the enemy garrison in New York City.[48] And, finally, after General William Howe evacuated the state in late June, Washington shifted his new army to Philadelphia in order to meet the anticipated Royal thrust there. By late summer, the stage was set for major combat exposure.

When the clash came, it was the sternest trial by fire the Second Establishment had faced. The British under Sir William Howe landed at Head of Elk, Maryland. They then worked their way toward Philadelphia. Howe's objective was not only to take the rebel capital but to draw the Continental Army into a general engagement and destroy it. Washington hesitated until September 11, when he elected to make a stand at Chadd's Ford on Brandywine Creek, a defensive position between the advancing redcoats and the city. The Patriot commander had chosen his ground well, and Howe refused an immediate assault across the Brandywine Creek. While keeping enough men at Chadd's Ford to worry the Continentals, he sent Major General Charles Lord Cornwallis on a wide flanking movement around the American right. By the time a surprised rebel command reacted, Cornwallis was bearing down hard, aided by a subsequent Royal attack over Chadd's Ford. The fighting was vicious on all fronts, and a number of Continental outfits handled themselves well. By evening, however, only the tough delaying action of Nathanael Greene's division prevented a collapse of Washington's right. The Patriot troops retired, soundly beaten.[49] Some two weeks later, unable to block British maneuvers, the Continentals allowed Howe's forces to march uncontested into Philadelphia.

The Continentals displayed determination, however, returning to fight tenaciously at Germantown on October 4, 1777, and at the Delaware River forts below Philadelphia during October and November. Howe never was able to land the knock-out blow that he sought. When the Continentals retired to winter quarters at Valley Forge in December, they were still a force of substance.

Brandywine was Bloomfield's only battle of the campaign, and it was almost his last ever. Fighting first at Chadd's Ford, elements of the New Jersey Brigade, including the young major's outfit, had shifted to the right to meet Cornwallis's attack. It was a brutal experience. Continentals went down all around him, and Bloomfield found himself swept backward, never able to make a permanent stand as the British bore in. But in the midst of the confusion, Bloomfield performed gallantly, saving the life of another officer. The major pulled his wounded comrade out from under enemy bayonets, barely rescuing him from death or capture. Shortly thereafter, he was hit himself, taking a bullet in his left arm from such close range that, as he recorded the incident, it "set my coat and shirt on fire."[50] The wound was serious, and it mended slowly. Returning to New Jersey to recuperate, Bloomfield was unable to rejoin his regiment permanently until late February 1778. Combat had proved a bitter experience indeed.

The defeats of 1777, however, never broke the spirit of Washington's regulars. Even in the grip of the Valley Forge winter, the soldiery responded well to the commander's attempts to improve training and organization. In the New Jersey Brigade, Bloomfield noted approvingly the efforts of Baron von Steuben to teach the army European tactics; Bloomfield himself worked directly with the Prussian as inspector of the New Jersey regiments, seeing to it that unit commanders faithfully drilled their men according to Steuben's instruction. Supply shortages, sickness, and unpleasant winter weather made the job no easier, but the hard work paid off handsomely with the opening of the next campaign. The Battle of Monmouth (June 28, 1778), as far as many Continental officers were concerned, was proof of the army's new fighting qualities. On the plains near Freehold, Continental and militia units, after some initial confusion, fought gallantly. Bloomfield was never more proud. He and his comrades had "engaged the flower of the British army," he noted, and had driven "the proud King's-Guards & haughty British-Grenadiers, & gained Immortal-honor."[51] The solid rebel performance at Monmouth perhaps served to erase the pain of Brandywine.

Monmouth also enabled Bloomfield to end his revolutionary military service on a positive note, for it was his final battle. The war had carried him back to New Jersey, and he decided to stay home. The reasons, in his mind, were compelling. His wound had not healed properly, which limited his effectiveness in the field. Perhaps more important was the fact that by 1778 a semblance of civil order had returned to the state. There were still skirmishes and local raids with which to deal and a pitched battle at Springfield in 1780, but New Jersey was no longer a major theater of war. The Patriot government was now fairly stable, and the courts were open. Bloomfield frankly admitted that prospects looked good in civilian life for a young lawyer. He also had made up his mind to wait no longer on marriage. Thus, when Congress voted to reduce the New Jersey Brigade to three regiments for the 1779 campaign, Bloomfield voluntarily stepped aside. "Accordingly, on Monday the 14th. Septr. 1778," he wrote in his journal, "I gave a handsome and elegant Entertainment to the Officers of the Third Jersey Regt. and those Officers who were nearly Connected to me in the Brigade." Although he was carried formally on the regimental rolls until February 1779, this was his last day as a regular. "So much," he concluded, "for my Life whilst a Soldier."[52]

Leaving the army closed this chapter in the formative stage of Bloomfield's career. He had been an effective citizen-soldier. As an officer, he demonstrated that he could learn and grow. With some exceptions, he got along well with his men, was adept at making friends, and generally found that others thought well of him, all traits that stood him in good stead over time. Bloomfield also remained a committed Patriot. While army life had enervating moments, especially when morale was low, the major left the service with his enthusiasm for the cause intact. Indeed, retiring when he did might have helped in this regard. He never labored through the acrimony of the half-pay controversy that later enraged the officer corps, nor did he suffer the privation of the bitter Morristown winter or witness the agony of the New Jersey Brigade mutiny of January 1781. His memories of the Third New Jersey were mostly good ones: sacrifice for patriotic ideals; service that brought him honor and praise; and the revolutionary spirit, to which he had made his first public commitment as a young adult.

Politics Calls

Bloomfield's transition back to civilian life was smooth, and the years following his military service offer the picture of a successful and happy man. He and Polly married in December 1778 and, after a brief stay in Haddonfield, settled in Burlington. They had no children, but they raised Polly's nephew, Joseph McIlvaine, as their own. The marriage was evidently a good one, and the Bloomfields enjoyed entertaining their friends and public figures over their many years together. Polly died in 1818 after almost forty years of marriage.[53]

His legal practice flourished as well. He argued cases in most of the state's county courts beginning in late 1778. Even before the end of the year, Bloomfield had received appointments as clerk of the state assembly and register of the court of admiralty. Indeed, between 1779 and 1782 he added positions in four South Jersey counties.[54] In civilian life as in Continental service, Bloomfield was quick to assert himself.

As he prospered in his legal career, the ex-major also became a political force to be reckoned with. Indeed, he rapidly incorporated public life into his personal routine, seemingly from a number of motives. Still a firm Patriot during and after the war, he never ceased to take seriously his duties as a citizen, and he saw civic duty as an obligation. As his personal fortunes advanced (and he was anything but poor to begin with), his conduct showed something of the sense of stewardship common to much of the early American elite. He wholeheartedly accepted the common premise that fortunate economic status implied social leadership as well, and he eagerly entered the political arena.

Like many former Continental officers, Bloomfield became a Federalist. He compiled an impressive record on behalf of that group. In elections during the 1780s and early 1790s he worked hard to turn out the vote, often in cooperation with old friends from the New Jersey Brigade, and in 1792 he served as a Federalist Presidential elector for George Washington.[55] He also sought office himself, serving as attorney general for almost a decade in the 1780s and as mayor of Burlington from 1795 to 1800. In 1792 he won a coveted appointment to be commanding general of the state militia. This may have been his most rewarding office, and he took the job in real earnest. In 1794 he personally led a New Jersey contingent to western Pennsylvania when the Washington administration moved to crush the Whiskey Rebellion. Thereafter, he preferred to be addressed in public as "General," and he took great pride in the title.[56] Just into his forties by the mid-1790s, Bloomfield had done well politically, becoming one of the most influential men in the state.

He had also become one of the wealthiest. His legal practice and various offices generated substantial income, and he inherited a generous share of his father's estate when old Moses Bloomfield died in 1791.[57] But Joseph Bloomfield did not confine his activities to the law or public office. He was equally diligent in his search for the main chance in other fields. Like many gentlemen-politicians of his day, he frequently used his connections to open the lucrative doors of financial opportunity. He speculated actively in western lands, relying heavily on the advice of his old comrade-in-arms Jonathan Dayton (the son of Elias), and he also was a partner in a Burlington nail factory while serving as attorney general.[58] At no time, apparently, did he suffer a financial reverse, and his lifestyle reflected his increasing wealth. Contemporary accounts leave little doubt that he lived the style of a cultured and financially comfortable gentleman, secure in his region's social elite.[59]

Bloomfield's prosperity and status, however, reflected more than personal ambition or commitment. Among many New Jerseyans he was a genuinely popular man. His knack for making and keeping friends, which was so evident in the army, remained a telling asset; he was apparently quite unpretentious about his high station in life. He had been, it is worth recalling, popular with his troops while an officer, and he was equally popular with New Jerseyans at home. In 1797, for example, when a Presbyterian parish of Newark seceded from its parent congregation, the church members sought a name for their new locality. After considering "Jefferson," "Randolph," and several other possibilities, one person suggested "Bloomfield." Some individuals at the meeting "bore testimony to the benevolence of his character, his kindness, and his disposition, as the soldier's friend." The group thus approved "Bloomfield" as the parish name (it became a separate town in 1812). In gratitude, the general appeared at the dedication and made a generous donation to the parish library.[60] No doubt such efforts worked well to enhance his reputation with voters generally.

Yet popularity and prestige did not result in complacency. Bloomfield was nothing if not politically astute. By the mid-1790s, political winds were changing nationally. The Federalists, dominant under Washington's two administrations, felt the first rumblings of opposition to key elements of their domestic and foreign policies (the Jay Treaty of 1795 engendered particularly partisan bitterness) during these years. Shortly thereafter, an effective Jeffersonian opposition, the Republican Party, emerged to struggle for power on the national and state levels. Bloomfield no doubt felt the change coming, and rumors spread that his allegience to Federalism was on the wane. He denied it several times, once as late as mid-1797. He even managed election as a Burlington

County freeholder and re-election as mayor of Burlington during the period (although these successes may have resulted from his personal popularity rather than any party affiliation). But some Federalists had their
doubts about him, which may explain why he was not named an elector
for John Adams in 1796. To be sure, he did not support Adams with the
personal enthusiasm that he had displayed for Washington.[61] Finally,
Bloomfield settled the matter: He openly renounced his Federalist ties
and joined the Jeffersonians in late 1797.

The decision shocked many of his contemporaries, prompting considerable speculation about his motives. "Violent" Federalists, as Lucius Q.
C. Elmer (the son of Bloomfield's revolutionary war subordinate Ebenezer Elmer) later recalled, "accused him of being a deserter," of trim-
ming his sails for the sake of political advantage and personal ambition.[62]
Carl E. Prince has argued that even some Republicans were cynical. In
fact, there were considerable grounds for mistrust. Relatively few members of the New Jersey elite allied with the new party, and even when he
did, Bloomfield still maintained good social and business relationships
with many Federalists. The new Jeffersonian also proudly remained active in the Society of the Cincinnati, an organization of former Continental officers (most of whom were Federalists) branded by many
Republicans as anti-republican, if not Royalist.[63] Over thirteen years later, after Bloomfield had served more than a decade as a Republican governor, one Jeffersonian leader still commented, "I did not suppose that
any one expected [*sic*] Bloomfield of belonging to the Republican party
from principle."[64]

There is not much direct evidence regarding why Bloomfield joined
the Republicans. To accuse him of crass opportunism is certainly an
overstatement. Too much testimony points toward a sincere conversion,
even if much of the case is circumstantial. There is, for example, the
matter of the depth of Bloomfield's original commitment to Federalism.
He was loyal to Washington, his old commander in chief, and to his old
army friends of Federalist inclination. But the major policy disputes that
led to the rise of the two-party system had not reached a critical stage in
the early 1790s. When they finally did boil over, "the General" frequently was not in the Federalist corner. He apparently had reservations
about the Jay Treaty, was less than enthusiastic about the nomination of
John Adams, and was openly hostile to such Federalist policies as the
Alien and Sedition Acts.[65] At the same time, he had some good Jeffersonian friends who no doubt encouraged his skepticism. A few were long-
standing acquaintances, such as Ebenezer Elmer and Aaron Burr (whom
Bloomfield knew from his army days), both of whom had no misgivings
about organizing political opposition based, if only rhetorically, on the

"people" and "democracy" rather than on stewardship of the elite.[66] Whether Bloomfield ever had any strong ideological attachments to Federalism in the first place, then, is open to question.

Besides, there is every reason to ask why Bloomfield would have feared a more "democratic" party, even without friends already sympathetic to such a position. "The people" (to use that oft-abused term) had been good to him over the years. His soldiers had viewed him as a fair and decent man, and the naming of Bloomfield parish could hardly have led him to distrust the general public.

There may have been another factor at work, although Bloomfield never expressed it directly. One wonders what the former Continental officer thought as many Federalist leaders adopted an increasingly pro-British stance during the 1790s. The American Revolution left him with few pleasant memories of Great Britain. It is possible that he saw no reason to forgive the old enemy so quickly. This is not to say that he viewed the pro-French leanings of some Jeffersonians as an acceptable alternative either. Indeed, as a member of the Society of the Cincinnati he signed a petition approving of Adams's tough posture against revolutionary France in 1798.[67] But given his family's experiences during the revolutionary war, he certainly had little sympathy for England, and he evidently feared that Federalist inclinations even imperiled the nation. "An adherence to Republican Principles and Republican men alone," he wrote to Ebenezer Elmer in 1800, was the only guarantee that "our glorious independence [will] be established and perpetuated."[68] Perhaps this was reason enough for forsaking his old political identity; if so, it was hardly an ignoble decision.

Whatever his motives, Bloomfield's shift of allegiance was a godsend to the emerging Republicans. His wealth and position lent considerable prestige to the new party. Furthermore, his skills as an organizer and his talents for working with people quickly emerged as vital factors for political success.

Governor and General

There seems little question that Bloomfield expected to be a Republican leader when he joined the party. He became one, and almost from the beginning. "The General" quickly established his impressive home as a party caucus headquarters. He emerged from these sessions as a central party figure, and he worked to bring unity and discipline to the Jeffersonians. His labors, in turn, yielded impressive results. In 1800, for instance, he chaired the party's first statewide nominating convention for the coming congressional and Presidential contests, which succeeded in building a surprising degree of Jeffersonian cohesion. Although the Federalists prevailed on the state level, the Republicans did well and Bloomfield, as Carl E. Prince has observed, garnered justified plaudits as "the titular leader of the party."[69]

The election of 1800 was only the beginning. In 1801, again with Bloomfield as a driving force, the Republicans captured the state government for the first time. It was an electoral breakthrough, marking a profound shift in state political fortunes. Now a majority in the legislature, grateful Jeffersonians who were fully aware of Bloomfield's critical labors on their behalf, elected him governor (a one-year term under the state constitution). The following year, a legislature deadlocked between equally numerous Federalist and Republican forces failed to elect a governor. Thus, under New Jersey law, John Lambert, vice president of the state council, performed the duties of the office during 1802.[70] But thereafter, the legislature returned Bloomfield unopposed to the governorship annually through the election of 1811. It was an astonishing testimonial to his popularity and political acumen.

The New Jersey Constitution of 1776 provided for a relatively powerless governor. Real authority resided in the legislature, a circumstance reflecting Whig fears about willful magistrates unchecked by a popularly elected branch of government. Limited to a one-year term, and with only minimal legal control over the legislature, a weaker personality would no doubt have been governor in name only. Bloomfield, however, was no mere figurehead. His actions ultimately made the office respected and effective beyond its constitutionally prescribed powers.

Bloomfield derived his powers not so much from the office itself, but from his position within the party. In particular, he became an active force in the Republican legislative caucus, which met frequently to determine party programs and actions in the assembly. Most members were legislators, but party leaders such as Bloomfield also took part, and in this environment Bloomfield excelled. He worked skillfully to mold legislative priorities and to avoid internecine party struggles, and he generally operated from a position of strength. He employed not only his own formidable powers of persuasion, but also his prestige as a spokesman for the state party in getting patronage positions from the Jefferson administration in Washington. His success in this regard was considerable. Jefferson initially felt that Bloomfield's federal job requests were excessive, but the President soon learned to respect the energetic New Jersey governor. As a result, Bloomfield consistently brought in patronage positions after 1801. State Republicans thus found it advantageous to cooperate with their governor.

During his long tenure in Trenton, Governor Bloomfield usually pursued a moderate political course. His party, as Ebenezer Elmer once put it, never dreamed "of destroying the natural inequality among men." Republicans were willing, however, to attack "moral and legal" inequities.[71] In this vein, Bloomfield did put the prestige of his office behind a number of causes. He fought a monopolistic private banking industry, for example, by advocating taxes on their stock dividends and by encouraging the creation of state-chartered banks.

He was also a vocal spokesman for antislavery, following in his father's footsteps. At the end of the American Revolution, Moses Bloomfield had publicly freed fourteen of his slaves, declaring bondage inconsistent with the ideals of the revolution. None of this was lost on Joseph Bloomfield, who declared early for abolitionism. In the 1790s he was an active member, and one-time president, of the New Jersey Society for the Abolition of Slavery. As governor he maintained his principles on the question and urged the gradual emancipation of New Jersey's slaves. Indeed, while many Jeffersonians, especially in the South, either hedged on the slavery issue or opposed emancipation, Bloomfield rallied considerable support for it in the state party. In 1804 New Jersey passed a gradual manumission act.[72] It was by no means a document of radical abolition, but it set the "peculiar institution" on a path to ultimate extinction in New Jersey.

Other affairs of state were not as grave, but they nevertheless served to keep the governor busy. Under the state constitution, for example, the chief executive also sat as chancellor of the New Jersey Court of Chancery. While he had been a well-trained and successful lawyer, Bloomfield never impressed his colleagues as a brilliant jurist. Rather, he received credit for "industry and probity" on the bench. His position as chancellor gave rise to one incident, possibly apocryphal, at least worth retelling. Perhaps touchy about criticisms concerning his conversion to Jeffersonianism, and seeking to persuade others of his republican zeal, he used the occasion of his first session of chancery court to ask that he not be addressed by the traditional title of "Your Excellency." Bloomfield soon had reason to regret it, when Samuel Leake, an old Federalist lawyer, solemnly said:

> May it please your excellency: your excellency's predecessors were always addressed by the title "your excellency," and if your excellency please, the proper title of the governor of the State was and is your excellency; I humbly pray, therefore, on my own behalf, and in behalf of the bar generally, that we may be permitted by your excellency's leave, to address your excellency, when sitting in the high court of chancery, by the ancient title of your excellency.[73]

On this field, at least, "the General" was beaten—"Your Excellency" he remained.

Such minor embarrassments aside, Bloomfield's first five or six administrations were generally tranquil. His command of the party was such that control of New Jersey's affairs never faced a major challenge. Indeed, when the real test of his leadership came, it was not on a matter of state politics, but had to do with the national government's handling of foreign relations. Serious problems in this regard arose in the five years prior to the War of 1812. In efforts to resolve differences with Great Britain and France, both the Jefferson and Madison administrations had resorted to a series of trade stoppages and diplomatic negotiations, but to little avail. Attacks on American shipping, including the impressment of sailors, and the encouragement of Indian depredations on the frontiers continued, provoking fierce political debate. For Republicans it was an especially galling situation. Jefferson's embargo clearly had hurt the economy in regions (such as New England) heavily dependent on the shipping industry, while the national government, which the Republicans dominated, seemed unable to defend either the general safety or the national honor. The situation had thrown the party off balance, and the Federalists had taken full advantage of circumstances. Charging that Republican policies were bringing only economic chaos and the possibility of conflict with Britain, they mounted a strong political resurgence in a number of states. In order to maintain control, Jeffersonian leaders had to marshal all the political skills at their command; in New Jersey, Bloomfield once again proved he could do just that.[74]

The governor spent these years carefully soothing the troubled Republican ranks. The foreign policy debate had split New Jersey party leaders badly. Some local Jeffersonians sided with the administration, and others moved closer to the Federalist position. Calling on his power of personal persuasion and his influence in the caucus, Bloomfield was at least able to keep the party from flying apart. The Republicans thus managed to maintain their legislative unity and majorities in Trenton, despite some important Federalist gains. Bloomfield himself stood with the national administration. He fended off charges that it was looking for war with Great Britain. At a time when Jefferson and Madison needed strong support, then, Bloomfield at least kept his state loyal.

For the governor, however, politics ended in June 1812, with the declaration of war against Great Britain. As hostilities flared, President James Madison recalled to active duty a considerable number of revolutionary war veterans to underpin the build-up of the piteously small American regular army. Thus, at almost fifty-nine years of age, Bloomfield resigned as governor in mid-term and accepted a commission as a brigadier general. He received assignment as commander of the army's Third Military District, with headquarters in New York. He took on his new duties with enthusiasm, displaying the pride he had always placed on his military service. His Republican friends were proud as well, and they gave him a rousing send-off on the Fourth of July: "When in the camp, on the march, or under the walls of Quebec," they offered in a departing toast, "may he never want the genuine character of a Jersey Blue."[75] But the party also missed him. With Bloomfield out of the governor's chair, the Federalists were able to elect a chief executive, Aaron Ogden, for the first time since 1800.

General Bloomfield was not destined for military glory. After overseeing the training of some eight thousand men, he marched with them to Plattsburgh, New York, with the intention of leading them as part of an American assault on Canada. Plattsburgh, however, was as close as he came to combat. He succeeded in calming some local fears concerning a British invasion of the region. But when operations against Canada began in the spring of 1813, his orders left him in command of the Plattsburgh area, where he continued training and garrison duties.[76] This was probably just as well, as the American forces, after some small initial gains, were finally thrashed in a series of British counterattacks. Some of Bloomfield's men, including his nephew, Moses Bloomfield, died in the fighting, as American senior commanders often displayed singular incompetence.[77] The invasion of 1813, then, was no more successful than that of 1775–76. For the second time, Bloomfield had seen New Jerseyans pay the ultimate personal price for military failure in the North.

Later in the war, younger commanders were finally able to repair some of the damage wrought in the early days of the war. Bloomfield, however, had no direct role in the effort. Transferred from Plattsburgh, he was put in charge of the defenses of Philadelphia. It was an inactive command, not involving field troops; but he did improve the defensive position of the city and, according to one report, even used some of his own funds when the exhausted federal treasury was not up to the task late in the war.[78] With the coming of peace in 1815, Bloomfield left the service as an undistinguished general. He had, however, served loyally and performed his duty when many of his countrymen had refused all support to the government.

Final Years

The War of 1812 was a logical place for Bloomfield to conclude a long and illustrious career. He was advanced in years, wealthy and respected, and able to look back on solid accomplishments as a citizen-soldier and gentleman-republican. His return to Burlington, however, was short-lived. Still acting as a Republican healer, he re-entered politics to assuage rifts among the party faithful. The effort induced him to accept nomination to Congress in 1816, and he served two terms (1817–21). His years in the House of Representatives once more demonstrated the aging general's pride in his military service. He took the lead in framing relief legislation for revolutionary war veterans, many of whom lived in desperate poverty. Bloomfield's work helped to produce a pension law in 1818, which offered some slight relief to the old soldiers. More important, it was an early building block in the modern veterans legislation system.[79] With this success, however, he saw his work as finished. Bloomfield declined renomination in 1820 and retired to his family estate.

Yet even his final two years were not without incident. Polly had died in 1818, after a long and happy marriage. Upon coming home, Bloomfield took another bride. On October 25, 1820, he married Mrs. Isabella Macomb of New York.[80] The general, however, had little time to enjoy domestic life. In mid-1823 he left home again, this time to see the lands he had purchased over the years in the area of Cincinnati, Ohio. It was not a good trip. His wagon overturned at one point, bruising the sixty-nine-year-old man very badly. His doctors bled him to induce recovery, and he never fully regained his health. Shortly after returning home to Burlington, he died on October 3, 1823.

New Jerseyans, whom Bloomfield had served well for most of his life, were genuinely grieved by his death. For decades, he had been New Jersey's citizen-soldier. Gentlemanly in manners and bearing, he thought of himself as a steward. He accepted republican ideals and the emerging democratic process and never lost the idealism that had initially attracted him to public life. If he was not "of the people," he knew full well that in a republic successful leaders had to draw their strength from them. With skill and conviction, he performed this important role. He served, whether knowingly or not, as a bridge between the elite-based factional politics of the past and the mass-based party politics of the modern age. Once committed to this profound change, he did as much as any American of his generation to fashion the party machinery that would allow the new methods to function well. On a personal level, he gained much from his labors. In public service, both in and out of uniform, he tried to give back as much as he had taken. Probably, Bloomfield would have approved the simple epitaph recorded in one notice of his death: "He was a firm republican in politics, and a brave soldier."[81]

Notes

[1] Notes on Bloomfield family history are in William Nelson, *New Jersey Biographical and Genealogical Notes . . . ,* Collections of the New Jersey Historical Society, vol. 9 (Newark, N.J., 1916), pp. 32–38.

[2] Lucius Q. C. Elmer, *The Constitution and Government of the Province and State of New Jersey . . . ,* Collections of the New Jersey Historical Society, vol. 7 (Newark, N.J., 1872), pp. 115–17.

[3] Nelson, *Genealogical Notes,* p. 36; Joseph Bloomfield's journal, April 1776. The journal is cited in this essay by date.

[4] On New Jersey's march toward independence see Larry R. Gerlach, *Prologue to Independence: New Jersey in the Coming of the American Revolution* (New Brunswick, N.J., [1976]).

[5] Quoted in Elmer, *Constitution,* p. 115.

[6] See, for example, Bloomfield's journal, January 1777.

[7] Gerlach, *Prologue to Independence,* p. 372; Nelson, *Genealogical Notes,* p. 35.

[8] These Cumberland County Whigs are discussed in Gerlach, *Prologue to Independence,* pp. 199–201, 445. Although there is no direct evidence of it, Bloomfield may have attended Green's academy with Thomas Ewing and Philip Vickers Fithian, who were deeply involved in local Whig activities.

[9] Sergeant was a College of New Jersey graduate, 1762, and a College of Pennsylvania graduate, 1763. He rose quickly as a New Jersey Whig and represented his state in the Continental Congress. Boudinot became one of the most prominent Jersey Patriots. He served in a number of important state and national positions, including commissary of prisoners for the Continental Army, and signed the Treaty of Paris in 1783 as president of Congress. For highlights of Sergeant's career see Gerlach, *Prologue to Independence,* pp. 267, 278–80, 349, 353–54, 372; for Boudinot see George Adams Boyd, *Elias Boudinot: Patriot and Statesman, 1740–1821* (Princeton, N.J., 1952) and Jane T. Boudinot, ed., *The Life, Public Services, Addresses and Letters of Elias Boudinot . . . ,* 2 vols. (Boston, 1896).

[10] On the Greenwich Tea Party see Frank De Witte Andrews, *The Tea-Burners of Cumberland County . . .* (Vineland, N.J., 1908); Joseph S. Sickler, *Tea Burning Town: Being the Story of Ancient Greenwich on the Cohansey in West Jersey* (New York, 1950); Robert G. Albion and Leonidas Dodson, eds., *Philip Vickers Fithian, Journal and Letters . . . ,* vol. 2: *Philip Vickers Fithian, Journal, 1775–1776;* 2 vols. (Princeton, N.J., 1934), 2:247–48.

[11] The eight surviving numbers of the "Plain Dealer" are in Special Collections, Alexander Library, Rutgers University, New Brunswick, New Jersey (hereafter, RUL). There is a privately printed version edited by William Nelson, *The First Newspaper in New Jersey* (n.p., 1894).

[12] The classic analysis of revolutionary republicanism is Gordon S. Wood, *The Creation of the American Republic, 1776–1787* (Chapel Hill, N.C., [1969]).

[13] [Jonathan Elmer?], "A Short Valedictory Address to Capt. Bloomfield's Company . . . ," "Plain Dealer" (Bridgeton, N.J.), March 26, 1776, RUL. Nelson speculates in *First Newspaper,* p. 4, that the author was Ebenezer Elmer. But since the latter was marching with the company, and the author was evidently not, Jonathan Elmer was more likely the author. See below, appendix 1.

[14] On the fielding of the First and Second New Jersey see Mark E. Lender, *The New Jersey Soldier, New Jersey's Revolutionary Experience*, no. 5 (Trenton, N.J., 1975), pp. 7–8. Commanding the First New Jersey was Colonel William Alexander, the self-styled Lord Stirling. William Winds later replaced Alexander when the rebel "lord" was promoted to brigadier general. The Second New Jersey was led by William Maxwell, who rose later to brigadier general and commanded the entire New Jersey Brigade.

[15] William A. Whitehead, *Contributions to the Early History of Perth Amboy . . .* (New York, 1856), p. 106.

[16] Worthington Chauncey Ford et al., eds., *The Journals of the Continental Congress*, 34 vols. (Washington, D.C., 1904–37), 4:47.

[17] On Dayton's colonial career see a campaign journal from 1764 and his military commissions in the Elias Dayton Papers, New Jersey Historical Society, Newark, New Jersey (hereafter, NJHS).

[18] Gerlach, *Prologue to Independence*, pp. 350, 456n; Dayton to Abraham Clark, July 20, 1776, Emmet Collection, Em. 9184, New York Public Library.

[19] Ebenezer Elmer, "Journal Kept during an Expedition to Canada in 1776," *Proceedings of the New Jersey Historical Society*, 2(1846):137.

[20] Bloomfield's journal, February–March 1776. A list of Third New Jersey officers is found in William S. Stryker, *Official Register of the Officers and Men of New Jersey in the Revolutionary War . . .* (Trenton, N.J., 1872). The actions of the Provincial Congress are noted in the *Minutes of the Provincial Congress and the Council of Safety* (Trenton, N.J., 1879), p. 354.

[21] Bloomfield's journal, February 19, 27, 1776; Thomas Cushing and Charles E. Sheppard, *History of the Counties of Gloucester, Salem, and Cumberland, New Jersey . . .* (Philadelphia, 1883), p. 37.

[22] "Farewell Address to Bloomfield's Company," "Plain Dealer." The "Address" is below, appendix 1.

[23] Bloomfield's journal, February 19, 1776.

[24] Elmer, "Journal," *Proceedings of the New Jersey Historical Society*, 2 (1846): 99.

[25] Bloomfield's journal, April 8–10, 1776.

[26] The northern campaign of 1776, including the retreat from Canada, is detailed in James Kirby Martin and Mark Edward Lender, *A Respectable Army: The Military Origins of the Republic, 1763–1789* (Arlington Heights, Ill., 1982), pp. 30–64.

[27] Bloomfield's journal, April 8–10, 1776.

[28] On the Mohawk area during 1776 see William W. Campbell, *Annals of Tryon County; or, The Border Warfare of New-York, during the Revolution . . .* (New York, 1831). The Iroquois are discussed in Barbara Graymont's fine study, *The Iroquois in the American Revolution* (Syracuse, N.Y., 1972).

[29] William Johnson's life is detailed in James Thomas Flexner, *Mohawk Baronet: Sir William Johnson of New York* (New York, 1959).

[30] A good account of the activities of the Johnsons and of Claus is found in Jonathan G. Rossie, "Daniel Claus: A Personal View of Military Loyalism in New York," in James Kirby Martin, ed., *The Human Dimensions of Nation Making: Essays on Colonial and Revolutionary America* (Madison, Wis., 1976), pp. 147–83.

[31] For Dayton's orders and instructions and Schuyler's letter to Johnson, which Dayton was to use as bait, see below, appendix 2.

[32] Details of the Third New Jersey's activities in the Mohawk can be traced in

Bloomfield's journal, May–October 1776, and in Elmer's "Journal," for the same period.

[33] Bloomfield's journal, May 17, 1776.

[34] Ibid., July 5, 1776, and passim; Elmer, "Journal," *Proceedings of the New Jersey Historical Society*, 2(1846):137.

[35] Bloomfield's activities in the Mohawk Valley are detailed in his journal entries for the summer of 1776. His Indian name appears in the August 3 entry. Details of the conference at German Flats are explained in Graymont, *Iroquois*, pp. 106–9. For another contemporary account of the council, as well as other events and individuals mentioned by Bloomfield, see Walter Pilkington, ed., *The Journal of Samuel Kirkland: Eighteenth-Century Missionary to the Iroquois, Government Agent, Father of Hamilton College* (Clinton, N.Y., 1980).

[36] See Bloomfield's journal, May 1776, as well as a roster of Third New Jersey officers, with attached comments by Dayton, in the Elias Dayton Papers, October 25, 1776, NJHS.

[37] See Bloomfield's journal during the Third New Jersey's stay in the Mohawk Valley. Bloomfield had a special dislike for drunkenness on duty, which Mohawk period entries also note. See also "Some Unpublished Revolutionary Manuscripts," *Proceedings of the New Jersey Historical Society*, ser. 2, 13(1894):17–18.

[38] Elmer, "Journal," *Proceedings of the New Jersey Historical Society*, 2 (1846):146; 3(1848):35.

[39] Bloomfield's journal, October 18, 1776.

[40] For the Burgoyne and St. Leger campaigns see Martin and Lender, *A Respectable Army*, pp. 78–87.

[41] Bloomfield's journal, November 1776.

[42] Quoted in John C. Fitzpatrick, ed., *The Writings of George Washington from the Original Manuscript Sources, 1745–1799*, 39 vols. (Washington, D.C., [1931–44]), 7:27–28n.

[43] Elmer, "Journal," *Proceedings of the New Jersey Historical Society*, 3(1848):90.

[44] Elmer, *Constitution*, p. 120.

[45] On the unsuccessful efforts to re-enlist the First Establishment see *Journal of the Proceedings of the Legislative-Council of the State of New-Jersey, at a Session of the General Assembly Begun at Princeton on the 27th Day of August, 1776, and Continued by Adjournments until the 11th of October, 1777* (Trenton, N.J., 1779), pp. 121–22; Fitzpatrick, ed., *Writings of Washington*, 6:85, 7:27; William Maxwell to the Governor, Council, and Assembly, October 18, 1776, in *Selections from the Correspondence of the Executive of New Jersey, from 1776 to 1786* (Newark, N.J., 1848), pp. 15–17; Elmer, *Constitution*, p. 104.

[46] Bloomfield's journal, November 15, 1776, March 20, 1777.

[47] Ibid., January 12, June 30, 1777.

[48] On the rebuilding of the Continental Line in 1777 see Martin and Lender, *A Respectable Army*, pp. 65–78.

[49] The fighting around the rebel capital is detailed in ibid., chap. 11.

[50] Bloomfield's account of Brandywine is in his journal, September 11, 1777. For Dayton's description of the battle see below, appendix 3.

[51] Bloomfield's accounts of Valley Forge and the Monmouth campaign are in his journal, March-June 1777. Greater detail on the New Jersey Brigade in the battle (it pulled out early, in Major General Charles Lee's initial withdrawal) is available in William S. Stryker, *The Battle of Monmouth* (Princeton, N.J. 1927).

[52] Actually, Bloomfield saw his men briefly in late September. He hurriedly re-

joined them to fight a British raid in the Newark area, but no major action developed. See the long retrospective entry in his journal, August 25, 1779.

[53] Elmer, *Constitution*, p. 114; Nelson, *Genealogical Notes*, p. 36; Bloomfield's journal, August 25, 1779.

[54] His appointed offices for 1779 were state prosecutor in Cumberland (February) and Salem Counties (March), surrogate of ordinaries court (May), state prosecutor in Gloucester County (June), and commissioner of loans for Salem County (August). In February 1782 he was appointed prosecutor of Burlington County—in all other counties, the attorney general represented the state personally.

[55] See Bloomfield to Elias Dayton, April 9, 1793, Joseph Bloomfield Papers, RUL; Bloomfield to Jonathan Dayton, February 28, 1789, RUL; Elmer, *Constitution*, pp. 122–23.

[56] Ibid., p. 122; Carl E. Prince, "Joseph Bloomfield," in Paul A. Stellhorn and Michael J. Birkner, eds., *The Governors of New Jersey, 1664–1974: Biographical Essays* (Trenton, N.J., 1982), p. 86.

[57] Nelson, *Genealogical Notes*, p. 35.

[58] Richard P. McCormick, *Experiment in Independence: New Jersey in the Critical Period, 1781–1789* (New Brunswick, N.J., 1950), pp. 98, 130, 230n; Bloomfield to Jonathan Dayton, March 7, 1803, March 15, 1806, Joseph Bloomfield Papers, RUL; Bloomfield to Dayton, February 23, 1789, Gratz Collection, Governors of States, Historical Society of Pennsylvania, Philadelphia; Bloomfield to Dayton, February 28, 1789, Miscellaneous Manuscripts, RUL.

[59] Joseph F. Folsom, ed., *Bloomfield Old and New . . .* (Bloomfield, N.J., 1912), pp. 44–46; Elmer, *Constitution*, pp. 114, 122

[60] Folsom, ed., *Bloomfield*, pp. 44–46. Less directly related to his feel for the general populace, but still indicative of the regard in which New Jerseyans held him, was Bloomfield's selection as a trustee of the College of New Jersey in 1793. He resigned this position when he was elected governor in 1801, as the governorship carried the ex-officio presidency of the trustees anyway. He was re-elected in 1819 and sat until his death in 1823. See Elmer, *Constitution*, p. 122.

[61] Carl E. Prince, *New Jersey's Jeffersonian Republicans: The Genesis of an Early Party Machine, 1789–1817* (Chapel Hill, N.C., [1967]), p. 37; Elmer, *Constitution*; pp. 124–26.

[62] Ibid., p. 124.

[63] Prince, "Joseph Bloomfield," p. 86. On his ties to Federalist friends see the letters cited in note 58.

[64] Quoted in Prince, "Joseph Bloomfield," p. 86.

[65] Prince, *New Jersey's Jeffersonian Republicans*, p. 37.

[66] Ibid., p. 36.

[67] Bloomfield was on a special committee of the Society of the Cincinnati organized to circulate the petition, and the document minced no words. It expressed "entire satisfaction" in the Adams administration's handling of foreign affairs, "in particular as it relates to the injuries and insults which had been received from the French Republic, as also of making assurance of our readiness again to take the field in obedience to any call of our country, in vindication of its national honor, and in support of that independence, for the establishment of which we patiently endured the toils, hardships, and dangers of an eight years' war." Quoted in Elmer, *Constitution*, pp. 124–25.

[68] Bloomfield to Ebenezer Elmer, December 28, 1800, Joseph Bloomfield Manuscripts, NJHS.

[69] Prince, "Joseph Bloomfield," p. 87. Unless cited otherwise, this section closely follows the work of Prince in ibid. and in his *New Jersey's Jeffersonian Republicans.*

[70] Bloomfield and Federalist Richard Stockton each had twenty-six votes on the first two ballots; on the third ballot, the Federalists withdrew Stockton in favor of Aaron Ogden but failed to change the result. They then proposed a compromise: As the legislature was also to elect a United States senator, they offered to split the offices. Each party then would have either a governor or a senator. The Republicans, however, refused. See Elmer, *Constitution,* pp. 132–33.

[71] Quoted in ibid., p. 132.

[72] Moses Bloomfield reportedly manumitted his slaves at a public Fourth of July ceremony in Woodbridge in 1783. Apparently, however, he kept at least one slave for his wife. His will, probated in 1791, directed that his "negro Festus" serve his wife Phebe "until the first of October, 1798, on which day the said negro shall be manumitted." Quoted in Nelson, *Genealogical Notes,* p. 35.

[73] The story is related in Elmer, *Constitution,* pp. 133–34.

[74] The Republican response to the foreign policy crisis is detailed in Prince, *New Jersey's Jeffersonian Republicans.* Federalist efforts in the state are traced in Rudolph J. Pasler and Margaret C. Pasler, *The New Jersey Federalists* (Rutherford, N.J., [1975]).

[75] Quoted in Prince, "Joseph Bloomfield," p. 88. The Jersey Blues had been colonial New Jersey's regular regiments, and the name remained attached to New Jersey outfits for some time after the American Revolution as well.

[76] Newspaper clipping [Bloomfield's troops near Plattsburgh], October 2, [1812], Ely Collection, NJHS. The daily activities of Bloomfield's command are found in his Orderly Book, 1812–13, Lloyd W. Smith Collection, Morristown National Historical Park Library, Morristown, New Jersey.

[77] On the death of young Moses Bloomfield see Nelson, *Genealogical Notes,* pp. 36–37. For a convenient survey of the war and the bungling in its early stages see Harry L. Coles, *The War of 1812* (Chicago, 1965).

[78] See laudatory obituary in the *True American* (Trenton), October 11, 1823. No confirmation could be found of this incident, but it would have been in character for Bloomfield.

[79] Bloomfield's law was the first to provide assistance to veterans solely on the basis of financial need. Previous statutes had demanded that the old soldier be physically disabled as well. The law provided between $8 and $20 per month, depending on former rank, to Continental (not militia or state) soldiers and sailors. On the pension laws see William H. Glasson, *Federal Military Pensions in the United States* (New York, 1918), pp. 65–67; U.S. Congress, House Committee on World War Veteran's Legislation, 79th Cong., 1st Sess., *Veteran's Legislation: Historical Statement of the Laws . . .* (Washington, D.C., 1945), p. 10.

[80] Nelson, *Genealogical Notes,* p. 36; Dorothy M. Stratford, ed., "Obituaries from the Mount Holly Mirror," *Genealogical Magazine of New Jersey* 38, no. 2 (1963): 53; *True American* (Trenton), November 4, 1820.

[81] Obituary notice, Joseph Bloomfield Papers (newspaper clipping filed with Bloomfield letter to Thomas Ritchie, May 27, 1784), NJHS.

Journal of Joseph Bloomfield

Volume 1
February 8–July 23, 1776

Journal; kept whilst in the Continental Service: Began the 8th. of Feby., 1776. and ended the 23d. day of July following, by Jos. Bloomfield Captn. in the 3d. New Jersey Regiment.

Recommendations of Cumberland County Committee and Field-officers of Joseph Bloomfield to raise a Company &c.

To the honorable the Provincial Congress, or during their recess, the Committee of Safety of the Province of New-Jersey.

We the Committee & Militia Officers of the County of Cumberland, expecting another requisition from the honorable the Continental Congress to our honorable Congress, to raise more troops in the Continental Service, beg leave to recommend the following gentlemen as persons well qualified & who would soon raise a Company for that purpose in the County of Cumberland, Namely Joseph Bloomfield Esqr. as Capn., Josiah Seeley as first Lieut. & Ebenezer Elmer[1] as 2d. Lt. These Gent. having behaved with Activity & Spirit as Militia officers in this County, we doubt not but that they will likewise conduct themselves with prudence resolution & bravery as Officers in the Continental Service; we therefore think them well worthy of our recommendation & hope they will meet with the approbation of the honble. Provinl. Congress of New Jersey. Decr. 12th: 1775.

Thomas Harris, Chairman of the County
   Commee.
Joel Fithian, Clerk of the said Committee
Ephm. Harris, Jona. Bowen Jr.,
Wm Biggs, Daniel Potter,
Abijah Holmes, Wm Kelsey,
Thomas Brown, James Ewing

Jonan. Ayres	
Theo. Elmer	Late Memb.
Jonn. Elmer	Members of
Saml. Fithian	Provinl.
Ths. Ewing	Congress

[1]EBENEZER ELMER (1752–1843). Born Cedarville, New Jersey. Physician. Ensign and lieutenant, 3rd New Jersey; surgeon's mate in the reorganized 3rd New Jersey, 1777; surgeon, 2nd New Jersey, 1778. Later active in state and national politics and served in the War of 1812. Last surviving officer of the New Jersey Brigade.

1776. February. Cumberland County, New Jersey. By the recommendation of the Continental-Congress, the Provincial Congress of New-Jersey directed a Regiment to be raised for the Continental-Service in the Province of New-Jersey, whereof Elias Dayton Esqr.[1] should be Colonel Anthony Walton White Esqr.[2] Lieut. Col., Francis Barber Esqr.[3] Major, to consist of Eight Captains Eighty five Men in a Company and Twenty four Subalterns, besides Staff-Officers.

The Committee & Officers of the two Militia Battalions in Cumberland County in the Western Division of New-Jersey unanimously recommended me with others to the Provincial Congress to raise a Company in Cumberland. I was Accordingly appointed by a Warrant dated the 8th. of February 1776 by the majority of Eleven Counties out of thirteen to raise a Company for the Continental Service, Mr. Josiah Seeley of Cumberland being appointed my first Lieut. Mr. William Gifford of Salem, second Lieut. and Dr. Ebenezer Elmer my Ensign. The County of Cumberland being 110 Miles distant from New-Brunswick where the Congress sett. we did not receive our Warrants till the 18th. of Feby., 10 days after they were Issued. Mr Josiah Seeley resigned his Warrant on Account of the Death of one of his Tenants and the advice of his Friends, upon which recommended Mr. Constant Peck (then a first Lieut. of a Minute Company) to the Provincial Congress to succeed Mr. Seeley as first Lieut. of my Company & who afterwards was accordingly appointed.

[1]ELIAS DAYTON (1737–1807). Born Elizabethtown, New Jersey. Active in New Jersey militia before the war. Named colonel, 3rd New Jersey, February 1776;

brigadier general, New Jersey Brigade, January 1783. Commanded New Jersey Continental Line after the resignation of William Maxwell in 1780. Also served as major general of New Jersey militia. Active in state politics after the war. Representative to the Continental Congress, 1787–88, and to the New Jersey Assembly, 1791–92 and 1794–96.

[2]ANTHONY WALTON WHITE (1750–1803). Born New Brunswick, New Jersey. Named major and aide-de-camp to George Washington, October 1775; lieutenant colonel, 3rd New Jersey, February 1776. Promoted to colonel, 1st New Jersey, February 1780, and ordered to command cavalry units in the southern department army.

[3]FRANCIS BARBER (1751–83). Born Princeton, New Jersey. Graduated from the College of New Jersey (now Princeton University) in 1767. Rector of Elizabethtown Academy, 1769–76. Named major, 3rd New Jersey, February 1776; lieutenant colonel, November 1776. Later served as assistant inspector general under General von Steuben and as adjutant general under generals Stirling and Sullivan. Wounded at the battles of Monmouth and Newtown and at the siege of Yorktown. Accidentally killed at the Newburgh, New York, cantonment.

19. [February]. See the 25th Augt. 1779. The *19th.* we beat up for Voluntiers and in Eight days, by the 27th. following we inlisted our full compliment of Men & four over, and the 2d. day of March following we had 106 inlisted when we were reviewed & passed Muster with great Credit & reputation, having inlisted many young Men whose Parents are Men of good Property, Family & Circumstances & who could not be induced to enter into the Service from Interest, but from Motives purely to Serve their Country. After being mustered I waited upon Saml. Tucker Esqr., President of the Provincial Congress of New-Jersey at Trenton, who had Orders to fill up the Commissions sent by the Continental Congress for the different officers Agreable to the date of their Muster-Roll and that the officers should rank accordingly, upon which I was honored with the following Commission (March 1776):

In Congress,
    The Delegates of the united Colonies of New-Hamshire, Massachusets-Bay, Rhode-Island, Connecticut, New-York, New-Jersey, Pensilvania, the Counties of New-Castle, Kent and Sussex, on Delaware, Maryland, Virginia, North Carolina, South-Carolina and Georgia, to Joseph Bloomfield, Esquire. We reposing especial Trust and Confidence in your Patriotism, Valour Conduct and Fidelity, Do by these Presents, Constitute and appoint You to be Captain of a Company in the third Battalion of the New-Jersey Troops whereof Elias Dayton Esqr. is Colonel in the Army of the united Colonies raised for the defence of American Liberty, and for repelling every hostile Invasion thereof. You are therefore carefully and diligently to discharge the duty of Captain bye doing and performing all manner of Things thereunto belonging. And we do strictly charge & require all Officers and Soldiers under Your Command, to be Obedient to

Your Orders as Captain. And You are to observe and follow such Orders and Directions from time to time, as You shall receive from this or a future Congress of the united Colonies or Committee of Congress, for that purpose appointed, or Commander in chief for the time being of the Army of the united Colonies, or any other Your Superior officer, according to the Rules and Dicipline of War, in Pursuance of the Trust reposed in You. This Commission to continue in force untill revoked by this or a future Congress. Dated this third day of March one thousand seven hundred & seventy six, 1776.

Attest.   By order of the Congress,
CHA. THOMSON, SECY.   JOHN HANCOCK, PRESIDENT

This is the Eldest Captain's Commission in the Regt. and makes me the Senior Captain & next in rank to the Major, and my Company the first in the Regimt.

Messrs. Gifford Peck & Elmer also had Commissions agreable to their Warrants of the same date with mine as officers of my Company. I also waited on Col. Dayton at head-Quarters and received orders to purchase Guns for & march my Company as soon as possible to Elizth.Town. Accordingly having Bought Guns, Blankets & Napsacks &c. for my Company, I marched the 27th. of March with Lieut. Gifford Ensign Elmer & my Company (Lieut. Peck being left sick) from Cumberland & the 4th. of April arrived at Head-Quarters in Elizth.Town. And after a few days I obtained leave to return to Cumberland to settle my *business* (particulerly with Miss McIlvaine)[1] as well as the Recruiting of my Company, as in my Profession of the Law which I practiced about 13 Months in Cumberland County [April 1776], and in leaving which (as I can say with Truth, I was respected, had the good will & Practice of the County in General, besides considerable business in the Counties of Salem, Glouster & Cape-May whose Courts I attended) that I have lost at least at the rate of £250 a Year, and this purely from Patriotic Principles. I trust of endeavoring to contribute my mite towards serving my Country, in defending her from the Invasions of Tyranny & Oppression. Actuated by this Noble Inducement, I hope I shall ever behave in such a Manner as to be worthy of the Post I fill, of the Confidence my Country has reposed in me & my Company by Inlisting under my Command. God Grant that the United efforts of the Colonies may be crowned with success & that they may be made a free great and happy People.

Lieut. *Peck* dyed in Cumberland the 9th. of April & Mr. Gifford succeeded him as my first Lieut. Dr. Elmer succeeded Mr. Gifford as second Lieutenant & Mr. William Norcross Quarter master to the Regmt. as my Ensign.

Whilst I was absent from My Compy. the whole Regiment marched to Amboy & Staten Island where they fortyfyed & were stationed for the defence of New-Jersey &c.

On Saturday the 29th. of April I returned from Cumberland [to Perth Amboy] & joined my Company which with the whole Regiment marched the next day to Elizth. Town & the day after embarked & arrived in New-York, where we were reviewed by Generals Washington, Putnam,[2] Sullivan[3] & Green[4] & Mustered by the Muster-Master-General & were esteemed & allowed by these Generals, to be the completest & best Regiment in the Continental service, which reflects Honor on the Province they were raised in, and I hope their Conduct will ever be such, as to Reflect Honor & be a Credit to the Province of New-Jersey.

[1]POLLY McILVAINE (d. 1818). This was Mary McIlvaine, daughter of Philadelphia merchant William McIlvaine. Joseph Bloomfield and Mary McIlvaine were married on December 17, 1778, and lived in apparent happiness until her death on December 2, 1818.

[2]ISRAEL PUTNAM (1718–99). Native of Connecticut. Farmer and tavern owner. Extensive experience in the French and Indian War. Commissioned as Continental major general, June 1775. One of the militia commanders at Bunker Hill. Involved in the Battle of Long Island, August 1776, and in the defense of the Hudson Highlands, 1777.

[3]JOHN SULLIVAN (1740–95). Native of New Hampshire. Lawyer. Served in the Continental Congress, 1774–75 and 1780–81. Named brigadier general by the Continental Congress, 1775; major general, 1776. Captured at Battle of Long Island, August 1776. Overrun at Brandywine, September 1777. Led successful expedition to New York against the Iroquois, 1779. Resigned commission same year. Later active in New Hampshire politics and served as a United States district judge, 1789–95.

[4]NATHANAEL GREENE (1742–86). Native of Rhode Island. Iron foundry operator. Commissioned brigadier general by the Continental Congress, June 1775; promoted to major general, August 1776. Became one of Washington's most valued lieutenants, serving as quartermaster general from 1778 to 1780 and then as commander of the army's southern department. Greene's maneuvering against Lord Cornwallis in 1781 became the basis for his reputation as an innovative commander.

May 1776. Whilst in New-York Col. Dayton's Regiment was put under the immediate Command of Brigadier General John Sullivan Esqr. whose Brigade are under marching orders for Quebec, and composed of the following Regiments,

Col. Reeds &
Col. Starks }   from New-England

Col. Wayne's & Col. Irvin's } from Pensilvania

Col. Winds & Col. Dayton's } from New-Jersey

New-York, Friday the 3d. of May 1776. The 3d. Regiment of New-Jersey Continental Troops Embarked in Sloops for Albany on their Way to Quebec with five other Regiments belonging to Genl. Sullivan's Brigade. My Company embarked at 12 [A.M.?] with William Gifford my first Lieut., Ebenezer Elmer 2d. Lieut. & Wm. Norcross my Ensign. Dr. Lewis Dunham, our Surgeon, & Mr. Edmund Thomas, Son of Col. Thomas of Elizth.Town, a Vol1untier in my Company, with Capn. Conway of the 1st. N.J. Regmt. & other Passengers, We all being in health & good Spirits anxious to get to Quebec. I have now 80 Men besides officers Not one haveing Deserted me since I left Cumberland & all free & Willing to March for Canada. My Muster Roll is as follows, vizt.

Sargants
Recompence Leake Junr.
David Dare
Street Maskell
Preston Hannah

Corporals
John Reeves
Carl Whitaker
Johnathan Lummis
Thomas Parker

Edmund Thomas, Cadet
John Kinney, Cadet
These Gentn. were promoted
  19th. of July, see hereafter.

Joseph Ryley, Drummer
  dischargsed 30th. Sept. on
  acct. of sickness
Lewis James, Fifer

1 Glover Fithian
2 John Jones
3 Clement Remington
  discharged on 30th. Sept. on
  acct. of sickness
4 Ezekial Brayman
5 Edward Russell

6 William Magraa
  died in Albany the 20th. of
  May 1776
7 Davis Bivens
8 David Martin
9 Charles Bowen
10 Daniel Ireland
11 Daniel Lawrence
12 Elijah Moore
13 William Tullis
14 Moses Tullis
15 John Major
16 Uriah Maul
17 Azariah Casto
18 John Burroughs
19 James Logan
20 Peter Burney
21 Abraham Hazelton
22 Isaac Hazelton
23 Otheniel Johnson
24 Henry Bragg
25 James Ryley
26 Benjamin Massey
27 James Burch
28 Richard Burch
29 Henry Buck
30 Daniel Moore
31 William Smith
32 Elnathan Langley
33 Davis Langley

34 Jonathan Davis
35 Ananias Sayre
36 Abraham Garrison
37 Bennet Garretson
38 Matthias Garretson
39 Joseph Garretson
40 Philip Goggin
41 Alexander Johnson
42 Ephraim Bennet
43 John Natter
  discharged 30th. of Sept.
  on acct. of sickness
44 Daniel Rice
45 David Ketchum
46 Samuel Dowdney
47 Samuel Potter
48 John Hays
49 Seeley Simkins
  Deserted in Albany
50 Benjamin Simkins
  [Ditto]
51 Ebenezer Woodruff
  [Ditto]
52 William Haines
53 Alexander Jones
54 John Casperson
55 Elijah Wheaton
56 William McGee

57 Charles Cosgrove
58 Charles McDade
  died in Albany the 25th.
  of May 1776.
59 John Barrett
60 James Ray
61 Philip Sheppard
62 Peter Sheppard
63 Robert Griggs
64 Read Sheppard
65 Benjamin Ogden
66 John Royal
67 Levi Thomson
68 Samuel Jackson
69 Abraham Dorchester
70 Joel Garretson
71 Thomas Gibson
72 Oliver Shaw
73 John Shaw
  left Sick in Cumberland
74 John McLoushuy
  Deserted in Cumberland &
  Inlisted in the Pennsylvania
  Provincial Troops.
75 Edward Christie
  [Ditto]
76 Robert Chambourn
  [Ditto]
77 James Veal

Note that George Ewing, James Newman & Frederick Shinfelt joined me in Albany & Michael Reynolds in Johnstown, also John Jaquis & James Yates at the German-Flatts.

72
 6 added
——
78
 2 dyed in Albany
——
76
  I now have my full Complyment
  Augt. 1776

J[OSEPH] B[LOOMFIELD].

The above Men compose my Family & for whom I feel an affectionate Regard. They are dear to me haveing put themselves under my Command. It behoves me to behave with Tenderness & humanity to them. I hope will ever mark the line of my Conduct. In short I will endeavor to behave in such a manner as to gain the Love & esteem of my officers &

Soldiers, to serve my country with care, Prudence & Fidelity & thereby fulfill the Trust reposed in me by my Country to their approbation, to the Credt. of myself & my Family.

3d. May 1776. We passed the Highlands on the North River about 9 O'Clock this Eveng. when we all retired to rest, except our Boatman. Sailed all Night.

Saturday 4th. of May 1776. All well aboard & in good Spirits. We promise fair to arrive at Albany by tomorrow Morng. Dined aboard of our Lt. Col. *White's* transport with Colo. Ogden, Capn. Conway, Capn. Patterson & his officers.

Sunday the 5th. of May 1776. This Morning abt. 4 our Sloop ran on a flatt opposite Cat's Kill where we lay all day without any prospect of getting off. Went ashore this forenoon at Cats kill on the west Side of the North-River about 34 Miles from Albany. In the Evening went ashore with Lt. Gifford at Livingston's Manor on the East Side of the North-River. Supped at Col. Robt. R. Livingston's[1] with my old Class-Mate Mr. Henry Livingston.[2] Returned to the Sloop by 12; found all enclosed in the *arms of Somnus.*[3]

[1]ROBERT R. LIVINGSTON (1746–1813). Born New York City. Lawyer. Graduated from King's College (now Columbia University) in 1765. Delegate to Continental Congress, 1775–79, 1779–81, and 1784–85; served on committee to draft the Declaration of Independence. Distinguished diplomatic career after the revolutionary era.

[2]HENRY B. LIVINGSTON (1757–1823). Born New York City. Lawyer. Graduated from the College of New Jersey in 1776. Served as aide-de-camp to Philip Schuyler. Secretary to John Jay, United States minister to Spain, 1779–82. Later was an associate justice of the United States Supreme Court, 1806–23.

[3]Somnus. The Roman god of sleep.

Monday the 6th. of May 1776. Our Sloop got off the flatt this Morning but the Tide & Wind being against us we lay in the Channel till 3 P.M. when we took the advantage of the Tide & got as far as Claverack.

This Morning went ashore at Cats-Kill & layed in Gammons,[1] Neats[2] Tongues &c. as stores for Canada. Lt. Elmer & Voluntier Thomas & a Sarjant went ashore to march to Albany to Inform Col. White of our Situation & the Reason of our delay. In the Evening 25 Men were landed at Claverack about 35 Ms. from Albany on the East side of the

North Rivr. to march for Albany, It being Wet & Rainy & the Men almost Stifled in the Vessel. Rainy all Night Very uncomfortable on board.

¹Gammon. Ham or haunch of a swine.
²Neat. Cow.

Tuesday the 7th. of May 1776. The Weather continues Rainy. The Men being Very uncomfortable in the Vessel & no Prospect of getting to Albany these 3 Days, went ashore at Luenburgh on the East Side of the North River with Ensign Norcross & 36 Men & marched about 18 Miles through the Village of Cosenhen to the Strand or Ten Eyck's Mill. There are two Saw Mills. Each have 14 Saws which makes them work amazingly fast. In our March this day we met with a Noted Tory of this Country who (for want of Tar and Feathers) we daubed with Clay, mud & leaves & then ducked him making him Acknowledge the supremacy of the Congress &c. &c.

Wednesday the 8th. of May 1776. Marched my Company by 6 O'Clock this Morning from Ten Eyck's, & on the Road overtook the division sent on [———]¹ & the whole arrived at Albany by 12 O'Clock after marching 15 Miles through absolute barren Country with Mud & sand over our Ancles & it raining hard all the time so that we were all wet to the skin & found no Accomodations was provided for my Men owing to upwards of 2000 Troops & 300 Indians (on a Treaty) being in Town. My Men badly provided for the whole Company obligded to lay in a Small Room. Lodged myself on board the sloop Lilly which arrived in Town this Morning. I now begin to feel more & more the Vicissitudes [of] a Soldier's Life, from home & no Friends.

¹Two words mutilated.

Thursday the 9th. of May 1776. *Albany.* After running all over Town I fora[y]de out to hire a Small Bed-Room for myself & Officers at an Extravagant Price. Layed on my Camp stool for the first Time. Engaged from 9 A.M. to 3 P.M. on a Genl. Court Martial whereof Lt. Col. Ogden¹ was President with 9 Capts. & 3 Subalt. of the different Regmts. in Town Members. Tried 3 Sarjants of Col. Irvins Regmt. for Mutiny, Disobedience of Orders, & Insulting Capn. Robinson. All the Charges not being supported we broke two reduced the other to the Ranks Mulched him of one Months pay & ordered him to be confined on Bread & Water for Six Days. At four Genl. Sullivan's Brigade composed of Col. Reed's & Starks Regmts. from New-Hampshire, Cols. Winds & Daytons from New-Jersey & Cols. Wayne[2] & Irvin's[3] from Pensilvania Paraded through the Streets to his Excellency Genl. Schuyler's[4] about a Mile from Albany where we were all reviewed by Genl. Schuyler & Sullivan. The Indian Chiefs & Savages that attended the Treaty, and all together made a most brilliant & warlike appearance to the Satisfaction of the Generals & applause of the Spectators. Col. Dayton's Regmnt. haveing the prefference of good looking Men & being the best Equipped of any in the Field which reflected Honor on the Province of New-Jersey.

[1]MATTHIAS OGDEN (1754–91). Born Elizabethtown, New Jersey. Attending College of New Jersey when the war broke out. Went along as a volunteer on Benedict Arnold's march to Quebec and was wounded in the assault on that city, December 31, 1775. Named lieutenant colonel, 1st New Jersey, March 1776; colonel, January 1777. Captured by British at Elizabethtown, November 1780. Exchanged and later granted a leave by Congress, April 1783, to visit Europe. Breveted brigadier general by Congress, September 1783.

[2]ANTHONY WAYNE (1745–96). Native of Pennsylvania. Active on Patriot committees in Pennsylvania protesting British policies before the war. Named colonel of the Chester County militia regiment that went north in 1776 to join in Canadian operations. Became a general in the Continental Army. Fought with Washington at Brandywine and Germantown, 1777, and Monmouth, 1778. Perhaps best known for his bayonet assault on Stony Point, 1779.

[3]WILLIAM IRVIN [IRVINE] (1741–1804). Native of Ireland. Educated at Trinity College, Dublin, and became a doctor. Served as a surgeon during the French and Indian War and then settled in Pennsylvania. Commissioned a colonel in the Pennsylvania Line early in 1776. Regiment sent to Canada where Irvine was captured at the Battle of Three Rivers, June 8, during the precipitous American retreat. Paroled in August 1776. Named brigadier general in 1779. Went on to have a national political career, serving in Congress, 1786–88, and the House of Representatives, 1793–95.

[4]PHILIP SCHUYLER (1733–1804). Born Albany, New York. Wealthy landholder and merchant. Fought in the French and Indian War. Represented New York in the Continental Congress, 1775 and 1778–81. One of four original major generals commissioned by Congress, June 1775. Served as head of the army's northern department, 1775–77, thus responsible for controlling Loyalists and maintaining relations with the Iroquois. Also named a member of the Board of Commissioners for Indian Affairs in the northern department, 1775. Served later in the New York Senate, 1780–84, 1786–90, and 1792–97, and in the United States Senate, 1789–91 and 1797–98.

Albany. Friday May the 10th., 1776. Engaged from 8 to 3 P.M. on the Genl. Court Martial which is Continued by order of the Genl. till the guard house is cleared of all the Prisoners, so that this Court is similar to the Court of Oyer & Terminer & General Goal Delivery held by the Judges of the Kings-Bench for the Trials of Criminals in the different

Counties of the Province. Tried a Soldier of Col. Irvin's Regt. for Disobedience of Orders & Insulting Capn. Robinson. Ordered that he receive 20 Lashes, Mulched One Months pay & confined a month upon Bread & Water and reprimanded at the Stake & recommended to the Genl. to Mitigate the 20 lashes upon Capn. Robinson's Intercession & then to ask Capn. Robinson's Pardon. Began also to try Ensign Wm. Nicholls of Col. Irvin's Regt. for abetting and assisting to rescue 2 Prisoners. By order of the Gen. Our Regm. began to Encamp on the Commons this afternoon.

Saturday the 11th. of May, 1776. Engaged all day on the Trial of the two Officers mentioned yesterday. We not finishing with the Evidence, adjourned over till tommorrow. Drank Tea this Eveng. in Col. Whites Markee[1] with Col. Dayton, Hartley,[2] Livingston, the Miss Schuyler's & other Ladies. Received a Letter this day from [no entry] & wrote one to my father by Mr McEllory.

[1]Marquee. A linen field tent pitched atop an officer's tent to distinguish it from other tents.
[2]HARTLEY. This was most likely Colonel Thomas Hartley, who later fought the Iroquois along the New York-Pennsylvania border.

Sunday, the 12th. of May 1776. Sat this day on the Court Martial till three when we finished the trial of Ensign Wm. Nicholl of Col. Irvin's Regmt. Ordered that the said Wm. Nicholl be Publickly reprimanded by Col. Irvin at the head of the Regm. & his Sword given to him afterwards to wait on Genl. Sullivan & ask Pardon for his Imprudent Behaviour. The Revd. Mr. Caldwell[1] our Chaplain haveing joined the Regmt. this day preached for the first time to the Regmt. & we attended Prayers Night & Morning.

[1]JAMES CALDWELL (1734–81). Native of Virginia. Graduated from the College of New Jersey in 1759. Ordained to Presbyterian ministry in 1761. Called to the pastorate of the First Presbyterian Church, Elizabethtown, serving there until 1780. Also chaplain to 3rd New Jersey until 1781, when killed by an American sentry in an apparent argument.

Monday the 13th. of May 1776. This day I was Capt. of the Main Guard & mounted Guard all Night with Mr. Hazelton & Clark Subalterns & 50 Men. Also this day payed off my Company.

Tuesday 14th. of May. Busy all day in preparing to March to Quebec tomorrow; much engaged in providing for my Men. Our Chaplain preached this afternoon to the general satisfaction of all that heard him. Our orders were this Eveng. countermanded.

Wednesday the 15th. of May (vid. 31st. Inst.) Last Night Seeley Simkins, Benjn. Simkins, Ebenezer Woodruff, Lewis Thomson, Uriah Maul & James Logan Deserted from me after Stealing a Watch & sundry other Things from the Company. William Magra also a Soldier in my Company died last Night & this Eveng. was buried in form, the whole Regmt. with the Field-Officers & Chaplain attending, who Prayed with & Addressed the Soldiers. Afterwards five Men fired three rounds over his Grave & the Men were Dismissed greatly admiring the respect Shewn one of their Brother Soldiers. Engaged on a Court Martial. Tried John Brewer of Col. Dayton's Regmt., Capn. Sharp's Compy. for Desertion. Sentenced to receive 25 Lashes & return to his duty. Robert Barry for Drunkeness & Disobedience of Orders Sentd. to receive 25 Lashes. Michael Calen for Theft, Embezzlement & Selling the Publick Stores Sentenced to be carried to the Post with a Halter about his Neck & to receive 39 Lashes for Theft, also 39 Lashes for making way with the Congress Stores, be carried back with a Halter about his Neck to the Guardhouse & be confined 8 Days on Bread & Water & return to his duty. Spent the Eveng. & Supped with Mr. Caldwell our Chaplain at Mr. Henry's.

Thursday the 16th. May. Set all day upon the Genl. Court Martial. Tried Thoms. Price for Desertion & Embezzleing the Publick Stores sentenced to receive the same Punishment ordered yesterday for Callen. Sundry others were tried some discharged & some Sentenced to receive Punisht.

Friday the 17th. of May. By directions from Major Genl. Schuyler, Brigadr. Genl. Sullivan Ordered our Regmt. to Parade at 6 O'Clock this morng. compleat in Arms & 350 of our best Men were picked out & supplied with flints Powder & Ball & five days Provisions on a secret Expedition. At 4 P.M. our Detachmt. of 350 Men with Col. Dayton, Major Barber, Capts. Potter, Patterson, Ross, Sharp, & myself with subalterns accordingly, our Surgeon, & Worthy Chaplain sett out & Marched as far as Cripple Bush Eight miles from Albany where we halted & Pitched our Tents. Lay this Night being the first time I ever slept in a Tent. This day was observed throughout the Continent as a Day of Fasting & Prayer by Order of the Congress.

Albany Saturday the 18th. of May 1776. Struck our Tents by 4 this Morning & Marched through a Scotch mist of Rain to Schenectady 18 Ms. from Albany where the Committee Desired the Inhabitants to Billet our Troops which was done & our Officers & Men were treated with great kindness. Dined with Dr. Prickett in company with Dr. Dunham & Mr. Gaulidet, appointed my Ensign on the present Expedition. At 3 P.M. crossed the Mohawk River opposite Albany & Marched eight Miles then Pitched our Tents & Lodged.

Sunday the 19th. of May. Proceeded on our March early this Morning. At 8 [A.M.] passed by the elegant Buildings of Col. Guy Johnson[1] & Col. Claus,[2] Son in Laws of Sr. Wm. Johnson,[3] & now in England doing America all the Mischief in their Power. At xi passed by the very Neat and Elegant Buildings that the late Sr. Wm. Johnson lived in, generally called Fort or Castle William on the East-side of the Mohawk river and within four Miles of the lower Castle of the Mohawk Indians called Fort Hunter, which we passed by 12 O'Clock alarming the Indians along this delightfull Country not a little & who appeared at a distance to be collecting. Here our Regmt. Landed & our Col. ordered advanced Flank & Rear Guards to our Partisan.[4] At 4 P.M. arrived at Johnstown, pitched our Tents at the upper End of the Town, our Troops being greatly fatigued with their march & heavy Burden of Provisions. Brought my Arms, Blanket, & Napsack with 6 days Provisions to Johnstown, being with Capts. Sharp, Ross, & Lieut. Mc.Mihell,[5] the only officers who did not on the road put their Napsacks in the Carriage Waggons. My Ambition was too great to see the Men loaded and myself, with no burthen, Nay I prided myself in Marching at the head of the Regmt. with as heavy if not heavier load than the Soldiery though I must Acknowledge my inclination frequently almost induced me to through [throw] my Napsack & Blanket into the Waggon. We were here informed that Sr. John Johnson had left John's Town with most of the Male Inhabitants & all the Highlanders, Dutch & Irish about it with 50 Indians, that they were embodied Armed and intended to Attack us Very probably this Evening. Col. Dayton ordered me to Mount Guard with 68 Men, Lt. Mc.Mihell, Lt. Mc.Donald & Ensign Anderson Subalterns, for the security of the Camp. Mounted guard all Night, visiting the 22 Centories [sentries] out at a time round the Camp every hour. The Vigilance now required made me forget my fatigue entirely. The officers & Men lay in the Tents on their arms. The forepart of the Night we could frequently hear the Indian Warriors yell the War-hoop or Alarum in a most hideous manner and this added to the Darkness of the Night, being in a strange Country surrounded with woods added greatly to our apprehensions of being attacked which made our Centeries as Watchful as Night-Owls. Though the Officers and Soldiers were anxious to engage the Enemys of their Country, yet they wished for the Day-light for such bloody business. The latter part of the Night all quietness, no alarms or Accident happening in the Camp.

[1]GUY JOHNSON (ca. 1740–1788). Native of Ireland. Probably the nephew of Sir William Johnson. Came to America during the 1750s and saw action in the French and Indian War. Also served as Johnson's personal secretary and in 1762 was named deputy Indian agent to the Six Nations. Served in the New York Assembly, 1773–75; replaced Johnson as superintendent of Indian affairs in the northern department in 1774 after his mentor's death. During the American Revolution worked to get Indians to make war on the colonists. Also command-ed Fort Niagara, 1780–82, before leaving the superintendency and moving per-manently to England.

[2]DANIEL CLAUS (1727–87). Native of Germany. Migrated to America in 1749 and eventually became associated with Sir William Johnson. Served as Johnson's deputy Indian superintendent for Canada during the 1760s. Married Sir Wil-liam's oldest daughter in 1762 and established an estate, Claus Manor, in the vi-cinity of Johnson Hall. Worked closely with Guy Johnson during the American Revolution in attempting to secure Indian support for the British side. After the war Claus joined thousands of Loyalist exiles in England.

[3]SIR WILLIAM JOHNSON (1715–74). Born in Ireland. Migrated to the Mohawk Valley in 1738. Steadily built personal influence with the Iroquois, especially the Mohawks, and acquired large amounts of land. Played key role in the defense of New York in the early stages of the French and Indian War and was knighted in 1755. Named superintendent of Indian affairs for the northern department in 1756. Lived in baronial splendor at Johnson Hall (completed in 1762) until his death, while managing white-Indian relations north of the Ohio River and Penn-sylvania.

[4]Partisan. Bloomfield uses the term to mean a member of a body of light troops who make forays against the enemy.

[5]WILLIAM MCMICHAEL. Little is known about this enigmatic 1st lieutenant of the 3rd New Jersey. He deserted to the enemy in August 1776, as mentioned by Bloomfield at a later point, and he was killed by Indians in September 1776.

Monday. 20. [May, John's-Town]. This morning the Commissioners appointed by Genl. Schuyler to treat with the Indians arrived in Town & at twelve, Abraham, the Indian King accompanied by the Sachems & Indian Warriors painted & dressed in their Warlike Manner also arrived and the Treaty was opened by the Indians demanding in a haughty man-ner of our great Warrior (as they called Col. Dayton) what He meant by coming into their country with armed Troops & whether He was for Peace or War? To which Col. Dayton replied that He came not to mo-lest our Brothers the Mohawks but to suppress the Highlanders & oth-ers who had taken up arms against the Congress & hoped our Brothers the Mohawks would not interfere in our Family Quarrel with great-

Britain. They replied that we came to take Sr. John's[1] Life, their good old Friend Sr. Wm. Johnson's Son, That they loved Sr. Wm. who was their Father, for his sake they would protect his son, that Sr. Williams blood ran in their Veins, was mixed with their Blood, and they would stand by him. After much more altercation the treaty was adjourned till tomorrow, the Indians first promising that their Warriors should be peaceable till the Treaty was over. It is worth remarking that the Interpreter after the Indians spoke delivered their Speech in Dutch to our superintendant & who delivered it to Colo. Dayton & the Commissioners in English. It is really surprizeing to see what an assuming behaviour those Savages put on whilst in Council. They sett in their Indian painted warlike dress with their Indian Tomahawks with Pipes (the handle of the Tomahawk being the Tube & the head of the Hatchet the Bole) and smoaking with such a confident air of Dignity & Superiority as if they were above all other beings mad[e] and their Authority extended over the whole Earth. My curiosity induced me to pay a Visit alone this morning to Johnson-Hall, which is a Very beautiful large & elegant Build[ing] with two Forts built by Sr. Wm. in the time of the last War about half a Mile from Town on a small eminance with a fine Stream of Water which runs about 5 Rod off before the Hall. My excuse to see the Hall was to Wait on Miss Peggy Watts (a Sister of Lady John Johnson's & who I was formerly Acquainted with) & who I said I understood was at the Hall. Lady Johnson[2] received and treated me with the greatest Politeness talked freely upon the present unhappy Times & seemed to have the greatest fortitude for a Woman considering the situation her Houshd. was in. She shewed me Sir Wm. Johnson's Picture, which was curiously surrounded with all kinds of Beads of Wamphum, Indian curiositys and Trappings of Indian Finery wh. He had received in his Treatys with different Indian Nations, Curiositys suficient to amuse the curious. She shewed me also the Johnson coat of arms, good old King Hendrick's Picture &c. &c. In short, I returned pleased with my feigned Visit, greatly pleased with Johnson-Hall and the worthy *Lady indeed* (though a Tory who is in Possession of it). Our Detachment parraded in the Evening and took Possesion of the Court-House, Goals, & Church for the security of the Troops in case Sr. John & his party should attack us & who we are informed are embodied to the number of 500 in the woods about five Ms. off & intend acting in a hostile manner, of repelling force by force. Pitched our Tents before the Court House & Church.

[1]SIR JOHN JOHNSON (1742–1830). Born Johnstown, New York. Son of Sir William Johnson. Served as a local militia captain; fought in Pontiac's uprising. Knighted in 1765 and created a baronet in 1774, the same year he inherited his father's vast estate, including Johnson Hall. Tried to organize Loyalists in the

Mohawk Valley region in 1775, using Johnson Hall as a munitions base. In May 1776 fled to Canada with numbers of his tenants. Commissioned a lieutenant colonel in Montreal, where he organized a body of rangers called the Royal Greens. Involved in border warfare until 1781, when he went to England, secured a commission in March 1782 to replace Guy Johnson as Indian superintendent, and returned to America. Spent later years in Canada, serving on the Quebec Provincial Council and working on behalf of Indian and Loyalist emigrants displaced by the war.

[2]LADY JOHN JOHNSON. Mary Watts, who married Sir John on June 30, 1773. In January 1776, Sir John agreed to a parole given by the Continental Congress in return for his guarantee that he would stop arming settlers and Indians in the vicinity of Johnson Hall. When he broke his parole in May and fled to Canada, Johnson left behind his wife, who was pregnant and could not travel easily. The decision was made to hold Lady Johnson as a hostage in an attempt to control Sir John, and Bloomfield later escorted her to Albany where she was put under the more watchful eye of provincial authorities.

Tuesday. 21 [May]. This morning the Indian Treaty was again Opened. Our great Warrior (Col. Dayton) told the Mohawks by the Interpretor that if they offered to take up the Hatchet or oppose his Warriors in their present Expedition He would break the Covenant Chain,[1] He would burn their upper & lower Castles on the Mohawk River, would burn all their houses, destroy their Towns & Cast the Mohawks with their Wifes & Children off of the face of the Earth; on the contrary if they would be still and let us alone in a Family Quarrel, his Young Men (meaning the Soldiery) Should not come near nor molest their Castles &c. At the same time our Detachment with the Drums & fifes were parrading & made a most martial appearance through the street. I believe this had a good effect, these savages cant bear to be supplicated, it makes them think they are of great consequence. The only way is to strike Terror into them. This is the way the brave & politic good old Sr. Wm. Johnson used to treat with them. Upon this the Indian Chiefs & Warriors withdrew for one hour, then returned appeared more mild, submissive & peaceable. Said they were determined not to meddle with our Family Quarrell; all they wanted was to be assured Sr. John should not be killed. We might do as we pleased with the Highlanders, upon which our Chief (Col. Dayton) told them not a hair of Sr. John's head should fall to the ground. We loved him also for his Father's sake, what we was a going to do would be for Sr. John's benefit. We should destroy [illegible] and those Indians who opposed us only, after which some friendly speeches past. The Covenant Chain was promised by both to be brightened and the Hatchet buried. Our Chief desired them not to let their Young Men imprudently come about our Camp, especially in the Night, for fear our Young Warriors & Young Men might be rash & take their Scalps. The Indian Chiefs promised that their Young men should stay at home & not hunt till we were gone out of the Country. Then this great & mighty Council broke up, after drinking plentifully of Toddy, which was the best drink the place good [could] afford. The Wine (if they ever had any) Rum & all the Provisions of the place were taken off by Sr. John & his Party, which makes every article of the Provision kind very Scarce & consequently extravagantly dear— Butter 3/6 per lb., Milk 1/6, Butter without Milk 1/4, Cyder /10 & small Beer /6 pr. Quart, Eggs 2/pr. Doz. and every thing else accordingly dear.

I will now give a description of John's-Town, with my sentiments of its importance.

John's-Town lies in Tryon-County New-York Government, forty five M. West-Nor:W. from Albany, four M. from the Mohawk-River between the upper (called Fort *Hendrick*) and lower (called fort *Hunter*) Mohawk Castles, Twelve Miles from Ionandago [Onadaga], from whence a Creek communicates with the North-River, and from whence there is a communication to Canada by land. The noted Tory rascals White & others went this way & were taken up by our Troops at lake Champlain.

By Examination of several Persons, Wigs & Tories it appears that Sr. John can raise of his own Tenants about 300, Scots and as many Dutch & Irish, that they have arms & ammunition. The warriors of the lower Castle are generally Tories & altho. they have professed themselves satisfyed yet they are not to be trusted, especially as they are much attached to Sr. John. The Missionary & school-Master in their Town: of this we had a most striking proof at the last treaty with Col. Dayton for notwithstanding their Warriors in their last speech gave the most solemn Assurances of their resolutions to abide by the Covenant made with the six Nations, their countenances expressed a Very different language, and evinced to every bystander that we are indebted to their Neutrality in arms to fear not to attachments.

The Town contains about 30 houses, mostly small half Stories. The Country round the Town is fertile & capable by cultivation to supply a great quantity of Provisions. It is well situated to connect the North & Mohawk Rivers to tamper with the Indians, to connect [the] Tories below with those above, And in case we should be unfortunate on either side to fall upon us—fall upon a Weaker party—cutt off a retreat and take the advantage of the fluctuating Passions of Mankind, that any circumstance might be improved against us. It [is] very evident Sr. John's Tenants are against us from the very circumstances of their being Tenants & otherwise in debt to Sr. John & dependant upon him, till their circumstances are altered they cannot nor will not be our Friends. There appears but two Methods of securing this Country in our Interest: The One, to keep a Garrison here to support the Wigs and over awe the Tories; The other, of planting Wigs in the room of Tories. The situation of the Town for a Garretson: For the middle and highest Part are a large Court house of Brick with a good well contiguous to it, and Church of Stone on opposite sides of the street about twenty rod distant from each other, about 100 rod from these and about 40 Rod from the upper part of the Town Sou: East upon ground much higher than the Town and the highest of any near it is a large Goal strongly built with stone, with three feet Walls with a well of good Water close to it. A little labour would render these places Very strong and whoever possest them first would not be easily dispossesed and from whence a Scouting Partie could be Sent through the Country to distress the Tories, To press Provisions if necessary &c.

A description of Johnson-Hall was given in Yesterday's Remarks &c.

A Proclamation was this day published & sent by Col. Dayton through the Country, warning the Scotch Highlanders[2] & all others who had taken up arms against the Congress to come in with their Wifes Children & Affects and they should be well treated; and all those who failed of immediately coming in should be dealt with the Utmost severity & suffer accordingly.

Lieut. Col. White came to John's-Town this Eveng. with the remainder of our Regt. & Proviss. for the whole. Lieut. Elmer of my Company being left in Albany with the care of the Baggage & Sick.

[1]Covenant Chain. A crucial question for both the British and the rebels concerned to whom the Six Nations would pledge their ancient covenents. Both sides claimed the tie of the covenant chain, relating to continued peace, brotherhood, and good will. The Iroquois carried a covenant chain belt with them to various conferences. It consisted of twenty-one rows of wampum beads. Bloomfield was hoping that the covenant chain would be linked to the Americans, indicating that the Iroquois would either be neutral or would actively join the Americans in their rebellion against British authority.

[2]Highlanders. Probably a reference to recent Scottish immigrants who became tenants on the Johnson estate.

Wednesday. May 22. I was early this Morning directed by Col. Dayton to take a file of Men & go to Johnson Hall with my side arms only & wait on Lady Johnson with a Letter, The substance of which was to demand the key of the Hall & drawers in the Rooms with directions for her immediately to Pack up her own apparel only and go to Albany, that an Officer & a Guard should wait on her Ladyship to Albany if she choses. Accordingly I went to the Hall & after directing the Sarjant of My Guard to place Centuries round the Hall & Fort I asked for her Ladyship who was then a Bed and after waiting an hour she came into the Parlour. I gave her the Letter with assuring her Ladyship it gave me Pain that I was under the disagreable necessity of delivering her a Letter that must give her Ladyship a great deal of uneasiness and which my duty obliged me to do in obedience to the orders of my superier Officer. She hastily broke open the Letter & immediately burst into a flood of Tears, wh[ich] affected me, so that I thought proper to leave her alone. After some time she sent for me, composed herself, ordered the Keys of the Hall to be brought in & given to me & which I desired might lay on the Table till the Coll. came. After which I breakfasted with her Ladyship & Miss Jenny Chew whose Father is in England Acting the part of a Violent Tory. After Breakfast Col. Dayton & Major Barber came & we in the presence of her Ladyship or Miss Chew Examined every Room & Every Drawer In Johnson-Hall & Sr. John's office, but found no Letters of a publick Nature inimical to the cause worth mentioning.

This search gave me an opportunity of fully satisfying my curiosity in seeing everything in Johnson-Hall. To give a particular Acct. would exceed the bounds of my Journal, only I'll say that we saw all Sr. William's Papers of all the Treaties He made with the different Indian-Nations, with Medals of Various sorts sent him from Europe & samples of others which He had distributed at his Treaties to the Indians &c., with innumerable Testimonials &c., all which placed Sr. William Johnson's Character in a Very important station of life and greatly merited the warmest thanks of his Country. But when we reflected on Sr. John's (his Son's) Conduct, it afforded a contrast not to be equalled. Whilst we admired and commended the Wisdom, Prudence, Patriotic Spirit, Ardor & Bravery of the Father, we could but detest and discommend the foolish imprudent, treacherous & base Conduct of the son, who, instead of Walking in the Paths of his good old Father in supporting the Liberty of America & thereby Merit the applause of his Country, He has basely endeavored and still is endeavoring to destroy the Libertys & Propertys of his Native Country, and to cutt the Throats of Those, who feared, loved & fought under the command of his Valiant Father, and who now (with a degree of Tenderness & Respect) are obligded to search the Hall built by the good industrious old Baronet (& in which He dyed) to discover and detect the the Young Profligate Knights Treacherous Villany. Lady Johnson treated us all with the greatest complaisance & Politeness, and begged of the Coll. to let her stay in the Hall for the present, assureing him that it was not in her power to send Sr. John any supply of Provisions, that she heard from Sr. John a Monday last, when she sent him a large supply of Provisions & that Sr. John informed her by Letter, He should make the best of his way with his Party to Niagara, which the

Coll. had reason to believe true as the Testimony of several on Oath both Wigs & Tories, confirmed the same & therefore He permitted Lady Johnson to stay in the Hall for the Present, Ordering Centuries to be kept around The house to prevent Provisions being sent from thence to Sr. John.

This afternoon the Coll. had his hands full with Examining Tories, Scotch-Men &c. &c. who came to deliver themselves up.

Thursday. 23. [May]. This day taken up in examining Scotch, Dutch & Irish Tories who came to deliver themselves to the Coll. It is not uncommon here to hear the different English Scotch, Dutch & Indian Languages talked at one time. P.M. Parties were sent out to secure some Tories & who were brought in Accordingly.

It is very surprizeing to see what a consternation & fright the Tories in this County are thrown into. Those miserable Wretches are afraid to be seen by any of the Soldiery, which is the Reasen we are so Scanty of fresh Provisions, Butter, Eggs &c. They behave with the greatest servility imaginable when brought to the Coll. & make all the Promises for their future good behaviour that can be desired, upon which they are usually dismissed.

The Committee of this County sitt every day & afford the Coll. all the Assistance in their Power.

Friday. May 24. John's-Town. This day taken up as yesterday in Examing Tories. At 6 P.M. I was ordered to take a Party of Men with Lt. Gifford & go to the house of the Noted Tory Rascal Alexr. White, Esqr. High Sheriff of this county and Examine his Papers & if I thought Necessary to bring him with me, which was no sooner said (as the old saying is) than it was done. I arrived at White's house on the Mohawk River 5 Miles from this place in 70 Mins. Searched his house found neither Letters Arms or ammunition. White assured me upon his Honor that He had not acted directly or indirectly in the present cause since he gave his Obligation not to, & had his parole from New-York Goal. After this examined two more Tory houses—Col. Butler's[1] for one, who is now in Niagara Superintendant of Indian Affairs, but without effect. Returned by xi with a good appetite for my supper. Capn. Sharp with 60 Men & two 2 subalterns were ordered on a Party to take Possession of a Mill about 20 Miles to the Northwd. to cutt off any Stores going from thence to Sr. John's Party &c.

[1]JOHN BUTLER (1728–96). Native of Connecticut. Saw extensive action in the French and Indian War, at which time he became associated with Sir William Johnson. Fled the Mohawk Valley area in the summer of 1775 with his son Wal-

ter Butler (ca. 1752–81), Daniel Claus, and Guy Johnson (under whom he served as deputy Indian commissioner). Later he and his son became known for their leadership of Butler's Rangers and their bloody sorties on the Pennsylvania–New York frontiers. John Butler's Loyalist-Indian forces were defeated by Sullivan's Continentals at the Battle of Newtown, August 29, 1779, as part of Sullivan's Expedition. After the war Butler helped to establish a Loyalist settlement in the Niagara region.

Sunday. May 26. John's-Town. This Morning we were informed Independency is declared by the Congress which greatly pleased our Regmt.

By direction of the Coll. I waited on the Church Wardens of the Church in Town; got the Keys of the Church, in wh[ich] the Revrd. Mr. Caldwell preached to our Regmt. true Wiggism for the first time I daresay & Prayed for the Congress, that ever it was done in this Church. Our officers took Possession of Sr. John's & the Governor's Pews which with the Pulpit &c. were hung in Black in mourning for good old Sr. William who built this elegant Church. It has a noble Steeple with a good Bell and an excellent sett of Organs which we also made use of, so that we had Presbeterism preached in an Episcopal Church in taste. O Tempora! O Mores! Qui Mutantur.[1] Mounted Guard this night. Lt. Tuttle, Lt. Coxe [Cox] & Ensign Patterson subalterns. Wet & Rainy. Went over to Johnson-Hall & relieved the old-guard myself.

[1]O tempora! O mores! Qui mutantur. A Latin expression meaning: Our times and ways. How they are changed!

Monday. May 27. John's-Town. By order of the Coll. waited this morning on Lady Johnson with a Letter directing her to prepare to go to Albany tomorrow morning. Breakfasted with her Ladyship who said she would be ready in obedience to the orders. P.M. waited on her Ladyship again desireing her to name the officer (as the Colonel intended one should Wait on) she would choose to Accompany her to Albany, upon which she desired me to attend her, to inform the Colonel she was most acquainted with & therefore preferred me before any other officer. This day our Regt. was reviewed by Col. Dayton Judge Duer[1] & the Committee of Tryon County who was greatly pleased with the Alertness of the Men & thought we were well disciplined Troops, when it well knew we are yet raw & unexperienced.

[1]WILLIAM DUER (1747–99). Born Devonshire, England. Educated at Eton College. After brief military service in India, migrated to New York and became prominent as a land speculator, cotton producer, and Patriot activist. Named a colonel and deputy adjutant general in the New York militia, 1775. Served in the Continental Congress, 1777–79; signed the Articles of Confederation; became assistant secretary of the treasury under Alexander Hamilton, 1789.

Tuesday. 28. [May]. Early this morning waited on Lady Johnson, Miss Mc.Donald (a Daughter of Donald Mc.Donald[1] the head of the Highland Clan and now a Prisoner in Pensilvania) and Miss Chew from Johnson-Hall to Mr. Adam's in John's Town where we breakfasted. At viii [o'clock] sett out on Horseback, with Lady Johnson & Mrs. Mulligan in a Phaeton. Attended by two Servants in livery & the overseer, Her two Children with the Nurse in a Waggon. Dined in Schenactady where a Pack of Tories came to Visit her Ladyship. At four proceeded on our Journey. About five miles from Albany I was attacked by four Men & ordered to deliver up my Horse Saddle & bridle, alledging that Lt. Col. White took the horse from one of them because He was a Tory. They swore I should not stir an Inch farther. By this time I was surrounded by upwards of twenty of those kind of Tory Animals who were determined to dismount me, upon which I took my Pistols out of my Pocket & told them I would be the death of two of them at least if they did not let go of the Reins of the Bridle immediately, that I would after dischargeing my Pistols, make use of my sword & sell my life as dear as possible before they should have the Horse. By this time Mr. Defendaff [Diffendorf] a Lieut. in Col. Van Schaick's Regt., came up drew his sword & said He wod. stand by me to the last, which struck such a Terror in those Cowardly Rascals that they left me to take the Road with my Horse as I pleased, which I did challenging them to come to Albany & I would give them satisfaction both with respect to themselves & the Horse, which in reality was arbitrarily taken from the Man because He was a Tory & had bought some of the Soldiers cloathing and encouraged them to desert. Overtook Lady Johnson arrived in Albany at viii [o'clock]. Waited upon Walter Livingston Esqr.[2] Chairman of the Committee with Col. Dayton's Letter & gave up the charge of Her Ladyship to the Commit[tee]. At 12 at Night dismissed my Servant John Royal with my Tory Horse that like to have brought me into a Hobble, to Johns-Town with directions to ride to Schenactady this Night & tomorrow morning deliver him to Col. White in John's-Town. Very much fatigued and unwell this Evening.

I forgot to mention a Man was murdered & robbed the day before yesterday near the place where I had my reincounter.

[1]DONALD MCDONALD. Probably the Scottish officer sent to North Carolina in June 1775 by British General Thomas Gage, where he organized a force of Scottish Highland Loyalists. Defeated at Moores Creek Bridge in February 1776; taken prisoner and exchanged at Philadelphia. Died in London after 1784.
[2]WALTER LIVINGSTON (1740–97). Native of New York. Delegate to the New York Provincial Congress, 1775; became commissary of stores and provisions for the department of New York, 1775, and also assumed the post, 1775–76, of dep-

uty commissary general of the Continental Army's northern department. Later took an active part in politics, serving in the New York Assembly, 1777–79, and the Continental Congress, 1784–85. In 1785 named commissioner of the United States Treasury under the Articles of Confederation.

Wednesday. 29. [May]. This morning waited on Lady Johnson & the Committee at their Request. Proposed Lady Johnson's Querys to the Committee & returned their answers in which they would do nothing in regard to the removal of my Lady or her furniture from Johnson-Hall, without orders from Genl. Schyler. Spent the Eveng. with Lt. Col. Ogden.

Thursday. May 30. Albany. Breakfasted this Morning with one Mr. Halstead, formerly of Elizth. Town & who has lived 14 Years in Quebec. He came out of Quebec with his wife & six Children in September last & lately made his escape when our Army shamefully retreated leaving £500 Ster: in Rum & all he was worth in the world. He was contractor Genl. to our Army there, is an Intelligible Man, says that three or four hundred Men could have taken Quebec in the Winter easier than 2000 can now & that if it is not taken in two Months, we never shall get Posession of it, as Troops will certainly arrive *from* England & the fortifications are daily made stronger & stronger. This gentleman & his Family sensibly feel the fortune of War, formerly lived in affluent circumstances, now reduced & dependant on his Friends, which must affect him & his Family Very sensibly.

An Officer from every Company with Waggons came in Town in the Evening from John's-Town to carry up the Baggage & rear guard. The officers told me I had gained a great deal of Credit by my spirited & resolute Behaviour last Tuesday when I was attacked by the Tory Gentry to rescue Col. White's Horse from me.

Very unwell all Day, my Mouth & Tongue is full of small Blisters & so inflamed that I can eat nothing but spoon-Victuals very cold, and that attended with the greatest Pain.

Friday. 31. [May]. Albany. Our Surgeon being absent, bled myself this morning & took a Dose of Salts. Very sick A.M. P.M. much better. Lady Johnson sent her Complymts. & Inquired this Eveng. how I did, A Condescention & regard that I could not expect from such a Violent Tory. Two of my Deserters James Logan & Uriah Maul were brought in Irons from Esipus[1] goal to Albany. Lewis Thomson another of my Deserters (see 15th. May) is also taken up & confined sick in Esopus goal.

[1]Esopus. Now Kingston, New York.

Saturday. June 1st. Much better today. Very busy in sending off the baggage of the Regmt. with the Deserters that were taken lately belonging to the Regmt. Had the agreable satisfaction of receiving 3 Letters from my Father & Brother this Evening, two of them dated but two days past, in which I was informed all my Friends were well, of the Election for Provincial Delegates, that my Father was one who had the greatest majority of Votes of any Elected in the County of Mddsx. [Middlesex] New-Jersey.

Sunday. June the 2d. 1776. There being no Preaching in Town except in Dutch which I dont understand kept my Room all day. P.M. was Visited by Lieut. Barberil & Mr. Goelet from Amboy, my old acquaintances & who informed me particularly of the State of affairs in the Jerseys. It is [a] Pleasure & satisfaction to meet a Friend at such a Distance from home.

Monday. 3. [June]. Engaged A.M. in writing my will & to my Friends. Dined with Messrs. Oliver Barberill & Goelet on board their sloop. Spent the Eveng. in Company with those Gentm. & Captn. Gradan & Mr. Stout from Philadelphia. Waited this Evening on Lady Johnson who received & treated me with the greatest Politness promising to do me all the service in her Power.

Tuesday. June the 4th. 1776. Busy A.M. in purchasing Stores & preparing to leave Albany. Dined with Walter Livingston Esqr. Dep. Commissary Genl. in company with Mrs. Montgomery[1] (relict of the truly courageous Patriotic & brave Genl. Montgomery[2]) & the two Miss Schuylers, daughters of Major Genl. Schuyler, who were all in Mourning for the Very worthy Spirited resolute & generous Montgomery, who, refused not to hazard & spend his useful Life in the glorious service of his Country. Mrs. Montgomery appeared to be a Very sensible good woman, & still Very disconsolate & overborne with Grief for her irreparable Loss, great indeed to her the partner of his Life, but still greater & of more consequence to America & her sons, who mention his intrepid Courage & bravery with admiration, & who will Acknowledge the singular service He has done his Country with Gratefull Hearts, praying that America may yet have more such men as Genl. Montgomery (which she greatly wants) to step forth & lead her valiant Sons to the field in defence of our invaluable Rights & Priveledges. After Dinner sett out on Horseback alone & got to Schenactady, where I lodged. Schenactady is a very neat pleasant & well built Town on the West side of the Mohawk-River & far preferable (though not so large) as Albany.

[1]JANET LIVINGSTON MONTGOMERY (1743–1828). Native of New York. Married Richard Montgomery, July 24, 1773. Through the loss of her husband at Quebec, came to symbolize women who had sacrificed almost everything for the Patriot cause. A woman of determined temperament, Montgomery managed estates under her control after 1775 and refused the hand of suitors, including General Horatio Gates in 1784.

[2]RICHARD MONTGOMERY (1738–75). Born Swords, Ireland. Attended Trinity College in Dublin, Ireland, and served in the British army. Moved to New York, married into the Livingston family, and was named a brigadier general by the Continental Congress in 1775. Served as second in command to General Philip Schuyler and led an expedition to Canada in the late summer of 1775. Took Montreal but died on December 31, 1775, in the abortive Patriot attempt to seize Quebec. Montgomery thus became one of the early Patriot military heroes.

Wednesday. 5. [June]. Sett out this Morning on my return to Johnstown, met & Dined with Lt. Col. White, Parson Calldwell & two Tory Prison[er]s at the neat, curious & elegant Seat lately occupied by Col. Claus, a son-in-law of Sr. Wm. & now in England. Whilst here, Capn. Potter & a Guard of 60 Men & two Subalterns passed bye with 52 Tory Prisoners taken in Tryon-County & now sent thus escorted by order of Col. Dayton to Albany. The most of those Unhappy Prisoners have left Wifes & Familys at home, who now might suffer greatly for the rash obstinate & imprudent Conduct of those deluded Men. After Dinner viewed the outhouses & gardens belonging to Col. Claus' seat, which exceeded for pleasantness of situation & useful conveniencies any I ever saw. In the garden is a Water-Spout which throughs [throws] the water from a Cistern underground, a considerable Height, & is very pleasing to the Eye. Col. Claus was a German & agreeable to the custom of his Country has introduced many other curious conveniences about his Seat, though he being a Violent Tory & having fled & taken up Arms against us, without doubt has forfeited to this Country all his Right to those Buildings &c. Col. Guy Johnson's House is about a Mile below & Castle Wm. two Miles higher up the Mohawk-River. Arrived at 5 in John's-Town. Was informed by the Colonel that in consequence of his Proclamation for the Torys & others disaffected to the cause to come in & deliver themselves up on Monday last, 195 came in accordingly, of whom the following is an Acct: English 11, Scots 32, Irish 6, Germans 74, Poles 1, Swiss 3, Prussians 1, Americans 67.

Fifty two of the most dangerous & incorrigible were sent to Albany-Tory-Goal. The rest—some signed the Association—gave Bonds for their future good Behaviour &c. &c. & were discharged.

Col. Dayton also informed me that some of our officers had imprudently (not to term it worse) last Night got the keys of & Plundered Johnson-Hall, of sundry goods & furniture to the amount of a considerable Value, that if those goods were not returned to the Hall this Night he would punish or rather prosecute those concerned with the utmost severity & of which He informed the officers of in general.

Thursday. June 6th. By order of the Col. Capt. Dickinson [Dickerson] & myself went this Morning to the Hall & took an Acct. of the goods returned, taken the Night before last from the Hall. After our Report the Coll. Judge Duer Mr. Adams & two Daughters (who have the care of the Hall) Capt. Dickeson & myself went to the Hall, saw that the goods & furniture were carefully packed & securely Stored in the Rooms, after which the Hall was Locked with strict directions for no Persons to enter without leave, which was particularly injoined on me to attend to as I mounted guard tonight. Mounted Guard all night, stayed myself In Johnson-Hall. Lieut. Lloydd Lt. Mc.Donald & Ensign Reading mounted guard at the Camp.

Friday. 7. [June]. On guard all day at Johnson-Hall. Spent A.M. in Playing Billiards at the Hall with Col. Dayton, the Major, Judge Duer & other officers.

The following is a list of the Officers of the 3rd. New Jersey Regimt.

Field-Officers
Elias Dayton Esqr. Colonel
Anthony W. White Esqr. Lt. Col.
Francis Barber Esqr. Major

First Company.
Joseph Bloomfield, Captain Promoted to a Majority this 20th of November 1776. 3d. Compy.
William Gifford, 1st. Lieut.
Dr. Ebenezer Elmer, 2d. Lieut.
William Norcross, Ensign.
Edmund Thomas & John Kinney, Cadets in the 1st Company, Promoted, see July 19.

Second Company.
Peter Dickinson, Esqr. Captain.
David Tuttle, 1st. Lieut.
William Gordon, 2d. Lieut. promoted
Joseph Anderson, Ensign D[itt]o

Third Company.
Samuel Potter, Esqr. Captain

Rynear Blanchard, 1st. Lieut.
Josiah Quimby, 2d. Lieut.
Cornelius Hennian, Ensign, promoted

Fourth Company.
Thomas Patterson, Esqr. Captain
John Mott, 1st. Lieutenant
William McDonald, 2d. Lieut.
Edward Patterson, Ensign
Nicholas Dean, Cadet in the 4th. Company.

Fifth Company.
Dr. John Ross, Esqr. Captain
Edward McMihell, 1st. Lieut.
Richard Coxe, 2d. Lieut.
William Clark, Ensign

Sixth Company.
Thomas Reading, Esqr. Captain.
Robert Hagan, 1st. Lieut. resigned
Jeremiah Billard, 2d. Lieut.
John Reading, Ensign.

Seventh Company.
Wm. Eugene Emlay, Esqr. Captain.
Richard Lloydd, 1st. Lieut.
Daniel Pierson, 2d. Lieut.
Edgar Gaulidat, Ensign.

Eighth Company.
Anthony Sharp, Esqr. Captn.
Samuel Flanagan, 1st. Lieut.
Samuel Hazelet, 2d. Lieut. resigned.
Nathaniel Leonard, Ensign.

Staff Officers.
The Revd. Mr. James Calldwell,
   Chaplain.

Lewis Ford Dunham, Surgeon
Samuel Sheppard, Adjutant
William Norcross, Quartr. Master.
Thomas Reed, Surgeon's Mate.

Promoted, killed &c. &c. &c.
Robt. Hagan & Samuel Hazelett
   [Hazlett] resigned, see e.g. July
   19th. hereafter.
Wm. Gordon, Joseph Anderson,
   Cornelius Hennean [Hennion],
Edmund D. Thomas & John
   Kinney, promoted, see roster
July 19th. &c.
Wm. McDonald, broke by a Genl.
   Court-Martial. vid: No. 3. Augt. 1.

Saturday. June 8. 1776. [Mohawk-River]. At the request of the Committee & Field Officers of Tryon-County Col. Dayton ordered three Captains subalterns accordingly & two hundred & twenty picked Men to sett out P.M. for the German Flatts under the command of Major Barber in order to oppose the Indians expected down to cutt off the Wiggs in that part of the Country. Accordingly 42 Men were picked from my Company & 20 from Captn. Dickenson's, Lieut. Gifford, Lieut. Pierson & Ensign Anderson being my subalterns, formed my Company, who with the rest of the Detachment marched at 4 from John'stown by the way of Conajoharee. Halted about 12 miles up the Mohawk-River at the beautiful Buildings belonging to Mr. Van Vackter who lodged the Officers & Soldiery & treated us with the greatest Hospitality.

Sunday. 9th. [June]. Marched at 5 this morning. At 10 passed the Mohawk-River about 20 miles from John'stown & marched the East-side of the River. At 5 P.M. passed by the Indian Castle called Fort Hendrick, in this place lives Miss Molly[1] (the noted Indian Squagh kept by Sir Wm. Johnson) & her Eight Children & who were all well provided for by the Vigorous old Baronet before his Death. Marched 10 Miles & Lodged at Col. Harkermers.[2]

[1]MISS MOLLY. One of two Indian wives of Sir William Johnson, after the death of his first wife, Catharine Weisenberg (mother of Sir John Johnson). The first Indian wife was Caroline, who had three children by Sir William; the second was Molly, a sister of legendary Joseph Brant and a Mohawk, who bore Sir William eight children and helped consolidate the Loyalist-Indian alliance.

[2]NICHOLAS HERKIMER (1728–77). Native of New York. Active in that colony's militia during the French and Indian War. Named brigadier general of

militia and put in charge of defending the Mohawk region against Loyalists and Indians, 1776. When the British invaded from Canada, 1777, Herkimer rallied the local populace but died as a result of wounds received at the Battle of Oriskany, August 6.

Monday. 10. [June]. Marched from Col. Harkermers and arrived at 9 & Pitched our Tents on the German Flatts opposite the ruins of Fort Harkermer about 40 miles from John'stown our Men being in good Health & Spirits, after this Very agreeable March. The Major gave out strict orders this Evening, that no officer or soldier should go a mile from the Camp & be [in] at 9 & lodge in their Tents. The Major with Messr. Gifford, Andersen [Anderson] Thomas & Kinney Lodge in my Tent with me.

Tuesday. 11. [June]. Exercised today as usual. It is common to hear High & low Dutch, Irish Mohawk, Oneida & English spoken amongst the settlers of this new, fertile & beautiful Country. Went in aswimming with the Major & other officers today in the Mohawk-River.

Wednesday. June 12. 1776. Obtained leave of the Major & went with Captn. Reading, Ensign Hennean & Mr. Kinney across the Mohawk-River to Kingland the upper part of the German Flatts & Crossed the Mohawk River back afoot to Fort Harkermer which lies on the West side of the Mohawk-River.

Thursday. 13. [June]. This day Mr. Dean[1] the Commissr. & Indian Interpreter for Indian-affairs went on Express from Genl. Schuyler with a Belt to summon the six confederate Indian Nations to meet next July in Congress to be held at this place.

[1]JAMES DEAN. Native of Connecticut. May have spent some of his early years living with local Indians and became adept at Indian languages. Attended Dartmouth College. Became a strong advocate of the Patriot cause and worked closely with Samuel Kirkland to secure favor with the Six Nations. Served as an assistant commissioner and interpreter at various conferences held with the Iroquois during the early stages of the war.

Friday 14. [June]. Obtained leave & sett out early this Morning for headquarters. Breakfasted at Col. Clarks & arrived (by the way of Stonerabby[1]) at John'stown by one P.M. Dined with Col. Dayton, Lt. Col. White & Parson Caldwell & Drank Tea with Mrs. Dr. Adams.

[1]Stone Arabia. A village on the north bank of the Mohawk River, ten miles from Johnstown.

Saturday. 15. [June]. Being very unwell & suspicious of haveing caught the Itch,[1] I was bled by Dr. Dunham. Took a Dose of Salt & began to anoint with Quicksilver-Ointment.

[1]Itch. Probably scabies.

Sunday. June 16. 1776. Breakfasted & Dined with Col. Dayton, & attended Publick-Worship.

Monday. 17. [June]. Sett out from John'stown & arrived at the German-Flatts by 4 P.M. after a disagreable ride, it raining the most part of the day. Called on the way at Hendrick Castle at the house of Miss *Molly* (mentioned before 9th. Inst.) & who by the generosity of her Paramour Sr. Wm. Johnson has every thing convenient around her & lives more in the English taste than any of her Tribe. She is now about 50 & has the remains of a Very likely Person. When I came to Fort Harkamer found that Major Barber had removed with the Detachment to Kingsland about a Mile & a quarter from the Fort on the North side of the River where they were encamped contiguous to the Church. Was also informed that a Soldier of Capn. Emlays [Imlay] Company was drownded last Saturday Evening in the Mohawk-River & burled Yesterday in Military form. Being unwell & my arm much swollen about the orifice. At the Invitation of Mr. Mc.Dougal a Merchant in this place I supped & Lodged at his house.

Tuesday. June 18. 1776. Breakfasted with the Major & Captn. Reading at Mr. Mc.Dougals. Exercised today as usual. It is customary on the Mohawk-River, particularly on the German-Flatts (the Settlers being mostly Dutch) to see the Women Rich & poor hoeing Corn & doing all kinds of servile Labor & astride when they ride on Horseback.

Wednesday. 19. [June]. About 5 this P.M. Col. Dayton & the rest of the Regimt. (except Capt. Dickerson & Emlay's Companys) with the Baggage of the Regiment arrived at Fort Harkermer & waded with the Col. at their Head up to their middles over the Mohawk-River where they were met by Our Detachment, the officers & Soldiers paying the usual Complyments as the Col. passed.

Thursday. 20. [June]. On guard today, Lieut. Pierson subaltern. Nothing Material.

Friday. 21. [June]. On guard as Officer of the Day, Lt. Coxe Subaltern. Put one Conoly of Captn. Potter's Comy. in the guard house for Disobedience of orders & mocking a Party on fatigue by my orders. In 25 Minutes after being in the guard house by his humble behaviour & Intreaties the Col. put him to do double fatigue with the Men I had ordered out. P.M. Struck & divided our Tents & pitched according to Rank in Military form.

Saturday. 22. [June]. Engaged in altering my Tent to a Markee. Lieut. Elmer Very unwell.

Sunday. 23. [June]. Attended Worship in the Dutch Church, the Rev'd Mr. Caldwell Preached A.M. & P.M., the Dutch Minister between, in High-Dutch. About 2 we had a Violent Gust of Wind & Rain accompanyed with sharp Lighting & heavy thunder. Many of the Tents were thrown down in this sudden storm & exposed the owners not a little to the storm & the diversion of the Choir of officers.

Monday. 24. [June]. Col. White with Capt. Ross from John'stown joined us today.

Tuesday. 25. [June]. The Militia in the German Flatts met on the opposite side of the Mohawk-River & draughted [drafted] 14 Men to go to Canada. Attended their meeting P.M. with Col. White, Captn. Hubble, the Parson, Lt. McMihell & Coxe & we were not a little diverted with their behaviour in recruiting & the Respect paid to Continental Officers as they called us.

Wednesday. 26. [June]. Pitched my Tent now converted into a Markee. Our officers attention was taken up this Morning in waiting upon two Dutch Militia-officers who for some affront Yesterday had challenged each other to decide the Dispute by a Duel. The Major was engaged as a second to one of the Champions & to humour their Passion encouraged them to fight. Loaded his Pistols with Powder & a Cedar Ball gave each one in the Presence of many spectaters, but they only altercated & swore at each other in the Dutch & Indian Tongue and finally did not fight, One being afraid & the other dare not engage & thus ended the sport of the morning.

Thursday. June 27. 1776. This day Mr. Duncan Mc.Dougal a Merchant in this place joined my Company as a Voluntier. P.M. In consequence of an Express from Genl. Schuyler to Col. Dayton to forward a

Letter to the Iroquois Nations, Col. Dayton dispatched me with Major Hubble (who is with us in Character of an Engineer) to go express to the Oneida Indian-Castle, to examine & see the situation & make Report of the state of Fort Stanwix &c. &c. Accordingly I set out with Major Hubble & a Dutch guide Mr. Weaver at six this Evening & rode through the Wilderness following each other through a blind foot Path. Crossed the Mohawk-River about 13 miles from the German-Flatts & rode till two O'Clock this Morning when we arrived at the Indian-Field's called Oresca Castle which lies 26 M. from the Flatts & where we begged a Lodgeing in an old Indian Hutt. Our Guest Hospitably given [gave] us a Dish of sour Bread & Milk & a Blanket to lie before the fire which we thankfully Accepted.

Friday. June 28. 1776. Arose from my humble Bed on the floor much refreshed with my two hours sleep, which was as sweet as if I had laid on a Bed of Down in the best of Palaces. Crossed Oresca-Creek at 5 & proceeded for & arrived at Fort Stanwix at Eight. Took a View of the Ruins of this Once strong & beautiful Fort, which is accounted to lie on the highest ground in all America; as it is the [source?] of the Mohawk-River which runs south to the North River & into the Atlantic Ocean, the head of Wood-Creek which runs directly North into the different Lakes to St. Lawrence N. by N.E. to the sea, The Oneida-Creek running directly West & the Waters on the East Canada & Fish-Creeks Eastward from the Fort. Fort Stanwix (so called after the general who built it in 1758) is large & well situated haveing a Glacis,[1] Breast-work Ditch & a Picket Fort before the Walls which are also well guarded with sharp sticks of Timber shooting over the walls on which is four Bastions. The Fort also has a Sally Port[2] Cevort-Way,[3] Bridge & Ravelling[4] before the gate at the entrance. The ruins of five houses & Barracks in the inside built for the Accomodation of the Stores Officers & Soldiery. At about a Mile distance is a Pickquet Fort called Fort Newport built opposite the Dam made over Wood-Creek for the main-guard quartered here for the defence of the Batteaus[5] &c. &c. The Examination of this fortification gave me a better Idea of the strength & Importance of a Fort than any thing I ever before saw or Read. There are 5 or 6 Families settled in this Rich & beautiful Campaign[6] Country not a Hill is to be seen around it which is also an Evidence of its being the highest Land in this part of America.

After breakfast we proceeded & arrived by 2 O'Clock P.M. at the Oneida-Castle & Delivered our Letters to the Sachems then setting in Council in a Miserable old long Hutt situated in the Center of their Town which lies on a large plain on the south side of the Oneida-River

Eight miles from the Oneida-Lake in a Very Rich beautiful Country. The Sachems and Indian Warriors received us with an Assuming air of Dignity invited us in their Council-Room, asked the News & treated us with the greatest Civility provided Lodgeing for us at the Revd. Mr. Kirklands,[7] their Missionary from the Presbeterian Synod & who is now at Albany. Towards Evening went with an Indian Interpreter & Visited most of their Huts in quest of Indian Whampum &c. Also visited their Chief Scanindoe who lives in a good house built in the Dutch fashion. This sachem & Mr. Spencer the Indian Interpreter spent the Evening with us & were Very good Company. It is the custom amongst the Indians for their Women to do all the servile Labor (such as cut Fire Wood, hoe Corn &c.). The Gentlemn. only Hunt & smoak at their Pleasure. They have one Very large cleared Field in which all their Horses & Cattle graise promiscusly [promiscuously]. The Oneida Castle is called Connowollakka & contains about 150 Warriors. They have other Castles & about 380 Warriors in the whole Nation & are esteemd the most Warlike & Politic Nation of the Iroquois & are now all true Wigs.

[1]Glacis. The parapet of a fort extended in a long slope to meet the surface of the ground.
[2]Sallyport. An opening in a fortified place for the passage of troops when making a sally or rush.
[3]Covert way. A covered way in a fortification.
[4]Ravelin. A triangular embanked area outside the main ditch of a fortress.
[5]Bateau. A flat-bottomed river boat.
[6]Champaign. Flat and open terrain.
[7]SAMUEL KIRKLAND (1741–1808). Native of Connecticut. Graduated from the College of New Jersey in 1765. Performed missionary work with the Seneca Indians, 1764–66. Became pastor of the Lebanon, Connecticut, Congregational Church, 1766. Shortly thereafter began a life-long career ministering to the Oneidas. Often given credit for keeping the bulk of the Oneidas and Tuscaroras attached to the American cause during the American Revolution.

Saturday. 29. [June]. Sett out early this morning. Arrived & spent the day at Fort Stanwix. Visited Wood-Creek, the upper-part of the Mohawk-River.

Sunday. June 30. 1776. Sett out from Fort Stanwix Early this Morning, breakfasted at Oresca castle & arrived at the German-Flatts at 2 P.M. I observed in my Journey particularly in the Oneida Country large Quantitys of Capillair[1], Gentian[2] & Liquorish Roots & other Medicinal Herbs.

[1]Capillair. Maidenhair fern.
[2]Gentian. A plant sometimes used as a tonic.

Monday. Tuesday. July 1, 2. Nothing Material. Officer of the Day.

Wednesday. July 3. Exercised as usual, attended Capt. Seber's Company being mustered this P.M.

Thursday. July 4. Capt. Sebers & Capt. Mc.Kean's Companys of Provincials & Capt. Eversland's Company of draughted Militia joined our Regiment today. Two men, one of Capt. Readings & one of Sharp's Company, received 25 lashes apiece for absenting themselves four weeks from Duty. We are daily Visited by Indians from the Oneida & Tuscaroras who attend & admire us when at our Exercise & whilst about our Camp are treated with the greatest kindness & Hospitality, They drawing Provisions & better than our Soldiers.

Friday. July 5. 1776. Engaged all day in Posting my Books &c. Exercised as usual. It is now after one O'Clock at Night all our Camp have been alarmed by the firing of 4 or 5 guns on our Centuries who returned the fire & gave the Alarm. The Drums immediately Beat & the Fifes Played to Arms, to Arms. At the same time the officers some in their shirts some barefoot calling their Men from their Tents & forming them in Front of their Tents ready on Orders & the Men turning out half dressed afforded a most serious & Martial appearance. When I first heard the Alarm from the Quarter Guards, immediately jumped out of my Markee with my Fusee,[1] Barefoot & my Cloaths in my Hands & raised my officers & Men to Parade which they and the whole Camp did with great Alertness, upon which I ordered advanced Guards in Front of my Company 60 Yards & divided my Company in three Divisions with an officer to each division & Placed the divisions so as to secure the right of of the whole Encampment. We remained in this situation impatient for Orders to scout for half an hour, when upon Inquiry we Imagined the Alarm was false & the Guns fired by Hunters or with a Design by the Inhabitants to try our Resolution, upon which the Captains were ordered to Dismiss & direct their Men to lay on their Arms all Night; which I have done to my Company & shall immediately lay on my arms in Tent. I write this at this later hour of the Night, for perhaps an attack made [may] be made & the writer hereof no more before Morning. I must observe that both Officers & Men turned out & shewed the greatest Spirit & Resolution on the Alarm & Beating to Arms.

[1]Fusee. The word as used here means fusil, a light flintlock musket.

Saturday. July 6. Slept late this Morning, consequently did not attend parrade, being sufficiently disturbed with last Nights Work. Captn. of the Guard tonight Lieut. Bellard [Ballard] & Ensign Clarke [Clark] subalterns.

Sunday. July 7. 1776. Very unwell this Morning did not attend Church. P.M. attended Meeting our worthy Chaplain Preached before the Col's Door under a Tree, we all setting under an orchard which afforded a fine shade. Officer of the day. Last Night, two Men were confined by my Order, one of Capn. Sebers another of Capn. Mc.Kean's for Drunkeness & being absent from their Quarters after xi O'Clock. The officer of the Main Guard confined a Soldier for sleeping on his Post. My guard Relieved by Capn. Potter.

Monday. July 8. 1776. Received 240 Dollars of Col. Dayton for the use of my Company. Gave my men two Dolls. apiece. This day a Court Martial sett & tried two Soldiers for sleeping on their Posts & Sentenced them to receive 25 Lashes apiece, but when the Men were Brought to the Adjutant's Daughter (the whipping Post so called by the Soldiery) they were pardoned by the Colonel.

Tuesday. 9. [July]. This P.M. we were reviewed in form by Col. Dayton who with the Spectators gave us the praise of performing admirably well. Both Officers & Soldiers have their hats neatly Bound, & have learnt to March both slow & quick steps Exactly by the Beat of Drum & the fife. And for the time we have been in the service have learnt most of the Maneuvres beyond the expectations of every Judge who has observed us Exercise.

Wednesday. 10. [July]. Captn. Emlay & part of his Compy. arrived from Johnstown. Nothing material.

Thursday. 11. [July]. Being officer of the day sett a Guard extraordinary from my Company over the Cannon Ammunition &c. & Batteries at Fort Harkimer which arrived with a Company of Artillery this Evening so far on their way to Fort Stanwix & for which Fort all our Regiment excepting my Company are ordered to get in Readiness to March tomorrow.

Friday. 12. [July]. Mr. Mc.Dougal (mentioned before June 27th.) having applied & obtained a Discharge from his Inlistment, and not haveing treated Mr. Edmd. Thomas a Voluntier in my Company with proper decorum, Mr. Thomas last Evening sent a Challenge to fight with Pistols for satisfaction & which was accepted in due form by his Antagonist who chose Major *Yates* for his second. Mr. Thomas chose Lieut. McMihell & at 7 the Champions took the field with their seconds Dr. Dunham & myself. After some altercation about the ground 15 Paces was measured off and as Mr. Thomas gave the challenge He offered Mr. Mc.Dougal the choice of his Pistols (which he borrowed of me) & the first Fire, upon which after desireing us to take Notice that if either of them should be killed they forgave the Survivor. Mr. Mc.Dougal takeing the signal from Mr. Thomas's second fired without killing or Wounding his Antagonist. Then Mr. Thomas takeing the signal from Major Yates fired & with as little effect, Upon which their two Friends interceeded to compromise Matters which was readily & eargerly [eager-ly] embraced by Mc.Dougal & as obstinately refused by Thomas who swore the Pistols had not half a Load in, to Charge them better & try what another exchange would do. By this time Lt. Col. White, Capt. Paterson [Patterson] & several other officers who had been Eye Witness to the sport at a little distance came up & told them their Honors were at Stake they must now fight till one or the other was killed, Well knowing at the same time that the Pistols were loaded with Nothing but a Paper-Wadd for a Ball, & the Duel was sett on foot by Col White himself to divert the officers & try the Resolution of our Heroes, & who before the first fire were Very sedate particularly Mc.Dougal who had not only wrote his Will, & wrote to his Brother but had said his Prayers (as his second reported) before he took the field. However, the Pistols were again loaded and Discharged with as little Bloodshed as at first. The Behaviour of the Duellists on this last fire excited the Laughter of the whole Parade which made them think, they were fireing only for our diversion. They now began to grow so courageous they had a Mind to fight 5 paces nearer & Thomas swore He would load his own Pistol And that Mr. Mc.Dougal might do the same. This the seconds opposed told them they had both showed their Resolution & they must now make Friends, which Mc.Dougal again offered to comply with, but it was as obstinately refused by my brave Voluntier. We finding matters began to grow more serious & that Thomas was determined to fight him some how or other at all events the Coll. & I put our Commands on him & after much Intercession made them shake hands & drink Friends. Thus ended this Mighty duelling Frolick; which served only & that sufficiently, to shew us the absurd folly of this piece of Gallantry. Never did I look upon duelling in such a contemptible light as I now do. This ridiculous custom serves only to shew the Passionate Temper & absurd Folly of those who expose themselves to satisfy their brutish thirst for what?

Why for nothing else but to keep the world from thinking they are Cowards, & to show that they have rashness enough to expose their Life as a testimony of their false Bravery.

Agreeable to Orders from Genl. Schuyler Col. Dayton with all his Regiment (except my Company) sett out at Ten with Capt. Sebeers & Capt. Mc.Kean's Companys for Fort Stanwix, the officers & Soldiers carrying their Arms & Accoutrements with four Days Provisions on their backs, the Ammunition Cannon Intrenching Tools & Stores of the Regiment being conveyed on the Mohawk-River by Batteaus by a Company of Batteau-Men inlisted for this purpose.

Upon Col. Daytons marching He gave me the following Orders:

German-Flatts July 12th. 1776.

Sir,
   You are immediately to Possess the Church with Your Company. Capt. Isinlord's[1] Company will be quartered in the Barn nearest the Church. You will be Very careful to keep proper Guard to prevent a surprize. Exert Yourself in disciplining Your Soldiers. Keep a Number of Men daily employed at the Well and apply to the Committee for any Material You may want in order to finish it.

   Twenty of Your best Men are to be equipped in the neatest manner and meet and escort the General to this place, when You get intelligence of his approach. See that the Soldiers be strictly subordinate & regular & endeavor that this Battalion be honorably represented by the Company under Your Command. Any Indians that want Provisions are to have it & to be kindly used.

I am Sir Your humble Servt.
ELIAS DAYTON

To Capt. Bloomfield

After the Regiment Marched I issued the following Order.

German-Flatts July the 12th. 1776.

Parole[2]: New-Jersey
Officer of the day tommorrow Lieut. Gifford
The Guard to consist of One Sarjant, One Corporal, & Twenty one Privates. Fourteen from Captn. Bloomfield's & Seven from Captn. Isinlord's Companys.
   Agreeable to Col. Dayton's Orders Capt. Bloomfield's Company are to lodge in the Church & Capt. Isinlord's will Occupy the Barn near the Church & by no means be absent after the Beat of the Tattoo, and both Companies will attend Roll-Call & Exercise together at the usual hours in the Morning & Evening in the Camp.
JOS. BLOOMFIELD

Immediately after the above Order was Issued my Company took Possession of the Church and all the Commissary's Provisions were removed from the Barn into the Church which is surrounded with a Breastwork & a tolerable good Pickquet Fort. Capt. Isinlord's Company also came

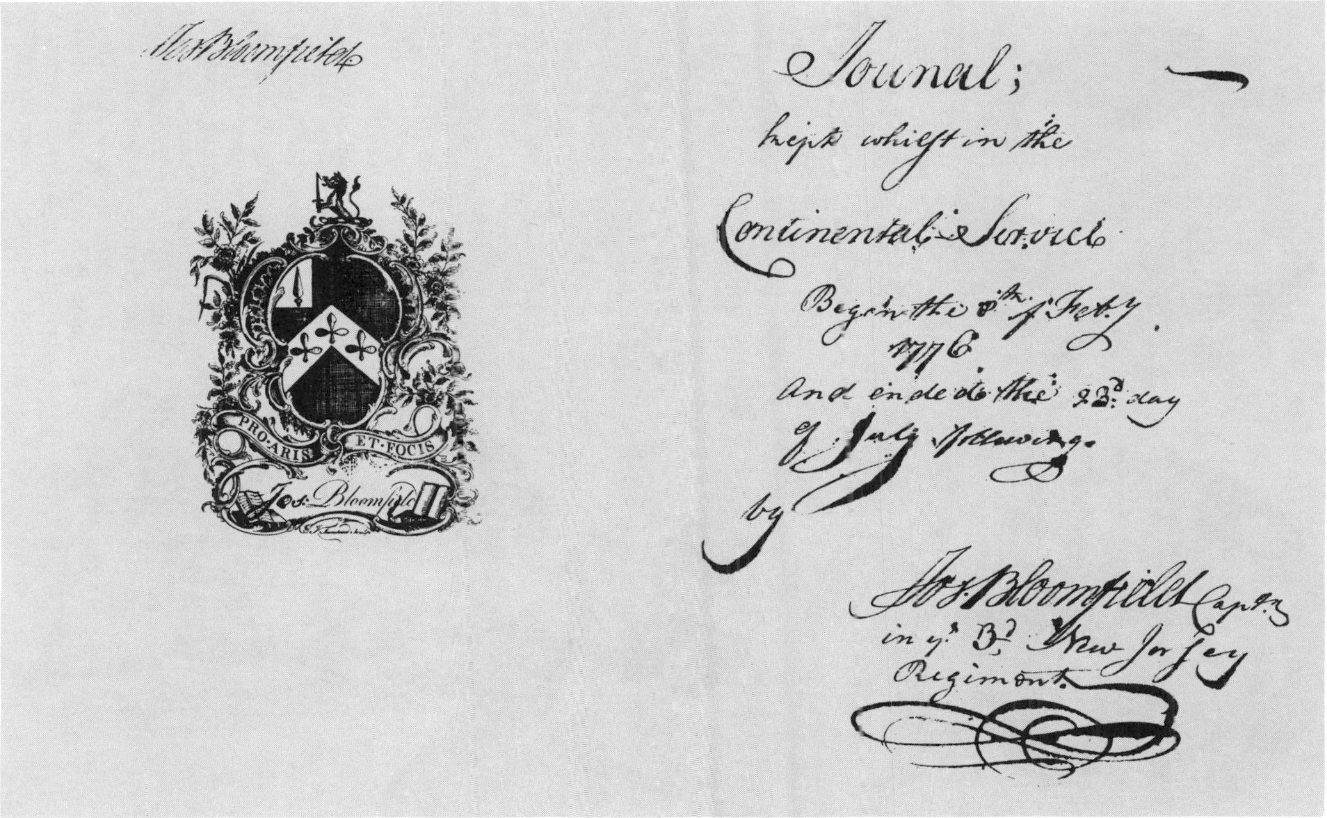

Fig. 1: Bookplate and title page of Joseph Bloomfield's war journal, 1776.

Fig. 2

Fig. 3

Fig. 4

Figs. 2, 3: Portraits of Joseph Bloomfield (1753–1822) in civilian dress and in his War of 1812 uniform. **Fig. 4:** Brigadier General John Sullivan (1740–95) led the American defense of the northern frontier in the summer of 1776. Bloomfield served under him at Fort Ticonderoga. **Fig. 5:** A 1771 map of New York State, showing the area where Bloomfield campaigned between May 1776 and January 1777.

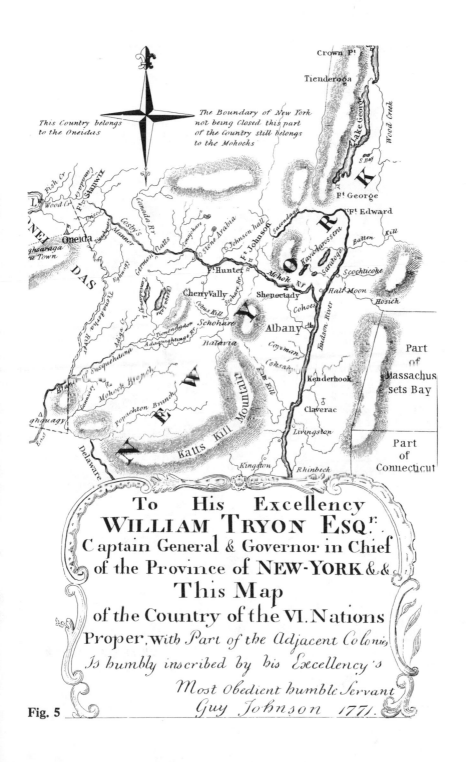

Fig. 5

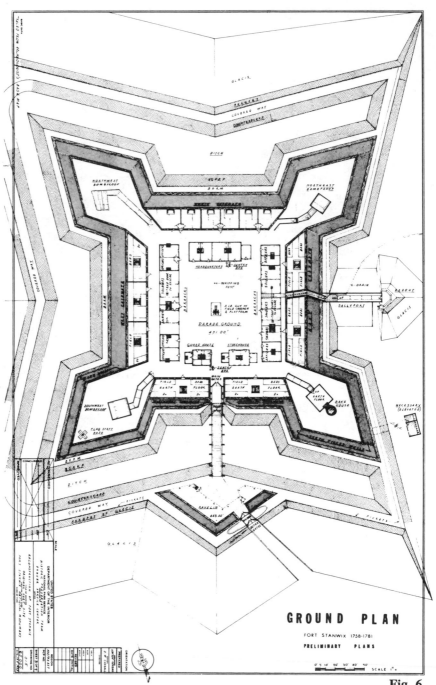

GROUND PLAN

FORT STANWIX 1758-1781

PRELIMINARY PLANS

Fig. 6

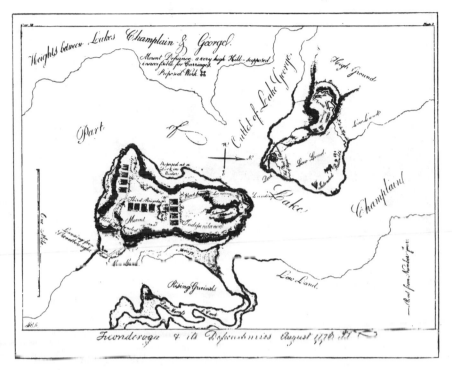

Fig. 7

Bloomfield was at Fort Stanwix, on the Mohawk River, in September and October of 1776 and at Fort Ticonderoga, on Lake Champlain, during the closing months of that year. **Fig. 6:** Diagram of Fort Stanwix, renamed Fort Schuyler. **Fig. 7:** Map of the Fort Ticonderoga area, August 1776.

Fig. 8

The Johnson family served as mediators between the British and Iroquois Confederacy both before and during the American Revolution. **Fig. 8:** Johnson Hall, the family seat, was built in 1762. **Fig. 9:** Sir William Johnson (1715–74) served as the British crown's Indian agent and retained the loyalty of the Iroquois during the French and Indian War. **Fig. 10:** Sir John Johnson (1742–1830), Sir William's son, was an active Loyalist during the American Revolution.

Fig. 9   Fig. 10

Fig. 11

Fig. 11: Major General Philip Schuyler (1733–1804) commanded the Patriot Northern Army in New York from 1775 to 1777. **Fig. 12:** In
conferences such as this both the British and Americans sought to win the
allegiance or at least the neutrality of the Iroquois Confederacy.

Fig. 12

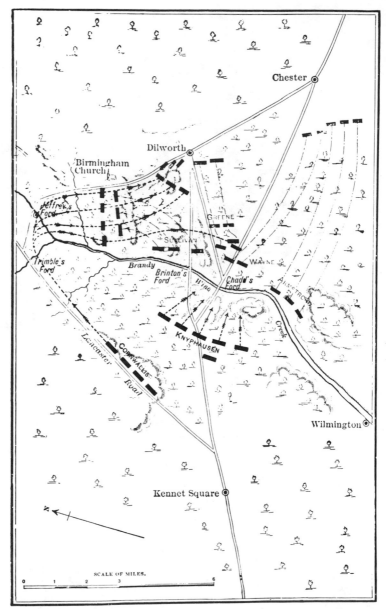

Fig. 13

Fig. 13: Bloomfield was wounded on September 11, 1777, at the battle of
the Brandywine, depicted on this map. **Fig. 14:** Colonel Elias Dayton
(1737–1807) commanded the regiment of which Bloomfield's company was
a part. **Fig. 15:** Bloomfield's troops participated in the battle of Germantown, October 4, 1777, where the confused action centered on the Chew
House.

GENERAL ELIAS DAYTON

Fig. 14

Fig. 15

Fig. 16: Bloomfield's company fought at the battle of Monmouth on June 28, 1778.

BRIGADE ORDERS.

HEAD-QUARTERS, CAMP, TRENTON, 18th *September,* 1794.

PAROLE, PERSEVERE—COUNTERSIGN, JERSEY-BLUES.

Officer of the Day to-morrow Captain *Price.* Same details for Guards and Camp-Duty as yesterday.

William Chetwood, Esq. is appointed Affiftant Brigade-Major, and is to be noticed and obeyed accordingly.

General Bloomfield *calls the attention of his Fellow-Citizens and Soldiers, who compofe the Jerfey Brigade which he has the honour to command, to the following Obfervations and Orders:*

NEXT to the collection and forming of the Infantry and Artillery of the Jerfey Brigade, *Military Difcipline* is the firft object which prefents itfelf to our notice. Every officer and foldier knows, that SUBORDINATION is abfolutely neceffary; that it confifts in a perfect fubmiffion to the orders of fuperiors; in a perfect dependance, regulated by the rights and duties of every military man, from the private foldier to the general. This fingle idea, which difplays itfelf to the leaft attention, fuffices to fhew its importance. Without *fubordination* it is impoffible that a corps can fupport itfelf; that its motions can be directed, order eftablifhed, or the fervice carried on. In effect, it is *fubordination* that gives a foul and harmony to the fervice—It gives ftrength to authority, and merit to obedience; it equally fupports the officer and the rank-and-file; it fecures the efficacy of command, and the honour of the execution. It is *fubordination* which prevents every diforder, and produces every advantage to an army. But if *fubordination* fecures the rights of fuperiors, it likewife makes them anfwerable for the confequences; and if it reduces inferiors to implicit fubjection, it at the fame time fecures them from all reproach; fo true it is, that in the failure of all enterprizes, the fault is laid on the commander alone—obedience juftifying the reft.

The EXERCISE is the firft part of the military art; and the more it is confidered, the more effential it will appear. It frees the officer and the foldier from the rufticity of fimple nature, and forms men to all the evolutions of war. Upon it depends the honour, merit, appearance, ftrength and fuccefs of the corps. For which reafon, General *Bloomfield* calls on every officer to make it his duty immediately—that the men be drilled and taught the manual exercife—particularly, expertnefs in loading and firing and ufe of the bayonet—attention to order—cleanlinefs in camp—different beats of the drum, and the fervice of the different guards.

It would be very ufelefs to enlarge, but General *Bloomfield* thinks it his duty to order, that the regulations for the order and difcipline of the troops of the United States by the Baron *Steuben* be executed with all poffible exactnefs. No excufe will be admitted for the leaft deviation from Baron *Steuben's* regulations and order of difcipline, and his inftructions to officers; with which every officer will make himfelf perfectly acquainted; for without this knowledge, it is impoffible that he can form the men or diftinguifh himfelf as an officer and foldier.

Fig. 17: Broadside issued to the Jersey Brigade just prior to General Bloomfield's departure for Pennsylvania to put down the Whiskey Rebellion of 1794.

Fig. 18: The First Presbyterian Church, in the New Jersey town named for Bloomfield, received both money and books from the general in 1797.

Fig. 19: After the American Revolution, he moved into this house in Burlington, New Jersey, where he died in 1823.

Fig. 20

Fig. 21

Fig. 20. Aaron Ogden, (1756–1839) and Bloomfield both served as Continental officers and were members of the Society of the Cincinnati (the portrait shows Ogden wearing the medal of the Society). When Bloomfield left the governorship for service during the War of 1812, Ogden became the first Federalist governor of New Jersey in over a decade.
Fig. 21: The State Capitol of New Jersey at Trenton was constructed under the Federalists around 1794.

Fig. 22: Mary McIlvaine Bloomfield, by Charles
Willson Peale. The portrait was painted in 1783, by
which time her husband Joseph Bloomfield was a
successful attorney. Peale portrayed her as a pleasant, well-dressed woman. Courtesy of the American Philosophical Society.

from their Quarters & Possessed the Barn contiguous to the Church. Struck my Markee my officers & Voluntiers their Tents & pitched them between the Church & Barn.

Our worthy Chaplain & myself provide now for ourselves Tea & Coffee Morning & Evening & Dine at Col. Belinger's of the Militia. My officers & Voluntiers Mess by themselves in their own Tents.

Several Indians from the Oneida & Mohawk Tribes came to Camp & were provided with Provisions to day. Lodged alone in my Marqee (Mr. Norcross my Companion being gone with the Colonel).

[1]JOHN ISINLORD [EISENLORD]. Probably Captain John Eisenlord of the New York militia. Stationed in the Mohawk Valley during 1776, he rose to the rank of major and was killed at the Battle of Oriskany, August 6, 1777.
[2]Parole. A password.

Saturday. 13. [July]. At five this Morning I had both Companies at Exercise & after Exercise cleared the Parrade of the Camp rubbish. The following Orders were Issued, which I enter in this Book that I may preserve them for my own Satisfaction.

German-Flatts July the 13th. 1776.

Parole: Woodbridge.
Officer of the day tommorrow Lieut. Cannon.
The Guards the same as Yesterday.

The Companys will take Notice that Voluntier Thomas is appointed to do the Duty of an adjutant, and Voluntier, Kinney of a Quatr. Master for the time being, And the Non-Commissioned officers are hereby strictly charged and the Privates left behind of those Companies that had marched to make proper Returns always at the Sarjants *Call* precisely at ten O'Clock when the Orders of the day will also be given out by Mr. Thomas.

Capt. Bloomfield recommends that every Officer & Soldier between the hours of Exercise clean their cloathing & Brighten their Arms & accoutrements in Order to wait on General Schuyler (expected tomorrow Evening) in as decent & becoming a Manner as possible. No Excuse will be taken if any of his *own* Company should come on parrade with their arms in any other Manner than will bear the strictest Examination whether the owners have endeavered By their Care & Industry to make them appear suitable to receive & attend upon the General.

At any alarm in the Night Capt. Isinlord's Company will immediately come to the Church & form within the Pickquet Fort before the Church-Door for their security & where they shall be properly provided with Ammunition.

The Treaty being near & but few Indians haveing arrived as is usual for them to come some time before upon such Occasions & those that have arrived behaving in an Insolent daring Manner in applying for their Provisions (which is given them out of the publick-Stores) and going away in a threatening Manner, makes me suspect their Intentions are not Very friendly. But those that Come under-Cover for Provisions are Tory-Spies, especially as one said: Bye in Bye we should see Indians come over the Mountains & Gun go Pop Pop this Way & dat [that] Way; take care You officer & Soldier, and much other such Language. Upon this we all removed from our Tents & are now in the Church within the Pickquet Fort. The guard & Centurys out are well-loaded & the Men lay on their arms. And I am now ready for an Attack—the sooner the better—as I am well provided with stores & ammunition for a Siege.

Sunday. 14. [July]. Attended Church A.M. P.M. rode with Mr. Calldwell & Capt. Sharp to meet the General. After riding a few Miles found He did not sett out till this Morning. Rode myself to Fort Hendrick 12 miles from hence, & got a Pair of Elegant Leggins made in the Indian Fashion by Miss *Molly*, & her Daughters mentioned before June 9th & 17th. Had the Pleasure of seeing the Young Ladys, one is Very handsome, both were richly dressed agreable to the Indian-Fashion. On my return received (by a Soldier from Johnstown) Letters from my Father dated the 2d. Inst. In Congress from Burlington, being but twelve days on their way, which informed me of *Independency* being declared the 4th. Inst. & much other News. Received Letters also from some of my other Friends. No Person, but what has experienced the satisfaction can tell the unspeakable Pleasure which arises from the Receival of Letters from our Friends at a Distance. Returned to Camp & Spent the Evening with Mr. Calldwell, Captn. Sharp & the officers, much pleased & satisfyed with the news from the Southward & smoaked Politics all the Evening.

By the Conduct of Lieut. Hagan I was under the disagreable Necessity of writing the following Letter to Col. Dayton, vizt.

German-Flatts 10 O'Clock
Sunday Night July the 14th.: 1776.
Sir,
I this day issued the following Order (vizt.)

July the 14th. 1776.
Officer of the Guard tommorrow Lieut. Hagan.
Parole: *Cumberland.*
No Officer or Soldier will presume to lie out of his Quarters as appointed by Col. Dayton under Penalty of the Punishment inflicted by the Ninth Article of the Additional Rules & regulations of War.
I was thus particular principally on acct. of Captn. Isinlord's Company. Yet notwithstanding this particularity and altho. Lieut. Hagan read the order, I have this Moment found He has gone out of Camp to Lodge. He did not so much as Intimate this resolution to me & only mentioned to

the Sergeant of the Guard that He was going out to lodge without telling him where He might call for him in case he should be wanted. I have appointed another officer in his Room and when He appears Shall put him under an Arrest and wait your further Orders.

I am &c.

JOS. BLOOMFIELD.

Immediately Issued an order as follows. Lieut Hagan haveing gone from Camp to Lodge & left the Guard without Leave, Lieut. Pierson is appointed Officer of the Guard in his room. After this I retired to my Marquee & about Twelve went to Bed.

Monday. 15. [July]. Orders of the day.

Parole: The United States of America.
Officer of the Guard tomorrow Lieut. Elmer.
The guard to consist hereafter of two sarjants, two Corporals & twenty one Privates, Centerys by day 3, by Night seven.

The Companys will Attend at the Beat of the Assembly at twelve Powdered and as well dressed as possible in order to Parrade & drink success to the United Independant States of America.

Accordingly at xii the Companys Parraded, the Gentleman in the Place & Indians attended, and the Declaration of Independency being read, the whole present signifyed their hearty & sincere Approbation by Three Cheers and cheerfully drinking the following Patriotic Toasts, (vizt.)

Harmony, Virtue, Honor and all Prosperity to the free and Independent United States of America.

Wise Legislatures, brave & Victorious Armies, both by Sea & Land to the American States. After this the Companies were Dismissed.

In the Evening sundry Indians of the Onidas & Cayugas Tribes came down when I issued the following additional Order. (vizt.)

The settlers in & about the Camp at the German-Flatts are desired not to sell or give any Liquors to any of the Indians attending the Treaty or to any Persons that will supply them with Liquors.

This Order is issued at the Request of the Oneidas & Cayugas Chiefs.

Mr. Dean & two other Indian Interpreters came & made an apology to the Indians for the General's not being here to day; He will attend by 8 tomorrow A.M. Lodged within the Stockade in the Church.

Tuesday. 16. [July]. At 7 A.M. parraded my own & Capt. Isinlord's Company, who were powdered & dressed as well as possible. Dispatched left [Lieut.] Gifford with 20 of my best Men & a Drum & Fife, to meet & Escort the General to this place which He accordingly did, The Men left behind being formed in Open Order; Received the Genl. in saluting & paying him the usual Compliments, the Gentlemen commending the appearance & behavior of the Men as superior to any they ever saw. I was introduced & Dined with the Genl. his Aid-de-Camp's, the Commissioners for Indian-affairs & other Gentlemen of the Army.

Informed his Honor of my Conduct with respect to Lieut. Hagan. He highly approved of Mr. Hagan's arrest & said He would recommend Him to resign. If He would not resign He would order a general-Court-Martial.

I then asked Genl. Schuyler for the Parole & Orders or who I should receive Orders from. The General said He should consider himself whilst at the German-Flatts in the Capacity of a Commissioner only: desired me to give out the Parole & Orders & Consider myself as the Commanding officer at this Place as well now as when He was absent. He said further, that He did not doubt but I knew my duty, would do it as a good Officer, and, as such (from the Character & Recommendation He had had of me) He should Confide in my Activity & Vigilance in Ordering the Guards & Centerys for the Security of his Person the Camp Ammunition & Stores. Exercised the Companies P.M. The generals aide-de-camps and other officers said that there were no Troops in the Continental Service equal to them in discipline. Sundry Indians of the Senecka [Seneca]-Tribe came to Town this Evening.

The following were the Orders of the day.

Parole, Schuyler.
Officer of the day tomorrow, Lt. Cloke.

A Court Martial will be held precisely at the hour of Nine wherof, Capn. Sharp is Presidant, Lieut. Cannon, Lieut. Elmer, Pierson & Cloke are members.

All Settlers in & about the Camp at the German-Flatts are hereby strictly charged not to sell any Liquors to any of the Soldiers quartered in this place Nor to any Indians attending the Treaty, nor to any Persons that will supply the Soldiers or Indians with Liquors.

All suttlers[1] & Retailers of Liquors are also forbid going carrying or sending any Liquors to Fort-Stanwix without the Express leave of the Commanding Officer at Fort Stanwix.

These orders are Issued by direction of Major-General Schuyler.
JOS. BLOOMFIELD.
The Adjutant for the time being will carry & Read these orders to every Suttler &c.

Lodged in the Court house.

I forgot to Mention that the Camp was alarmed last night by one of the Centerys of my Company firing on a Soldier of Capn. Isinlords Company, who was going out of the Camp upon *urgent Business*, & never answered the Centery when called upon three times. Both Companys formed agreable to orders of the 15th Inst. After inquiring into the Matter I commended the Centery, put the Culprit in the Guard-house &

dismissed the Men after applauding them for their activity in turning out.

¹Sutler. A trader who follows an army and sells provisions and liquor to the troops.

Wednesday. 17. [July]. Orders of the day.

Parole, Elizth. Town.
Officer of the day tomorrow Lieut. Gifford.
Lieut. Gifford with 20 Men the Drum & fife-Major well equipped & Neatly dressed will parrade before the Generals Door in order to attend his Honor as life-Guards over the Mohawk-River. A Sarjant & four Men from my Company are constantly to attend the General by day. Guards as usual.

A.M. waited on the General who was much engaged with the Senecka Tribe who came to salute the Genl. & ask the News, &c. at xii [o'clock]. Attended the Genl. with the Commisss. & Gentlemen of the army to reconitre a proper Place for a Fort. Crossed the Mohawk in Batteaus & returned by 3 P.M. no place being thought proper on the other side of the River. Agreable to the orders of yesterday the following return was made.

At a Regimental Court-Martial held by order of Capt. Bloomfield at the German-Flatts 16th & 17th of July 1776.
Capn. Anthony Sharp, President. Lieut. James Cannon, Ebenezer Elmer, Daniel Pierson, & Jacob Cloke, Members.
Jonathan Lummis & Thomas Parker Corporals, Charles Cosgrove Private in Capn. Bloomfield's Company Charged with going from Parrade & being absent during Exercise without leave in the Evening of the 15th Inst. in disobedience of Orders, Lying out of Quarters & being absent one mile from Camp without leave, and absenting themselves from Roll-Call & Exercise in the Morning of the 16th Inst.
Upon examination of Corporals Lummis [and] Parker it appears by their own Confession they are guilty of the above charge except that of being one mile from Camp.
The Court Martial considering the above Crimes sentence them to be reduced to the ranks & Confined seven days upon bread & Water.
Upon examination of Charles Cosgrove it appears by his own confession he is guilty of lying out of his quarters & not attending Roll-Call. For which the Court sentenced him to be confined seven days on bread & Water & reprimanded at the head of the Company by Capt. Bloomfield.
ANTHONY SHARP, PRESIDENT.
I approve of the above sentence except the Prisoners Confinement & being fed on Bread & Water, which is hereby remitted.
JOS. BLOOMFIELD.

Accordingly at Evening Exercise Lummis & Parker were sent for under-guard & sent into the Ranks with orders to go on Centery to Night. Cosgrove was reprimanded & also ordered on Centery.

Major Ranselear[1] one of the Genls. Aid-de-Camps waited on me this Evening informing me that Genral Schuyler had Ordered Capn. Veeders & Capn. Vosburgh's Companys of Provincial Troops from Col. Wincoops Regt. to join my Corps & do duty in Garrison under my Command. Soon after I was introduced to the two Capts. who said their Men were much fatigued with their march arriving only to Day & hoped they could be excused from duty tonight which was complyed with.

Seventy two Indians from the Canojaharee Castle or Fort Hendrick of the Mohawk-Tribe came in in Indian-file this Evening fireing & hallooing & dancing after the Indian-Manners out of Respect as they said to the General.

Lodged in the house contiguous to the Camp with the General & his Life Guards of Officers.

Very unwell & took Physick this afternoon.

[1]JAMES VAN RENSSELAER (d. 1827). Aide-de-camp to Major General Philip Schuyler, June–August 1776. A New York Continental who began his service in 1775 as an aide to ill-fated Brigadier General Richard Montgomery.

Thursday. July 18th. Orders of the day.

Parole, General Heard.
Officer of the day tomorrow Lieut. Pendleton.
Capt. Veeders & Vosburghs Companys being ordered by Major-Genl. Schuyler to join the Troops & do duty in Garrison, are hereby directed to attend Roll-Call & Exercise in Camp at the beat of the Drum Morning & Evening.
    Capt. Bloomfield's Company will form on the right at their usual place. Capt. Veeders on the left Capt. Vosburgs on the right in the Center & Capt. Isinlords on the left in the Center.
    In case of any alarm, All the Companys will immediately form & repair to the Church & Parrade within the stockade where they shall be properly supplyed with Ammunition & receive further Orders.
    The orderly sarjant of the day from every Company will attend at the Sarjants *Call* precisely at Ten O'Clock in order to make Returns of their Companies & receive the Orders of the day from Mr. Thomas appointed adjutant for the time being.
    The Guards will consist of three Sarjants, two Corporals, & forty Privates, 11 from Bloomfield's, 10 from Feders [Veeders], 8 from Vosburgs & 11 from Isinlord's Company's. A Sarjant & four Men from my Company will hereafter attend the General by day.

By Invitation Dined with the General & Commissioners &c. No Exercise P.M. it raining Very hard.

I have been so hurryed with business & being unwell withall that I havn't been able to mention every particular daily as it occurs, but will now take Notice that on Tuesday [July 16] P.M. the day the General arrived, One Peter Rikerman an Indian Trader [came?] from Niagara Accompanied by twenty one Senecas. He left the Fort under pretence of going out to shoot Pigeons, accompanied by his Son a young Man but had previously communicated his Design to a few of the Indians who conducted him safely. He informs that the Fort at Niagara is exceeding well fortifyed & the Garrison consists of about 2100, expected to have been invaded in the spring & that had any considerable body of our People appeared the Garrison instead of opposing would have gladly received them owing chiefly to a scarcity of Provisions for several months which continued to the eighth of May when supplys arrived from Detroit. They have but few Indians there & those few are detained by almost constant Intoxication. Five days march from Niagara Mr. Rickman met a Captain three Lieuts. three Soldiers & a guide who had made their Escape from Pensilvania haveing broke their Parole & were then going to Niagara. By Mr. Rikman we also hear that Sir John Johnson suffered greatly on his march to Oswegacha, many of his Party dyed, some say fifteen and that it was said that he was gone to Montreal. The Seneka Tribe Mr. Rickeman thinks are friendly. They are more attached to us than several tribes nearer us. They have taken great pains to draw off the few who are at Niagara but strong Liquor is too powerful for their Arguments & Entreaties. Tuesday P.M. Mr. Dean the Indian Interpreter & Mr. Kirkland the Minister that lives amongst the Oneidas set out for Oneida & Onondago to hurry the Indians down to the Treaty.

And yesterday arrived 174 Indians chiefly of the Onenhoghgwage [Onondaga] Tribe of Oneidas, part of them were Tuscaroras who living in the Neighbourhood chose to Accompany them rather than their own Nation. Mr. Crosby a Worthy Minister who is Missionary to those Indians accompanied them. They are Very Civil & almost all profess the Christian faith. They very soon made themselves little Houses or sheds covered with Bark which shelters them from the Rain. Generally two of those sheds 10 or twenty feet long faced each other, Contained several families & one fire in the middle supplyed both. They have their Squaa's & Children with them. The Squaa's are generally at work makeing Mockinsons & such other Things as they use themselves or expect to sell to us. They are here almost as much at home as any where else especially as we supply them with Provisions.

Friday. 19. [July]. Major-Genl. Schuyler's Orders. (vizt.)

Head-Quarters German-Flatts
July 19th. 1776.

General-Orders,

First Lieut. Robert Hagan & second Lieut. Samuel Hazelett both of the 3d. New-Jersey Regimt. Commanded by Col. Elias Dayton, being by sickness rendered incapable of doing duty in the Regiment & haveing requested leave to resign their Commissions, the General has accepted their Resignations which causing a Vacancy & Promotion in the Regiment, the General has been pleased to promote second Lieut. William Gordon to the rank of first Lieut. Ensign Joseph Anderson & Cornelius Hennean to the rank of Second Lieuts. in the said Regimt. He has also been pleased to appoint Messrs. *Edmond Disney Thomas* & John Kinney Voluntiers in said Regimt. to be Ensigns therein.

By order of the General.
JAMES VAN RENSELAER
Aid de Camp.

Lieut. Hagan finding He must be tryed by a genl. Court-Martial in Consequence of his behaviour & arrest mentioned (July 14th.) that He could not be Acquitted with Honor & Very probably be broke, desired me to make application to the General for leave to Assign the Reason mentioned in his resignation with Mr. Hazelett who in reality is incapable through sickness of doing duty, which was accordingly done, We all being glad to get rid of an Indolent slothful officer who Valued himself more upon the Cock of his Hat & the Powdering of his Hair & strideing about the Camp than doing his duty as a good officer.

If He had done his duty He would not have been Arrested. If it had been the first time He had been remiss when on Guard, it would have been looked over with a reprimand only.

The General Issued his General-orders in Consequence of these Gentn. resigning & made the Promotions upon Mr. Calldwell's, Capt. Sharp's & my Application. P.M. I waited on the Genl. & Introduced Messrs. Thomas & Kinney when the General gave me the orders mentioned, at the same time informed the Young Gentn. of their appointment wishing they might derive Crdt. & Honor from their Commisss. as He did not doubt they would by the recommendations He had had of them.

And at the same time commended me for my spirited bahaviour with respect to my Arresting Mr. Hagan.

After drinking a glass of Wine or two we left the Genl. after Returning him our thanks for his Friendship.

After the Evening's Exercise I informed the Companys of the Promotions by reading the Generals Orders, & directing the Soldiery that as Messrs. Thomas & Kinney were now Ensigns in the Regt. they should Respect & treat them as such accordingly. Orders of the day.

Parole: The States of New-Jersey
Officer of the day tomorrow, Lieut. Solsberry.
Guards as usual.

The Rev'd Mr. Calldwell our Worthy Chaplain this P.M. visited one of the Indian Incampments & brought seven Chiefs of the Onenhogh-gwagaa Tribe & their Minister to drink Tea with us. They could not speak English but were Very social & pleasant among themselves & with us as far as we could converse by an Interpreter. After Tea, a Drink of Cyder & a Pipe or Two. Good *Peter,* one of their Chiefs, addressed Mr. Calldwell in the Indian Language to this effect, "Father, we all thank you; we did not expect this invitation & this kind Treatment, it makes us Glad; You have our best Wishes & thanks." Mr. Calldwell replied, "that He was Very glad to see them: He loved them as Children, and when they returned to their own homes He should still feel the Heart of a Father for them." After shaking us heartily by the hand they bid us fare well in their Dialect & retired.

I forgot to mention that in the forenoon 12 of their Principal Men had waited upon the Commissioners with a short congratulatory address, to this effect, "Brothers We are glad to see You here, asesing You are engaged in War. We all Pity, Our Women & Boys Pity You. All will catch Your Tears & with this string will wipe Your Blood if any should be shed." Suitable replys were made & after some social Chat with us & one another, & Cautioning the General not to give any Liquor to any shooting Indians who might Come from their Camp, and cautioning one another they withdrew.

Saturday. 20. [July]. Parole, Montgomery. Very unwell A.M. Took ziss de Sal. Glauber. [Glauber's salts][1] which did not agree Very well with my Bowels. Lt. Solsberry of Capt. Vosburgh's Company dined with me. Was Visited by the famous Capt. Soloman & his Lieut. Deputies to the Treaty from the Stockbridge Indians. This Capt. Solomann has been to Europe & Introduced to his Majesty. His behaviour is quite different from the rest of the savages being Polite & remarkable free & Easy in conversation. He talks English Very fluently.

This Evening the Seneka-Nation of Indians had a Dance before the Generals Door for his Entertainment, which was very diverting. See July 23d.

[1]Glauber's salts. A compound of hydrated sodium sulfate used as a cathartic.

Sunday. July 21. 1776. Parole: Cato. Attended Church with all the Companys in*firm*, the General & all the Commissioners & his officers also attending. When our Worthy Chaplain delivered us two Sermons Very pertinent & suitable to the Occasion & altered one of Watt's Psalms so as leave out the King & Britain & bring in the "United States of America" to the great satisfaction of his Audience. See 145th. Psalm. Dined with the Genl. & Commissioners &c.

Monday. 22. [July]. Orders from the Genl.

> Head-Quarters
> German-Flatts July 22d. 1776.

General Orders

A picket fortification is to be erected near the Church at this place. Capt. Bloomfield will superintend the work, and make out a Detail of the Number of Officers & Men each Corps is daily to furnish, and the commanding Officer of every Corps will accordingly furnish his Quota agreable to such detail, The men to work eight hours a day to begin and leave off, work at such times as Capt. Bloomfield shall direct; Three pence a day will be allowed to each Non-Commisioned-Officer & private in lieu of Rum to encourage them to go on with the Work with Alacrity & Dispatch to be weekly paid by Capt. Bloomfield who will be furnished with money for the purpose.

By order of Major-Genl. Schuyler

> JAMES VAN RANSALAER.
> Aid de Camp.

In consequence of the above, the following orders were issued.

Parole: Ticonderoga.
Officer of the day tommorrow, Lieut. Bates.
The Guards hereafter are to consist of Two Sarjants 2 Corporals & 24 Privates.

Every officer & Soldier except those upon guard shall appear upon the parade in the morning at the Revallie beating, at which time such a Number of Officers & Soldiers from each Company as may hereafter be directed shall repair to their working Posts diligently to labour two hours; and then retire to Breakfast. After one hour & a half every one as Afd. [aforesaid] shall parrade again & repair to labor three hours, & then return to Dinner.

After two hours intermission all are to parrade again as above, Labor three hours more & be dismissed for that day.

For Fatigue or Working Party Captn. Bloomfield's Company will turn out 26 Privates daily, Captn. Veeders 9, Capn. Vosburghs 6, Capn. Isinlords 19, the whole Consisting of 60 Privates. Every 15 privates are to be officered with One Commissioned & two Non-Commissioned officers who will turn out & labor as before directed.

Lieuts. Gifford & Solsberry & Ensign Thomas will go out upon fatigue with the working Party tomorrow.

> JOS. BLOOMFIELD

Agreable to the Generals-Orders, I had the ground surveyed & with the Assistance of Mr. Calldwell laid out the ground & Lines & sett the Officers & Men to work. We began to brake ground to fortyfy by ax & dug the Intrenchment for the Pickets fort one Line this day, the officers & Soldiers working with the greatest cheerfulness & activity, in endeavoring to outvie each other in the different tasks assigned them. P.M. Col. Dayton arrived from Fort Stanwix & lodged with us.

Tuesday. 23. [July]. Notwithstanding it is mentioned to have been wrote the 23d of July, I have sett the accts. down as my time & business wd. allow. The following is a brief description of the Indian-Nations attending the Treaty, by the various Accounts I have collected, vizt.

The five Nations consist of so many Tribes or Nations joined together by a league or confederacy like the united Provinces, and without any superiority. This union has been time immemorial. They are known & distinguished by the Mohawks, Oneydaes [Oneidas], Onondagas, Cayugas, & Seneka's. The Tuskaroras, after a War it is said they had with the People of Carolina, fled to the five Nations, and are incorporated with Them; so that now, indeed, they properly consist of six Nations. Each of them is again divided into three different Tribes, who distinguish themselves by three different arms, viz, the Bear, the Tortoise and the Wolf; The sachems put that belonging to their Tribe to every publick Paper.

They think themselves by Nature superior to the rest of Mankind, and assume the Name of Ongue-honwe, that is, Man surpassing all others. This Opinion gives them that carriage, which has been so terrible to all the Nations of North-America; and that Opinion they have taken such care to [impress?] on all their Neighbours, that on all Occasions they yield to them the most submissive Obedience. They have such absolute Notions of Liberty, that they allow of no kind of Superiority, and banish all servitude from their Territories.

An old Mohawk Sachem, in a poor Blanket & dirty shirt, Issues his orders, with as arbitrary an authority as a Roman dictator. The Authority of their Sachems who govern in publick affairs as well that of their Captains consists wholly, and is only obtained by the good Opinion the Nation have of the Wisdom & integrity of the former, and of the Courage & Conduct of the latter; and they loose it by a failure in those Virtues.

Their Instruments of War are Muskets Hatchets, and long sharp-pointed Knives; these they always carry about with them. The Hatchet in war-time, they stick in their girdle behind; and they have the art of directing & regulating its motion, so, that though it turns round as it flies, the edge always sticks in the tree, near the place they aim at. The use of bows & arrows is not entirely laid aside, except among the Boys, who use them with surprizeing dexterity. Their Castles or Towns are generally square surrounded with Pallisadoes, without any bastions or out Works. They express peace by the metaphor of a Tree & fire, and all Indians make use of a Hatchet or ax as an emblem of War.

Wampum is the current money among the Indians, it is of two sorts, white & purple; the white is worked out of the inside of the great Conques [conch], into the form of a Bead, & perforated, to string on Leather. As the Indians live far from the Sea, our people make & sell the Purple or exchange them for Beaver-skins &c. and many, at Albany particularly, make a handsome living by that Trade. The purple is worked out of the inside of the muscle [mussel] shell; they are wove as broad as one's hand, & about two feet long; these they call belts, & give and receive at their Treaties, as the seals of Friendship; for lesser matters, a single string is given. Every bead is of a known Value and a belt of a less Number is made to equal one of the greater, by so many as are Wanting, fastened to the belt by a string.

One hundred of those Beads are usually valued at 4/. per 200, 8/. & so on, & in this manner they trade & barter with each other & with all that deal with them.

I will now describe the Indian-Dance mentioned a Saturday Evening July 20. The Indians were painted after their usual manner, Red, Black, blue & every colour in their power. Those who dance are Naked, except their Breach-Clout & Ornaments. Those who dance are the Youngest Men. The Chiefs are Spectators & Conductors. The middle State conduct the music. One beats upon a Keg over the head of which is streached a skin. The others round him join their Voices, He who beats setting the tune. Their Notes are few, but soft, & all keep time & Tune with the greatest exactness. Every one who sings has two little sticks which He beats together in concert with the Drum. Round these the Dancers perform after their manner, which consist of Violent exertions & according to some rules. Once in the space of two Minutes, they step with a shout in which they exert their Voice to the Utmost. The Singers are grave & the Dancers full of pleasantry. After a little pause the Music begins & the dance goes on they stomp violently upon the ground & Exert themselves to great fatigue. This dance seems calculated to enure to harden & to render the Muscles Vigorous. In the midst of the dance one of chief Warriors who was a spectator steps forward & strikes with a stick, which produced a instant pause. In a short speech He related his warlike exploits, the Prisoners & Scalps taken from other Nations appealing to those who were Witness, and then finished with a present of a

little paint wrapped up in paper which he had received from the Commissioners for that purpose. This was received by all with great marks of
applause. Some time after, another Chief & then another did in like manner. This custom is intended in the time of their mirth to Inspire them
with a thirst for War & an emulation to have the like Opportunity
publickly to relate their gallant deeds. The Seneka's are taller & better
proportioned than the other Indians present or the whites, And from
their healthful fleshy appearance, are more temperate & better fed than
the other Indians.

Every Indian-Nation has something peculiar in their own Customs &
Manners different from each other.

The Indians in general are tall & straight in their limbs, beyond the
proportion of the whites. Their bodies are strong; but of such a species
of Vigour, as is rather adapted to endure much hardship, than to continue long at any servile works: it is the strength of a beast of prey, rather
than a beast of burthen. Their Bodies & heads are flattish, the effects of
Art fro[m] the Squaa's carefully brace their Children or papoosses's till
they walk alone on a Broad board to which they lace the Infant with
broad Cloths carrying them on their shoulders in all their Journies, for
Most of them for the sake of the Presents given at the Indian Treaties,
take their whole Familys with them, carrying & lugging such
Papooosse's as are unable to walk in this slavish manner. The Cottages
in the meantime, are shut up & there being no furniture to lose, a string
or thong of leather serves for a lock. Their features are regular but their
countenances fierce; their Hair (those that wear it) long in general Very
black, lank & Very strong. They have no beards owing to custom of
continually drawing it out by the roots with twisted wires. The colour of
their skin a reddish brown, admired amongst them; and improved by the
const. use of Bear's fat & paint. They in general go naked except a Clout
which they wear to cover their Nakedness, Once in a While throwing a
Blanket over their Shoulders. The Squaa's dress in the same manner,
only they always wear a striped Blanket, striped with Red or Yellow
ferryiting [ferreting][1] or Ribbons agreable to their quality in life & and
those stripes are generally on the middle of the Blanket & covered with
silver & brass Broaches of all sizes.

Their only Occupations are hunting & War; Vide Friday June 28th.
remarks. Agriculture is left to the Women. Merchandize they contemn.
When their Hunting Season is past, which they go through with much
patience, & in which they exert Ingenuity, and their Provisions laid up,
they pass the rest of their time in an entire indolence. They sleep half the
day in their Tents, they loiter & jest among their Friends, and they observe no bounds or decency in their eating & drinking. They are exces-

sive fond of spirituous Liquors, and the desire of acquiring these is a principal End they pursue in their Treaties with us: & from this they suffer inexpressible Calamities, for haveing once begun to drink they can preserve no measure, but continue a succession of drunkenness as long as their means of procuring liquor last. In this condition they lie exposed on the ground to all the Inclemency of the seasons, which wastes them by a train of the most fatal Disorders. They perish in rivers & marshes, they tumble into the fire, they quarrel & Very often murder each other. And in short excess of Drinking, with us highly Criminal, & which is not generally Very pernicious in its effects as among this uncivilized People, who have not art enough to guard against the consequences of their Vices, is a public calamity. The few among them who live free from this evil, enjoy the reward of their temperance in a robust & healthy old age. The Disorders which a Complicated Luxury has introduced & supported amongst us are strangers to the Savages.

The Education of the Indians from their Infancy is solely directed to fit their Bodies for this mode of Life, & to form their Bodies & Minds to endure the affliction of the greatest evils.

As I said before, Almost the sole Occupation of the Indians is war, or such Exercises as qualify him for it. His whole Glory consists in this: and no man at all is considered till he has increased the strength of his Country with a Captive or adorned his Hut with the Scalp of one of its Enemies. And these Scalps are so many evidences of the Trophies of their Bravery.

The Character of the Indians is striking. They are grave even to sadness, upon any serious Occasion; observant of those in Company, respectful to the old, of a temper cool deliberate, by which they are never in haste to speak before they have thought well on the matter, & are sure the person who spoke before them has finished all he had to say; they have therefore the greatest contempt for the vivacity of our People who interrupt each other, & frequently speak altogether.

Nothing is more edifying than their behaviour in their public Councils & Assemblies; every man there is heard in his turn, According as his Years, Wisdom, or service to his Country, have ranked him. Not a Word, not a Wisper, not a murmur is heard from the rest, whilst He speaks; no indecent condemnation, no ill-timed applause. The younger sort attend for their Instruction. Here they learn the History of their Nation; here they are inflamed with the songs of those who celibrate the Warlike Actions of their Ancestors; and here they are taught what are the Interests of their country, & how to pursue them.

Their habitations are Very small, consisting only of a little cottage, in the middle of which is their fire-place: here both they and the Animals they breed, live promiscuosly. They have a particular fondness for Dogs, & never are without three or four little curs in their huts; a hog or two, and a little poultry, with some earthen ware, as pots and jugs, & the Cotton which their Wifes spin, constitute the whole Inventory of an Indian's effects. Their beds consist of two or three sheep-skins, without Pillows or any thing else; and on these they sleep in their usual squatting posture; and as they never undress, appear always in the same garb.

The above Acct. of the Indians must serve for the present, as I shall be daily more & more acquainted with their manners. I will sett down hereafter promiscusly such observations as Occur & strike my fancy, considering at the same time, my *time* & business.

Awoke & arose to business agreable to Orders of Yesterday & with our Worthy active Parson, laid out the lines of the Fort & sett the fatigue-Party to work, & who by Night finished the lines being (2 feet wide & 4 feet deep) so as to be ready for the Pickquets, which began to be brought in this Evening being large heavy & 20 feet long. These Pickquets when put up will defend our Lines, and with the Natural situation of the Place & a deep Ditch in front of the stockade will make our fortification formidable to our Enemys; especially as on the different angles will be placed small Artillery to secure the Lines in case of a close Attack. Within this stockade is included a convenient House suitable for the officers & a Very large Barn which will serve for Barracks for the Soldiery, also a Very good Well. 500 Men can fight at once on the Lines & it is so constructed as to be defended by half that Number of Men.

In the Evening went to the General's Bowry. Whilst there an Express came to the General, from Genl. Washington informing him all was well at New-York.

Also the Rev'd Mr. Kirkland & some of the principal Chiefs from the Oneida-Castle, particularly the Chiefs *White-Skin* & *Grasshopper*, who treated me with a good deal of kindness when at the Oneida-Castle (see June 28 antea).

After the usual salutation of *Sago*-ongh Ottachagousola (How do you do Brother, or Friend?) & shaking of hands they sat down beside the General & Commisss. The Genl. ordered Liquor & Pipes immediately, Light his Pipe & drank to them, by wishing them Welcome & signifying He was glad to see them in health & peace, which was interpreted to them. They in their turn by their Chief *Grasshopper* (which is his name in their languague being Cheeastawaliosottee) said "They were glad to see the General & Commissioners that God had permitted them to meet again in [Health?] to drink one another's health & smoak a friendly Pipe together."

White-Skin drank their Health & the United States wishing them prosperity. After smoaking a Pipe or two & hearing the News, they retired, it being first Settled that the Treaty should open in two days hence, as all the Onendagoes & Tuscaroras will then arrive.

Returned to camp with my fellow-Lodger who are at present—Col. Dayton being down from fort-Stanwix otherwise called Fort Schuyler, Mr. Timothy Edwards[2] one of the Commissioners of Indian-Affairs, The General's aid-de-Camp being Major Livingston from Elizth. Town, and the worthy Mr. Calldwell my Assistant in fortyfying Fort [entry incomplete].

The following being the *Lord's-Prayer* in the Mohawk Tongue, may serve as a specimen of the Indian-Language in general, there being but little Variation, except in the pronunciation. (vizt.)

The Lord's Prayer: Ra, odereanayent ne Royaner.
Songywanika ne Karongyage tighsideron, wasaghnadogeaghtine. Sara-yert sera iewa, tagserra Eighniawewan, siniyought Karongyagough, oni oghwansiage. Niyadwighniseroge taggwanadara nondaghsik nonwa: Neon-itondag warighwiyoughston, siniyught oni Jakwadadouighwiyoughstan i: Neonitoghsadaghgwasarineght, dewaddatdennageraghtangge nesane sed-jadagwaghs me Kondighserokeanse, kea sayanertsera ne naagh, Neoni, ne kaeshatste, Neoni ne Onweseachtakne siniyeheinwe Neoni siniyekeinwe. AMEN.

The *Mohawk*-Nation pronunce their Words long soft, full, low & with suprizeing sweetness. The *Oneydoes* on the contrary pronunce their words very short harsh & with a great deal of roughness. The Seneka & Cayugas Language differs considerably from both.

[1]Ferreting. A narrow piece of tape used to bind or edge a fabric.
[2]TIMOTHY EDWARDS. On July 13, 1775, the Continental Congress named Philip Schuyler, Joseph Hawley, Turbutt Francis, Oliver Wolcott, and Volkert P. Douw members of the Board of Commissioners for Indian Affairs in the northern department. Edwards must have joined this group shortly thereafter, probably as a deputy commissioner. Besides the German Flats conference under consideration here, Edwards was present at a conference held at Albany, April 1776, and at one which also met in Albany, September 1777. In that latter conference, the Oneidas and Tuscaroras, as well as a smattering of Onondagas and Mohawks, accepted the war hatchet on behalf of the Americans.

June 20th. 1776. A Report of Captn. Bloomfields Company in Camp on the German Flats. This report was carefully taken by Lieut. Elmer at my desire & Returned to the Coll. by me. Jos. BLOOMFIELD.

	Subalterns	Voluntiers	Serjeants	Corporals	Drum & Fife	Privates
Present fit for Duty	3	2	4	3	2	55
On Duty, Capt. Bloomfield	—	—	—	—	—	5
Sick, Present	—	—	—	—	—	2
Sick, Absent	—	—	—	1	—	5
Deserted	—	—	—	—	—	7
Dead		—	—	—	—	2
Present	3	2	4	3	2	62
absent sick deserted etc:	—	—	—	1	—	15
Totals	3	2	4	4	2	77

Total absent,   16
Total Present,   74
                 90

Tents to be Drawn for, Exclusive of Voluntiers 72 Soldiers which is 12
Tents allowing Six men to a Tent,   12
Officers,   2
Voluntiers including Mr. Dean,   1
For Capt. Bloomfield's Company
Tents,   15
I have 3 Washer-Women besides.
Jos. BLOOMFIELD.

Volume 2
July 24, 1776–February 12, 1782

JOURNAL: kept whilst in the Continental-Service: Began the 8th. of February 1776. and continued in this Book from the 24th. of July 1776. and ended the [12th] day of [February 1782] by JOSEPH BLOOMFIELD, Major of the 3d. New-Jersey Regt. & Inspector to the Jersey-Brigade.

Wednesday. July the 24th. German-Flatts on the Mohawk-River. Arose Very early this Morning. Immediately attended & have been engaged all day in overseeing the fortification now erecting in this place, by direction of Major-Genl. Schuyler, as before mentioned July 22d. Col. Coxe's Militia drew Pickets all day. Dined with the General Commissioners & officers of the Army, who had a Visit paid them after Dinner by the Chiefs, Sachems & Warriors to the amount of near 100. of the Oneydoes, who arrived to day, & came to pay their Respects & Return the belts which summoned them down, to the General.

Genl. Schuyler made them a speech, which they readily answered, Complimenting one another Very highly, after which the Genl. ordered Pipes, Tobacco & Grogg (as is usual upon such Occasions) to Drink each other's Health, at the same time, thanking the supreme being that they were permitted to meet, & smoak a friendly Pipe together & prepare to kindle a Council-Fire. After much conversation in which they shewed a great deal of Wit & pleasantry, as it was interpreted to us. They parted in the Evening with the usual Greetings.

The following may serve for a description of this Country.

The German-Flatts lye on the Mohawk-River about 40 or 50 Miles above John'stown, is one or two miles wide & 5 or 6 long, exceeding rich & fertile. On either side are very high mountanous Hills, over these Mountains the Land is flat & rich. The Mohawk-River seems to run all the way from Schinactaday to Fort-Schuyler, which lies at the head of the River through a ridge of Hills & Mountains with a rich Valley between, which is very rich & fertile & where the Dutch the Inhabitants of this fertile Country raise Vast Quantitys of Peas which they carry down the Mohawk-River in Batteaus to Albany, & is what we call the *Albany Peas*. At the Head of these Flatts is my present Post, where on the North-side of the Flatts a Creek makes out called Lower-Canada Creek about one third as large the River. Upon both sides of this Creek & up & down the river lies the famous Tract of 120,000 Acres of the finest Land in America, belonging to Sr. William Johnson's Estate; whose Family by being Tories, have forfeited his & their other Estates to the Colonies.

This Country, particularly this Place is remarkable for Fogs. Almost every morning a Fog like a Cloud ariseth from the rivers or Mountains & falls like a fine Rain, or if it does not fall in this mist it generally falls in heavier Showers before Night.

Here I see that passage of the Psalmist (mentioned 104th. Psm: 8th. Verse) remarkably fulfilled: where speaking of the Waters, He saith, *"They go up by the Mountains, They go down by the Valleys, unto the place thou hast founded for them."*

Here we see the vapour rise, sometimes in smaller Columns and sometimes in larger; and presently form a Cloud, which breaks over the Mountains & pours down upon us. By this means the Country is watered.

These are some of the wonderfull Works of God, of whose Goodness the Universe is full.

Thursday. July 25. 1776. Engaged all day in overseeing the Picquets brought in as yesterday. Wrote home to my friends today, by an Express from Genl. Schuyler to Genl. Washington.

Invited Joseph an Indian Sachem & 2 others of the Onandagoes & Abraham, a Lieut. of the Stockbridge Indians, to drink tea with me, which they Accepted & behaved with a good deal of Modesty. This Joseph was in the American-Army at Boston last Summer & staid some time this spring with Genl. Washington in New-York where he was greatly caressed & Dined every day with his Excellency.

Friday. 26. [July]. Began this morning & Engaged all day in raising the Pickets & securing the stockade. I forgot to mention that last Evening I restored Jonathan Lummis & Thomas Parker mentioned before (July the 17th.) to their former station of Corporals. Spent the Evening at the Generals.

Saturday. 27. [July]. Necessity drove me to order a Court-Martial today wh. made the following report.

At a Regimental Court-Martial held by order of Capt. Bloomfield at the German-Flatts July 27th. 1776. Capt. Garret Veadder President, Lieut. Wm. Gifford, Pendleton, Cannon & Elmer members.

Michael Reynolds of Bloomfield's Coy. accused of Lodging out of Camp in disobedience of orders, Nonattendance at Roll-Call this morning & attempting to leave the Company without leave. (after mentioning the Evidence) The Court Martial considering the above crimes do sentence him, to be led to the post stripped & tyed thereto for the space of a quarter of an hour & afterwards dismissed to his duty with the stoppage of One Weeks pay from his wages.

GERRIT S. VEEDER
Presdt. & Capn.

Which was approved in the following manner. "I approve of the above Sentence & order it put immediately into Execution." JOS. BLOOM-FIELD.

At the Roll-Call in the Evening the Companies were drawn round the Adjutant's Daughter (the Whipping-Post so called), The Prisoner tyed up & was exhorted by our Chaplain for his base Conduct & the Soldiery warned against bringing themselves to such a shamefull Punishment. I also spoke to my Company & the Prisoner, told them it gave me a great deal of Pain to see One of their Brother-Soldiers punished; but, at the same time, when I reflected He was not originally Inlisted with me but taken up as a Deserter from the 2[d.] Pennsylvania Battn., it was some alleviation of my Anxiety &c. &c. &c. After Prayers the Prisoner was released & Expressing himself in a haughty manner that He was punished, through spite, I ordered him immediately to be again Confined in the Guard-house. vid. July 31.

Sunday. July 28. Attended Meeting (with the Companies under my Command in form) & heard the Revd. Mr. Kirkland Indian Missionary from the Presbeterian Synod preach to the Indians in the Oneida-Language, the Oneidoe's being professors of the Christian-Religion & Presbeterians, attended in general. The Mohawk Nation, who are Episcopalians, also attended, & the Gentlemen of the Army, & some few Indians of the other Nations out of curiosity.

Mr. Kirkland first sang an Indian-Psalm, Prayed first in English, & then in Indian, Sang another Psalm in Indian & then Preached to them from [blank] (as he afterwards told us). After Sermon and Anthem well sung in the Oneida-Tongue & then the Congregation was dismissed after Prayers & the Blessing both in the English & Indian-Languages.

The great attention serious, solemn & devout Behaviour of those poor Savages, with the sweetest, best & most harmonious singing I ever heard, excited the steady attention & admiration of all present, & was an Example to the whites & at the same time a Reproof to the Christians, who haveing the Gospel allmost daily preached to them, pay no great attention (it being an old Story) & frequently behave with the greatest Rudeness during Divine service. The Oneydoes excel in singing. They carried all the parts of Music with the greatest Exactness & harmony.

Though I did not understand a word that was said, Yet I never paid greater attention or was more improved in attending divine Worship.

When I observed & Reflected with what reverence & solemnity the almost naked Savages, (the Men haveing a Clout only round them & the Women a skirt & Blanket wh. they covered themselves except their faces entirely) unless some few of the Heads & Chiefs & their squaas who were elegantly dressed with mockinsens Leggins &c. &c. after their Indian Fashion, I say, their devout Behaviour struck me with Astonishment & made me blush with shame for myself and my own People. In short we all came away after service greatly pleased with the Indians & Conscious of our own Inattention & want of Reverence during divine services in general. P.M. Attended Divine service with the Companies as in the Morning; when our Very Worthy & Patriotic Chaplain Preached (in the Presence of Genl. Schuyler & the officers of the Army & sundry Indians who returned our Complyment paid them in the Morning by their also attending Divine Worship deliverd in the English Language) from 2 Sam: X.12 "Be of good Courage, & let us play the Men for our People, & for the Cities of our God; & the Lord do that which seemeth him good." This Text being very suitable to the Occasion, was Delivered with a great deal of Judgement & applied particularly to those who bore the Military Character in such a Manner as to engage the attention of his Audience & Edify all present.

It is worth remarking that Very early in the Morning I heard the Dutch Domine preach in the High-German-Language, so that I heard Divine-Worship Delivered in three Tongues today. Besides I heard in the different Companies I was in, the following Languages spoke—1st. English, 2d High-Dutch, 3d. Low-Dutch, 4th. French, 5th the Mohawk, 6th. Oneydoes, 7th. Senekas, 8th. Cayugas, 9th. Tuscaroras & 10th. the Onondagoe-Languages. The most of those Tongues I heard daily spoke and one Person in particular a frenchman can speak French, English Low-Dutch & the five Indian-Languages.

I must also observe, that whilst the Religious Oneydoes were at their worship in the Morning, the Atheistical Seneka's Onondagoes & Cauyugas who believe there is no God & make a jest of all Religion were beating their Tub singing, Dancing & Carrusing in the most profane Manner. The Tuscaroras are Papists by Profession but in fact have no Religion. In short, the various scenes of this day I shall never forget, & hope whenever I reflect on it will excite a grateful sense of thankfulness to the supreme being who has placed me in such a situation in Life as to enjoy so many advantages above those poor Savages.

Monday. July 29. 1776. Engaged all day in overseeing the Erecting Pickets at the Fortification &c. &c. Two Grand matches were made up between the Oneydas & Tuscaroras at Ball, or what the Scott's call Golf. Near 100 Dollars worth of their Ornaments were staked each time, which were gained by the Tuscaroras. The Oneydas had been used to beat them at all set matches for many years till this day. At these Matches the Ornaments staked are generally collected from the Women who generously give some of their wampum, silver, Bead Bracelets, others their Earrings, nose-Jewels & Pins. Others give Necklaces, belts &c. & all kinds of Indian-Ornaments. They are remarkably fair in their play. Nothing that has the appearance of Cheating nor any Wrangles are seen on these Occasions. When the boys play together, or shoot for Coppers, all is fair & honest, & Courteous. The Indians when sober are remarkably cautious. They will hardly ever say or do a Thing that will give offence. If one supposes he has ground of offence or has received an Injury he will not shew it unless Drunk & has an opportunity for Revenge. This caution undoubtedly arises from their form of Government or rather being without Government. We are not afraid of offending because secured by the force of Government from revenge. This security they have not, & most therefore screen themselves by caution.

The Genl.-Officers of the Army; & all the Indians, Men & Women, attended at the matches at Ball to day.

This day I also saw in the field an Indian Squaa with two Babes, born in her hutt about three days before, & soon after her arrival. She was now out with them more than half a mile from Camp. The Mother & Infants appeared Very well. They were both bound upon their Boards or Cradles according to Custom, & one of them was carried by the Mother & the other by a little sister. The same Woman a few Years ago was taken in Travail upon the Road to a Treaty. She only halted by the wayside a few Minutes with another female friend till they received the stranger, bound it up, & marched after in the rear of the Company. With many of them it is a Custom to send the Newly delivered Woman out to Chop a Load of Wood & Carry it home upon her Back. This they say brings all the Joints & Bones to their place again. And their Women have been seen to be taken in Labour while out cutting their Wood. They lay down their ax wrap the Papoosses in their Blankets & bring them home upon their loads of Wood. I shall be more particular in giving an Acct. of the Indians & a description of their Play, before mentioned when my time will permit. See hereafter August 29th.

Tuesday. 30. [July]. Engaged between the hours of 2 & 3 P.M. on a Genl. Court-Martial for the trial of Lieut. Wm. McDonald (vid. Aug. the 1st.) This P.M. rode out in the Generals-Coach with Major Livingston, the Generals Aid-de-Camp, the Genl's Secretary Mr. Larson, Capt. McGee & other Gentmn. on Horseback. After riding over the German-Flatts we crossed the Mohawk-River 3 miles from this place. Drank Tea at Mr. Shoemakers & returned at 6, when the General & Gentm. of the army were much engaged in observing a total Eclipse of the Moon being most of the Time Visible.

Wednesday. July 31. 1776. Engaged on the Court-Martial as Yesterday. This day Tesconindoe[1] the Head-Warrior of the Oneydoes Dined with me. He made me a present of a Red-Belt or sash worked with beads as a Testimony of his regard, ariseing I suppose from my Visiting him when at the Oneyda-Castle & treating him with familiarity since He has been here. I forgot to mention or rather had not time to enter the Proceedings of a Regimental-Court Martial on Monday last.

At a Regimental Court-Martial held at the German-Flatts July 29th. 1776. by order of the Commanding Officer, whereof Capt. Vosburgh is President, Lt. Pendleton, Bates, Solsberry, & Ensign Thomas are members. (after mentioning the Evidence which is very lengthy.) The Court takeing into Consideration the Cases of the abovementioned Persons John Cook, Luke Jinnins, & James Newman do adjudge them guilty of Gameing & Cards to the Value of £7:00:0 & upwards & Order that they immediately make each other as good as they were before & pay four Shillings fine & be returned to their duty.

To which the following Assent was given:

I have Considered of the Sentences of the Court against the respective Prisoners within mentioned & do approve of the same except the fines imposed on John Cook &c. which is hereby remitted except so much as will pay for every Pack of Cards at the rate of 1/. [shilling] per pack that is as will be hereafter publickly destroyed by order of the officers of the respective Companies in this place agreable to the orders of this day.
                                        JOS. BLOOMFIELD. 29th. July 76.

Michael Reynolds mentioned 27th. Inst. haveing shewed great contrition for his misbehaviour &c. &c., he meant the Soldiers & no officer; was discharged.

[1]SKENANDOA (1706?–1816). Bloomfield's Tesconindoe was the long-lived Oneida chief Skenandoa (or alternate spellings). Reportedly a drunkard as a young man, reformed to become one of the most respected Iroquois leaders. Firm friend of colonists during French and Indian War, tried first to keep Iroquois neutral during the American Revolution. Later was influential in persuading many Oneidas and Tuscaroras to fight for the Americans. He was a devout Christian and friend of missionary Samuel Kirkland.

Thursday. August the 1st. This morning the Genl. Court-Martial held by order of Genl. Schuyler whereof Col. Van Dye is Presidt., Major Barber, Capts. Bloomfield, Sharp, Vedder, Vosburgh, Isinlord, Lieuts. Van Ransalear, Tuttle, Flannigan, Pendleton, Solsberry Cannon & Elmer are Members, finished their Proceedings with regard to Lieut. Wm. Mc.Donald, who was charged before the Court, "for behaving in a manner unbecoming the Character of an Officer & a Gentlemen, by takeing or Assisting in takeing out of the house of Sr. John Johnson at John's-town sundry effects, the Property of Sir John, or other Persons unknown & for aiding & abetting others so to do, & for Assisting in concealing effects so taken; as also for Disobedience of orders, to which Lt. McDonald pleaded not guilty. The Court for two days past have been engaged in Examining Evidences as well in support of the Charge as in favor of Mr. Mc.Donald.

The Court after reciting the Charge & Evidences made the following Report to Major-Genl. Schuyler.

> Whereupon the Court after the most serious & mature deliberation, were unanimously of Opinion that Mr. William Mc.Donald is guilty of the whole Charge exhibited against him & consequently guilty of a breach of the 27th. article for the Government of the Continental Troops as also of the second & last Article of the Amendment (that part of the Charge of the 2d. article expressed by the Term *Fraud* being only excepted); & therefore this Court do Sentence the said Wm. Mc.Donald to suffer the Penalties thereunto annexed.

Upon which, Genl. Schuyler's Genl. Orders were read in the presence of Mr. Mc.Donald by the Aid-de-Camp to the Troops at Roll-Call approving of the Sentence of the Court-Martial & after reciting the articles above referred to the orders say:

> The General therefore by Virtue of the said sentence & the said Articles of War hereby discharges the said Wm. Mc.Donald from the Continental Service, as a person unfit for further service as an officer & Orders that any Pay due to him be detained.
> The General with great satisfaction observes from the Proceedings of the Court-Martial that the Gentlemen haveing conducted themselves with a regularity that reflects Credit on them, & haveing no further Business for them dissolves the Court & they are dissolved accordingly.

This day another Match was played for near 60 £ between the Oneidas & Tuscaroras, when the former were successful.

Friday 2d. [August]. I forgot to mention that yesterday P.M. Mr. Kirkland brought 6 Men & about 12 Squaa's of the best singers of the Oneida-Nation to entertain the Col. & Company. They sing exceedingly well & were greatly admired by all present. Yesterday Evening also I attended a Dance at the Seneka-Camp & was greatly diverted with their odd manner of Dancing, which I have already described before.

This A.M. the General & Commissioners attended a Race for sundry Articles made up by them for the Indians to run for, in order to prevent their betting so high at Ball which might end in a quarrel &c. The Stakes being exposed to Public View all the Indian-Nations were invited to enter the Lists & run over the Ground which was 40 Rod over a Mile. At length near 20 started & ran over the ground in 5 Minutes & a half. The foremost was a Meningoe Indian, the second an Oneydoe & the third Prize was taken by a Tuscarora. P.M. Lieut. McMikell of Col. Dayton's Regt. came from *Oswego* (being sent with three Soldiers of his own Choice from Fort Stanwix on a scout) & brought intelligence that no Troops have yet arrived at Oswego but was informed by three Indians who came directly from Oswegatohea & two also from Niagary, that Col. Butler with all the Indians intended meeting Col. Johnson from Oswegatohe who was to be at Oswego by the 10th. Inst. with two Regts. of Regulars sundry Tories & Indians, when they were to fortify Fort *Oswego* & prepare for a treaty with the six Nations & afterward invest Fort-Stanwix. Lieut. Mc.Mikall passed for a Deserter.[1] Col. Dayton, Major Barber & Parson Calldwell sett out for Fort-Stanwix this P.M.

[1]Bloomfield evidently inserted this reference to Lieutenant McMichael later, as that officer was still with the army to have tea with Bloomfield on August 4 (see below). He must have deserted shortly thereafter (see entry of August 16).

Saturday. 3d. [August]. Three more Prizes given by the General & Commissioners were run for to day by 15 Indians of different Nations. The first Prize was won by a Senika the 2d. & 3d. by Oneydoe Indians.

One Cassady of Capt. Isinlords Company havg. been caught asleep on Century, I ordered a Court-Martial wh. reported the Prisoner Guilty & ordered him to receive 20 lashes which sentence was approved of in the usual form. At Roll call in the Evening the Prisoner was brought out & tyed to the stake & just as the Drummer was about performing his duty I sent the following Note to Lieut. Elmer acting Adjutant for the time being:

> Lieut. Elmer, you are hereby directed to postpone the Punishment of Edward Cassady till next Monday Evening when you'll see the sentence Executed.

This I did at the request of the officers of his Comy. See Monday next.

P.M. I was visited by sundry Oneydoe Indians, two of which were sachems sons, & had been Educated under Parson Wheelock[1] in New-England. They understood my Name was Bloomfield, and after consulting together they said they would give me my Sir-name in the Oneydoes-

Language & one of them wrote as follows—Bloomfield, or, a *Field*-in-Bloom, in the Oneydoes-Language, is Yo, chee, chiah, raw, raw, gou. And is pronounced Yoe gee geaau law law go*hh*.

They said they should hereafter call me by my right Name in their Language. I thanked them & told them I was much pleased with it & would carefully remember the Name. I ordered some Bottles of Porter & drank to them, they in return Calling me by my Indian Name Drank to me, and after learning how to pronounce this long Name by their frequently repeating it to me & makeing them Very merry they parted highly pleased with their Entertainment saying they should esteem me hereafter, as Teca otatago neons ol*aa,* as a "Brother & a Friend" in English.

[1]ELEAZAR WHEELOCK (1711–79). Native of Connecticut. Graduated from Yale College in 1733. Became pastor of the Lebanon, Connecticut, Congregational Church, 1735. Developed a consuming interest in the conversion and education of Indians. In charge of Moor's Charity School for Indians, 1754–68, and founded Dartmouth College with the same purpose, 1769. Served as president and was the dominant force at the college until his death.

Sunday. Augt. 4. 1776. Mr. Calldwell being at Fort-Stanwix & Mr. Kirkland Returned to Visit his Family we had no preaching today. Every One did what was right in his own Eyes. Lt. Mc.Mikall, Mr. Hagan & Mc.Donald dined with me today. P.M. was Visited by sundry Indian-Ladies to drink Tea with me.

Monday. 5. [August]. Engaged in the Morning in moving Ananias Sayres two miles over the Mohawk River on acct. of his haveing caught the small-Poxe. About 12 attended the funeral of one Mr. Helmer & Son who died Yesterday & were buried in one grave. The Son was 16 Years old, an awfull sight & which affected all present. After the Interrment I was Invited to go home with the Friends, which I accepted. We first had a sermon delivered to us in a Barn & their singing in High-German. After this went to the Widows of the deceased where we were Entertained with a Dinner under a Tree to the amount of 40 or 50 Persons in the most plentifull manner both with regard to Victuals & Liquors which was served up & the Attendants behaved more like Guests at a Wedding than sincere Mourners for such and a reflective dispensation of Providence. The Widow also attended & behaved with the greatest Calmness on the Occasion.

I forgot to mention that it is customary for the High-Dutch to sing all the time of the burial of the Body which was the case today, & always to prepare a sumptuous Entertainment for those who attend the funeral.

One Mr. Ichabod Bonney who said He formerly lived with my Grandfather & had married the Deceased's sister was present with his Wife & three Children who attended Table & were Masters of the Ceremony. Bonney tells me that He was taken Prisoner at Oswego & Carried to Oswegathea where he met with Mrs. Bonney who was also a Prisoner with all the Family of the Helmers being taken Prisoners & carried off when the German-Flatts was cutt off last War. There he got acquainted with her & after their return from Captivity they married, & settled on a tolerable good Farm, about 3 Miles up the River & live as I am told Very comfortably. About 230 Indians of the Seneka's & Cayugas came in this Evening. The Commissioners [told] me that there are now 1719 Indians including Women & Children in this Place & draw Rations accordingly.

Cassady mentioned the 3d. Inst. was brought to the stake & after being stript & tied to the Post was pardoned.

Tuesday. 6. [August]. Major Barber and Mr. Calldwell returned from Fort Schuyler formerly called Fort Stanwix but named last Week after Major-Genl. Schuyler by Col. Dayton & his officers in form, by manning the lines, fireing Cannon & Small Arms &c. &c. & Proclaiming the Fort which is now finished & called Fort Schuyler.

Spent the Evening at the Generals.

Engaged all P.M. in makeing out my Pay-Roll &c.

Wednesday. Augt. 7th. At Twelve, Major Genl. Schuyler Peter V. Dow[1] & Timothy Edwards Esqrs. the Commissioners for Indian-Affairs appointed by Congress proceeded in form attended by all the officers of the army in this Place neatly dressed with their side-arms to the place appointed & opened the Treaty with the six Nations. The Commissioners after Informing them of former Friendships & Treatys, mentioned wherein the six Nations had broken the Covenant Chain & now insisted upon their telling the Colonies what Part they intended to Act. If the six Nations would be still & take no part in our Family Quarrel we would treat them like Brothers & Protect them from our Enemies on the other side of the Water. On the Contrary if they intended to take up the Hatchet against us to tell us of it plainly. We would like them the better for it. We would let them go to their own homes, after that they must take the Consequence. The Commissioners also pointed out to them the advantages of their being in Friendship & as one People with the United States to defend their great Island from our Enemies on the other side of the Water &c. &c. &c. &c.

[1]PETER V. DOW [VOLKERT P. DOUW]. Local leader and gentleman politician in the area of Albany before and during the American Revolution. Served as the mayor of Albany, as a delegate to the New York Assembly, and as a local justice of the peace before the outbreak of war. Named a member of the Board of Commissioners for Indian Affairs in the northern department, 1775.

Thursday. 8th. Augt. 1776. Nothing material. The Indian sachems are much engaged in preparing to answer the Commissioners speech. In the Evening the Seneka-Warriors entertained the General with a Dance. Near 1200 Indians were present.

Friday. 9. [August]. Very unwell, took a Dose of Rhubarb. Towards evening the Sachems & Chiefs of the Six Nations Assembled & sent for the Commissioners who attended them with the Officers of the Army in form. But little or nothing was said more than to let the Commissioners know They were ready to answer their speech but as their Ancestors never spoke of Peace in the Evening they would answer next Morning. After some complyts. were passed in which they are Very artful & always speak in such A manner as to insinuate a little Liquor would be agreable, The General takeing their hint told them as they had been setting in Council all Day their Throats must be dry & heads confused that they would drink a little Toddy together to moisten their Throats & clear their Heads & smoake a friendly Pipe together, so as to be able to meet together in the Morning in Peace with clear heads & sound hearts. After this they parted. Dined at the General's today.

Saturday. Augt. 10, 1776. Arose at 4 & Engaged till 7 this Morn. in playing at the Game played by the Indians with Bats & Ball with a sett match of twelve officers chosen 6 of a side last Night. Lost one & won two Games. Attended at the General's last P.M. in [ord]er to [w]ait upon him with the officers to the Treaty. But the Indians were not prepared till 2 P.M., when we all attended the Commissioners to the Treaty.

Abraham the Mohawk-Chief answered for his Nation. His speech was full of trifyling Evasive answers & showed that the Mohawks acted more from fear in being still than Inclination. The Onondagoes & Senekas delivered their answer together & shewed very plainly that they were for Peace only when it was for their Interest to take up the Hatchet that they would not be answerable for the Conduct of their Young Warriors. The Cayugas in their speech said they were now for Peace but could not be answerable for the behavior of their Warriors. The Honest *Oneydoes* & *Tuscaroras* spoke together & said they were for Peace & always keeping in Friend-ship with their Brothers on this great Island, that they did not intend to interfere in our Family Quarrel, that they should remain quiet at home & what they said they intended to follow, & called God to witness the sincerity of their Intentions. They all said they were sorry for the Imprudence of their Warriors & that they would bury the Hatchet, by giving a Belt, under a Rock immoveable.

After this Drinking & smoaking as usual concluded the day. Several Belts were given by each Nation in confirmation of what they said. A Belt was given by the Commissioners with the 13 United States represented by as many squares on one End of a large Wampum Belt & the Six Nations by as Many squares on the other End. Two Persons shakeing hands in the middle represented the Unity & M[utual] Friendship of the 13 United States & the Six Nations.

Sunday. 11. [August]. Rainy & Very uncomfortable all Day. Dined with the Genl. Towards Eveng. went to Church with the Companies & received a Lecture & Prayers from our Worthy Chaplain.

[Monday]. 12. [August]. At one P.M. The Commissioners met the Indians & replied in a Very spirited manner to their answer but concluded with Saying the[y] could Through [throw] all what was past behind them, bury the Hatchet & look upon them as Friends & hoped they would Abide by their Plighted Faith &c. &c. &c. After sundry speeches both sides & passing 24 Belts the Council-fire was raked up till tomorrow-morning.

Dined at the Genls. In the Evening went over to the River & Visited Capt. Patterson.

Tuesday. 13. [August]. The Genl. & Commissioners were much engaged [to]day in takeing leave of the Indians & distributing the Presents to the amount of upwards of £2000, amongst them, The Presents consisting of Blankets, coarse Cloths, Linnen, Knives, Tobacco Boxes &c. & about 12,000 Dollars which was delivered to the Sachems & Warriors in Publick. The Commissioners left them, and they divided the whole by Nations, the different Nations by their Tribes & Castles & then by Familys in a Very little time & without the least Noise or Contention. The Squaas attended & Lugged home heavy Loads of Blankets, their Children besides on their Backs whilst the Gentlem. walked in state after them smoaking their Pipes & Looking like Men of great Consequence. The Commissioners distributed 1000 Doll[ar]s. in private Gifts to the Sachems & Principal Warriors of all the Nations.

The Revd. Mr. Calldwell our Very worthy Chaplain took leave of us & sett out this A.M. on his return to the Jerseys. Spent the Evening at the Generals.

Wednesday. 14. [August]. Arose early this morning. Collected the Companies together & Received the Genl. on his return with the usual Complyments. He gave me directions to finish & garrison the Picket fort now building with my Company Capt. Isinlord's & Capn. Sabres Companys to keep up strict discipline & subordination, that I must stay here till further Orders from him, after which the Genl. Mr. Edwards & the Gentn. of the army their Attendants took their leave of us. Capt. Sabre's Company joined me early this Morning & Capt. Vosburghs & Veadder's Companys were ordered to Albany, & Capt. Mc.Kean's to Johnstown. Engaged the rest of A.M. in Assisting in discovering a Ploth [plot] Entered into by sundry Persons (three of our Regt.) in order to Join the Enemy. Apprehended Alexr. Stewart who swore against several one officer & two Sarjants of our Regt. in Consequence of which an Express sett out (Mr. Kinney) for Fort-Schuyler.

Thursday. 15. [August]. Ordered the Pickets pulled up round the Church & sett up at the fortification. Lieuts. Pierson & Paterson came from Fort Schuyler & confirmed the Acct. of Lieut. Mc.Mikell, Sarjant Smith & one Ridley's deserting Yesterday to the Enemy.

Friday. 16. [August]. By another Express from Fort-Schuyler were informed of Mc.Mikell & his party haveing been seen by the party sent after them crossing the Oneidas Lake, also of Sarjant-Major Younglove, Sarjant Aaiken & Mr. Gemis were killed on their Return from a scout from Oswego & that Freeman was wounded & One Bell made their escape. Lieut. Gifford & Elmer struck their Tent & removed into the house within the Garrison & began again to mess with me.

Saturday. Augt. 17. Nothing material. Orders of the day: Parole Major Barber. Officer of the Guard tomorrow Lieut. Gifford. The Officers will be punctual in attending Parade & Exercise with their Companys hereafter within the Garrison & always oversee the fatigue partys from their Companys, The Officer of the Guard only excepted, who will diligently attend his duty as officer of the Guard.

The Officer of the Guard is hereby directed once every half hour after the beatting of the Tattoo till the Revolle to call the Sentry at the Guard house "Alls-Well": The Sentry next him to pass the call to the next Sentry on the right & so on from Sentry to Sentry till the whole have cryed "Alls-Well."

Sunday. 18. [August]. Sett out early this Morning & rode to accompany Major Barber now Very unwell on his Return to Fort Schuyler. Rode about 16 Miles & returned in the Evening.

Monday. 19. [August]. John Nutter returned from Albany & brought Letters from New-Jersey & the latest Papers which afforded us much Pleasure & satisfaction. Ensign Kinney returned in the Eveng. with Letters & Papers also from Albany, with a Letter from Major-Genl. Schuyler directing me to apprehend & secure one Simpson, formerly a Suttler to our Regt. for takeing things from Johnson Hall, And directing me about finishing the Picket-Fort in this place.

Tuesday. 20. [August]. Engaged in Examining Simpson, who I sent under the direction of Lt. Clok to the Genl. in Albany. Wrote to the Genl. Major Livingston & my Father.

Wednesday. 21. [August]. Wet & Rainy A.M. Went over the Mohawk-River to [illegible]. The fortification ordered to be built in this place (see antea No. 2. July 22d.) being enclosed. P.M. was taken up in Erecting a Pole upward of 60 Feet high on which was fixed a Staff with the Name *Fort Dayton* & Liberty on one side & *Fort Dayton* & *Property* on the other with a blue Pennant. After this the Men were ordered under Arms, manned the Lines & fired by Companies through the Post-Holes. Afterwards were drawn in a Circle in which was Brought a Barrell of Grogg & success to Fort-Dayton being Named by the Officers was drunk accompanied by Nine Cheers from the Soldiery. The whole then parraded without round the Garrison & after coming within the Fort the same quantity of Liquor & other Patriotic Toasts were drank accompanied by the same Acclamations of Joy. The Men were then dismissed with strict orders for No officer or Soldier to lye without the Camp. Captns. Isinlord & other Company drunk Tea with me. Very tired this Eveng.

Thursday. 22d. [August]. Nothing Material.

Friday. 23d. [August]. P.M. Attended with the Companies & buried a Soldier of Capt. Sabres Company in Military form, the High-Dutch at the same time singing Psalms according to their Customs. Lieut. Patterson came from Schenactady & Lodged with me, also Capt. Sabre & Isinlord began to Lodge in Garrison.

Saturday. 24. [August]. Busy in settling my Acct. of Guns &c. Towards Evening had a Game of Indian Ball with the officers. Reced. Letters in the Eveng. from Col. Dayton, Major Barber &c.

Sunday. 25. [August]. Wet & Rainy Most of the day. In the Morning walked up Canada-Creek with Lieut. Gifford above the settlement. Returned to Dinner. In the Evening Capt. Hubbard arrived at the Fort escorted by a Subalterns Guard with 25,000 Dollars to pay the Troops in this Nor:Western Department, & Lodged with me.

Monday. 26. [August]. Rainy most of the day. Lieut. Elmer sett out with a Guard to Escort the Paymaster & Money to Fort Schuyler. Busy in settling my Books. Exercised the Men in the Evening.

Tuesday. 27. [August]. Continues rainy. A Court Martial was held today.

Wednesday. 28. [August]. Rainy by spells all day. P.M. attended & saw a ludicrous Beating up for Voluntiers by a High-German appointed Capt. who can neither read nor write. The oddity of the Capt., his officers & Recruits with their dress excited the Laughter of all our officers. In the Eveng. engaged in Settling a fray between the Soldiers & Inhabitants.

Thursday. 29. [August]. This afternoon the Guard returned from Fort Schuyler. At Roll call agreable to the sentence of the Court-Martial held on Monday last one Passaffy of Capt. Sabres Compy. was tied to the Post & though ordered to receive 20 Lashes was pardoned He being Very penitent. Also one Henderson of Capt. Isinlords Company was tyed Naked & stood at the Whipping post half an hour agreable to the orders of a Court-Martial which I approved of.

Friday. 30. [August]. 1776. Engaged in paying my Men four Months pay for May, June, July & Augt.

Saturday. 31. [August]. A Court Martial by my order sett this Morning for the Tryal of Charles Cosgrove of my Company for Drunkeness, abuse to his officers & absenting with out leave from the Guard. After being confined & to all which He plead Guilty, & the court ordered him to be punished with 39 Lashes for the charge, 39 for the second & to be Drummed out of the Army for the Third which I approved of for the present & ordered him (after being stript & tied to the Whipping post) to be suspended till further directions.

In the Eveng. Lieut. Elmer with the Paymaster arrived from Fort-Schuyler.

September 1st. Sunday. Haveing notice that some of my Company were Drunk over the River & been absent all Night from Garrison, I ordered a Corporal & four Men to order all Soldiers to the Garrison & to bring those who did not immedly. come or were drunk with them & to forbid any Liquors being sold by any Suttler whatever except Lt. Col. Belinger who had permission to sell being this side [of] the River & near the Garrison. The Guard in Obedience to orders went over the River found John Barret & Isaac Hazelton Drunk & 3 other Soldiers at the Suttlers. After telling his orders the Corporal ordered the Guard to bring Barrett & Hazelton along. Barrett swore He would not come till his frolick was over. After much more altercation the Guard proceeded to their Duty but met with opposition by the five Rascals at the Suttlers by their drawing their Bayonetts & making use of Clubs &c. &c. The Corporal of the Guard haveing knocked Isaac Hazelton [down] as they thought dead intimidated the Villains in such a manner as to give themselves up & obey orders. Haveing heard the Guard were not able to do their duty by the resistance they met with I immediately Dispatched Lieut. Elmer & some Men over the River & soon after followed on myself But found them returning with the Guard. Upon seeing Barrett run from the Guard I followed him Dismounted drew my Sword & threatened to run him through the Body upon wh. He fell on his Knees & plead for mercy. But He being the Ring Leader of the fray & haveing exasperated me in such a manner by his & his Companions disorderly Conduct I could not help bilabouring him with my sword, which I did so effectually that I believe He will ever remember it. After this I ordered them all closely confined. I am thus particular, as this Rascal is the first Man of my Company that I ever laid the Weight of my hand on & had I been present when they opposed the Guard I certainly should have been the Death of some of the seditious villains, two of whom were of Isinlord's Company.

It is strange when men have Money that are fond of Drink, what Pains they will take to stupify themselves & then when in Liquor murder their best Friends if denyed the pernicious Liquor.

Drunkeness is undoubtedly the *primum Mobile* of all mischief & disorderly Conduct.

Monday. 2d. [September]. A.M. a Court Martial sett for the Tryal of the Seditious Soldiers mentioned Yesterday & Reported the Evidence with their Opinion that the Crimes committed were of so high a Nature that they could not be Tryed by a Regimental Court Martial but that Cognizance thereof came only for the Punishment within the Limits of a Genl. Court-Martial. Upon which rather than to proceed to the riguor of the Martial Law which for Sedition would extend to the Life of the Principal Barrett & by the recommendation of my Brother-Officers I ordered the guard to bring them before the Companies on the Parrade & after mentioning the Crime they had been Guilty of & tryed before the Court-Martial & the Consequence of my further Prosecuting them I Reprimanded them very severely & ordered them to return to their Duty & if their Behaviour was such as to evince their hearty Sorrow for what they had done I would forgive them. Otherwise they might expect the severest Punishment. Their humble & thankfull Behaviour was immediately expressed. Abm. Hazelton went to the Hospital to take care of his wounded Brother by the Blow He received over the head in the fray Yesterday. Hamilton was ordered to Join his (Capt. Isinlords) Company & *Barrett* the Principal was kept still confined. After which the Companys were Ordered to be in readiness to secure Col. Elmer & his Regt. which I heard was over the River. Went over & introduced myself to Col. Elmer[1] & the Coll. introduced me to his officers. The Coll. & four companies were piloted by me to Fort Dayton where they were received by us. The Companies Lodge in the Church. The Coll. & officers after refreshing themselves with a Drink of Toddy at my Invitation retired to their Quarters.

[1]ELMER. This officer is obscure. He was perhaps a New York militia officer, or Colonel Samuel Elmore, who raised a Connecticut regiment for northern duty in 1776. He was no known relation to Bloomfield's subordinate, Ebenezer Elmer.

Tuesday. 3. [September]. Engaged all Day in preparing to March for Fort-Schuyler. Col. Elmer & sundry of his Horses spent forepart of the Evening with us in Garrison. Released Jno. Barrett from Confinement in order to march with us.

Wednesday. 4. [September]. Sett out early this Morning with Lt. Gifford & my Company for Fort-Schuyler. Waded through the Mohawk-River Ten Miles above Fort Dayton, before we arrived at old Fort-Schuyler where we Halted & Dined. Charles Cosgrove mentioned 31: ult. being again Drunk crazy & stupid attempted to shoot himself but was prevented by the Sarjant of the Rear-Guard. Arrived about sunset at Oresca-Castle where we Lodged keeping a Sarjant's Guard for our own security all Night.

Thursday. 5. [September]. Renewed our March early this Morning from Oresca. After marching six Miles we met Lieut. Paterson going Express from Col. Dayton to Genl. Schuyler with Intelligence of 700

Indians being at Oswego & Scouting parties of the Enemy now Lurking about Fort-Schuyler. Upon which I ordered my Company to Load & divided the Cmp. into two Divisions. A Sarjant & four men went 100 yds. in Front as an advanced Guard. I followed with the first Division, Lieut. Gifford about 30 yds. after with the second Division & a Sarjant & four Men 50 yds. in the Rear as a Rear Guard. In this manner We marched with the greatest silence till We arrived about x [10 o'clock] at Fort-Schuyler. My company were ordered to Occupy a Barn for Want of Tents. Dined with the Col. & Major. Lodged at the Colonels.

Friday 6. [September]. Engaged this A.M. on Parrade & Exercise. P.M. in Receiving & takeing care of my Baggage which arrived with 7 of My Company in Batteaus from the Flatts. Began to lodge at Rooss.

Saturday. 7. [September]. Officer of the day. This morning a Scout of 4 Oneida-Indians & Mr. Stout sett out on a Scout to Oswego. P.M. Rainy. Nothing Material.

Sunday. 8. Sepr. 1776. Fort Schuyler. Unwell with a Pain in all my Bones owing to a Cold I have caught after the use of too much Mercurial Ointment for the Itch, a troublesome Pestilence prevalent throughout the whole Camp amongst both Officers & Soldiers. The fatigue Partys are busily engaged at their respective Works without any regard to the Day which is no ways distinguished from any other day in the Week unless by the hoisting of the Flagg & flaming Sword of Liberty within the Fort. Every man that is not at work doing wht. is right in his own Eyes. A Scoutt of 100 Men was sent out today.

Monday. 9. [September]. Engaged A.M. on a Court-Martial being Presidt. Lieut. Mott Hagan, & Coxe & Ensign Reading Members of the Court. Tryed one Fletcher of Captn. Ross' Compy. for Disobedience of orders & Sentenced him to be confined five days to Hard Labour. Also confined one Cox a Carpenter for selling strong Liquors contrary to orders. Ensign Gaulidet Dined & Capt. Sharp Drank Tea with me in my Markee.

Tuesday. 10. [September]. Officer of the Day. P.M. the Revd. Mr. Kirkland & Lieut. Patterson arrived here with accts. of an Engagement betwixt the American & British Troops on Long Island about a Week past. The Scoutt that went out Sunday Returned without any Intelligence of the Enemy.

Wednesday. 11. Sepr. 1776. Unwell. Took Physick. An Express arrived from below in the Evening with Accts. that all the Militia in Tryon & Albany Countys were in Arms ready to come to our Assistance hearing a formidible Army was on their March against us from Oswego. Strange how Accts. are exaggerated by travelling. Wrote in the Evening a long Letter to my Parents.

Thursday. 12. [September]. Capt. Sharp's Brother arrived here on a Visit from the Jerseys. Nothing Material.

Friday. 13. [September]. Engaged on a Court of Inquiry all Day.

Saturday. 14. [September]. Engaged as Yesterday. The Scout mentd. this day [last] Week Returned from Oswego & Say no Indians or any of the Enemy are there.

Sunday. 15. [September]. Engaged in Writeing Letters to the Jerseys. P.M. heard the Revd. Mr. Kirkland preach.

16. Monday. 17. Tuesday. 18. Wednesday. [September]. Engaged on the Court of Inquiry Ordered by Col. Dayton whereof Major Barber is Prest., Capts. Bloomfield, Potter, Reading & Emlay [Imlay] are Members. To Inquire by hearing Evidences of the Conduct of Lt. Col. White, Capts. Patterson & Ross touching their plundering Johnson-Hall, which Evidence being taken before the Court was Certifyed & transmitted to Albany to be laid before the Genl. Court Martial ordered for those Gentlemen being tryed. The Court also on Inquiry found one Mayres Guilty of Toryism & Committed him to the Main-Guard. Messrs. Jonathan Dayton[1] & Wm. Barber[2] arrived here from the Jerseys. Mr. Sharp sett out on his Return home.

[1]JONATHAN DAYTON (1760–1824). Born Elizabethtown, New Jersey. Son of Colonel Elias Dayton. Graduated from the College of New Jersey, 1776. Served as paymaster of the 3rd New Jersey. Commissioned a captain, 1780. Present at the siege of Yorktown. Went on to have an extensive political career as a member of the New Jersey Assembly, 1786–87, 1790, 1814–15; a delegate to the Constitutional Convention of 1787; a delegate to the Continental Congress, 1787–89; a representative to the United States Congress, 1791–99, during which time he served as speaker, 1795–99; and a United States senator, 1799–1805. Dayton, Ohio, was named after him.

[2]WILLIAM BARBER. Commissioned an ensign in the 3rd New Jersey, October 1776. Named a lieutenant and aide-de-camp to General William Maxwell, January 1777. Promoted to captain, April 1777; major, May 1778; major and aide-de-camp to Lord Stirling, October 1778. Wounded at Yorktown, October 1781.

19. Thursday. 20. Friday. [September]. We were alarmed these Nights by the fireing of our Centuries at some Messasauga Indians who attempted to surprize & take off some of our Men. They have been tracked by our scoutts but can not be taken. I am now & have been ever since my arrival at this place Very unwell, owing to my annointing with Quick-silver Ointmt. for the Itch (a Disorder Very prevalent amongst both Officers & Soldiers of our Regt.) & My exposing myself on my March from Fort Dayton by wadeing through the Mohawk-River, Oresca-Creek &c. The Glands about my Face & Throat are so swollen that I can take no other Nourishment than spoon-Victuals.

Saturday. 21. [September]. Took a Dose of Salt A.M. Towards Evening the Regt. parraded & were Reviewed by the Colonel. *After* Attended by a Number of Sachems & Warriors of the Oneida-Tribe & who in the Eveng. had an Interview with the Col. and informed him of the certain Arrival of Sr. John Johnson & a large Army at Oswego that they were determined to take no part in the Quarrel & desired that none of their Young Warriors would be sent any more on any Scout for us.

Sunday. 22. [September]. The Colonel replied to the Delegates, Chiefs & Warriors of the Oneidoes this Morning but being Very sick did not attend the Council. After this the Indians returd. home.

Monday. 23d. [September]. Lodged this Night in Garrison with the Major.

Tuesday. 24. [September]. Capt. Sharp, Lieut. Elmer & Anderson sett out with 60 Men on a scout to the Oneida-Lake. Engaged on a Court-Martial today with Lieuts. Mott, Bellard [Ballard], & Hennion & Ensign Kinney Members. Tried three Prisioners Mc.Neil, Cooper & Wills & who were discharged at Roll-Call this evening. Skeanenden the first Chief of the Oneida-Tribe came Express from Cannowollchen with information that Sr. John Johnson & his Army mentioned the 21st. Inst. had left Oswego & gone over Lake Ontario. Skeanonden & other Inds. spent the Evening with the Major, Parson Kirkland & Myself. This Skanondo (before mentioned July 31st.) Said He would give me his present true Name which He would ever hereafter call me by & desired Mr. Kirkland to write it down which is as follows, Aoghweanjondawetha & is thus pronounced, Aw-vogh wun joon daw wat haw. Sconendon Lodged with us in Garrison.

Wednesday. 25. [September]. Officer of the Day. I this day Visited the house made use of as a Hospital & found that the Sick greatly suffer for the Want of those Necessary Articles which are allowed their Attendants to Cook with & make the sick Comfortable, which I reported in my Return of the Guards & Visiting Rounds nearly in the above Words with this addition to the Colls.: "That unless provision is made in this Respect, it is Vain for Medicine to be administered." My Report had the desired effect. The Colonel made immediate Inquiry about the sick, Visited them himself & ordered the Necessary Conveniences.

Thursday. 26. [September]. 1776. One Elwell a Soldier of Capt. Sharp's Company dyed last Night, & was this Evening buried with the Honors of War, the Coll., Chaplain, Surgeon, Officers & Regimt. attending. The Scout mentioned 24th. Inst. returned from the Lake.

Friday. 27. [September]. One Woodruff a Soldier of Capt. Dickersons dyed last Night & was buried in form today.

Saturday. 28. [September]. Very unwell. Nothing material.

Sunday. 29. [September]. Rainy all day. Had no Prayers or preaching. Capt. Woodbridge of Col. Elmers Regt. came with a guard from Fort-Dayton with 16 Batteaus. Drank Tea & Lodged with me.

Monday. 30. [September]. The Batteaus returned. This day Clement Remington, Joseph Ryley & John Nutter were discharged from my Company by the Colonel, being rendered incapable through sickness of doing Duty.

Tuesday. Octr. 1st. Officer of the day. Lt. Anderson officer of the 2d. Guard in Garrison spent the Evening with me.

Wednesday. 2. [October]. Engaged A.M. on a Genl. Court-Martial whereof Major Barber was President, Capts. Bloomfield, Potter, Reading & Sharp, Lieuts. Mott, Flannagan, Hagan, Hennion & Anderson of Col. Dayton's Regimt. Funnewel [Furnival] & Savage of the Train of Artillery Members. Tried Two Corporals of the Train for Desertion. Sentenced one How to be reduced to the ranks & punished with 39 Lashes. The other one Mc.Evy haveing shewed great Penitence & in being inveigled to Desert through How's persuasion, was sentenced to be reduced to the Ranks only & punished with 15 Lashes & afterwards on Petition of the Company of Artillery was pardoned by the Colonel. How was at

Roll-Call paid his Just due. P.M. The Gentm. who composed the Genl. Court Martial met at the President's Room & not only Drank Seven Bottles of Wine for those who had'nt served before on a Genl. Court-Martial but Nine in addition with great Mirth & Social Friendship. Before breaking up The Company diverted themselves with an Indian-Dance, performing of which several shewed great Dexterity & the effects of the *Yocktaryencrar*. Perhaps my Reader May think, I partook too freely of the luscious Juice of the Grape. No, my being an Invalid excused my fullfilling all the Punctilio's required usually in Jovial Company. I Retired to rest by xi [o'clock], with a clear head.

Thursday. 3. [October]. Engaged in fixing Accomodations for my Room in the Fort. Spent the Evening in the Major's Room & was agreably Entertained with Vocal Musick by Parson Kirkland & two Oneida-Indians in their Language. One was Hangoes frequently mentioned before in my Diary, & Thomas one of Kirkland's Deacons. Better this Evening.

Friday. 4. [October]. Was well enough to day to Visit the sick & play one heat of Indian-Ball.

Saturday. 5. [October]. In consequence of a Letter from Genl. Schuyler, Major Barber, Lieuts. Mott, Anderson, Pierson, Ensign Reading & others were ordered & sett out in Batteaus for Albany as Evidences in the Tryal of Lt. Col. White Capts. Patterson & Ross. It seems if this imprudent plundering of Johnson-Hall will never be settled but that our Regimt. is to be convulsed during their being by this rash Action & not to call it worse.
P.M. Visited the sick with Capt. Potter & saw them removed near the Garrison. Capt. Potter & his officers (Lieuts. Quimby & Hennien [Hennion] & Ensign Kinney) removed into the room contiguous to mine. We all supped & spent the Evening Very agreably together.

Sunday. Oct. 6. 1776. Parson Kirkland being gone to Oneida to preach to the Indians, The day was no farther regarded than the hoisting of the Liberty Flagg. Dined with Lieut. Paterson [Patterson].

Monday. 7. [October]. Officer of the Day. In the Evening Capt. Potter, his Officers, Dr. Dunham Mr. Norcross & Mr. Jona. Dayton spent the Evening till 12 in my Room very agreably.

Tuesday. 8. [October]. P.M. Played the Indian-Ball (which our officers call Shinney) with all the officers & five Indians from Oneida.

Wednesday. 9. [October]. Engaged all Day on a Regim. Court-Martial being President, Lieuts. Savage Elmer, Hennion & Ensign Kinney members. Tried Quartr. Master-Serjeant Hacker for abuse of Lieut. Funnewel of which He was Aquitted, also one Grant Cottle, a Papist Sutler for sundry Crimes, who was ordered immediatly from this place. Spent the Eveng. in Dr. Dunham's Room. Parson Kirkland returned with the Colonels son from the Oneida-Castle.

Thursday. 10. [October]. Nothing material.

Friday. 11. [October]. The Scout sent this day Week to returned from Oswego & report that no Indians or any of the Enemy are or have been lately there. Nothing more material.

Saturday. 12. [October]. This P.M. Lieut. Gifford & Ensign Thomas returned from Albany with the News & Letters from my Father &c. & orders from Genl. Schuyler for the Removal of our Regt. to Tyconderoga. Col. Elmer now at Fort-Dayton is to be stationed at this Post. Mr. Kinney & myself invited this Eveng. for the Scotch-Fields.

Sunday. 13. [October]. Parson Kirkland preached twice to the Regt. today. Dined with the Colonel 2d time.

Monday. 14. [October]. A.M. Lt. Col. White & Capt. Ross arrived from below. P.M. five Tories were brought in that were taken up at the Oneida-Castles by the Indians on their way to the Enemy. Engaged in the Eveng. in assisting the Coll. & takeing those Rascals Examination.

Tuesday. 15. [October]. Obtained leave with Capt. Potter (being Invalids) of the Colonel to ride to Schenactady where our Regt. is ordered to rendevous 'till further orders. After dining at the Colonels, sett out on our Journey. Got to Oresca about 4 to the Oneida path where are the ruins of old Fort-Schuyler by sunset. We here crossed the Mohawk-River after swimming our horses some distance & nearly escaped being drowned, with the Loss of my Saddle Bags in which was my own & fellow Travellers linnen &c. to the amount of 40 Doll[ar]s. Being wet all over we put up a log hut just by the River where with difficulty we made out to dry ourselves by the fire & take our Lodgeings on a dirty muddy floor.

Wednesday. Octr. 16. 1776. We sett out early this Morning & rode through the Wilderness to Thomson's by viii time enough to take leave of Col. Elmer & his Officers now on their march to relieve Col. Dayton. Spent A.M. at Thomsons with Lt. Gordon whilst a hired servant went to the Hut I lodged at at last night for my Pistols which I had carelessly forgot. We Dined with Capt. Henk. Masings who treated us with a great deal of kindness & Civility. At four sett out & got to Col. Bellinger's on the German-Flatts by day light where we took our Lodgings.

Thursday. 17. [October]. Spent the Morning with Major Barber now on his return from Albany to Fort-Schuyler, & in Visiting my Sick left in this place, P.M. In visiting Fort-Dayton lately built under my direction (see [blank]). Capt. Isinlord & his Officers Unwell in the Evening.

Friday. 18. [October]. This day is my Birthday being 23 Years of Age, old enough to be better & Wiser than I am. This day Twelve months [ago] I was engaged in my Profession of the Law enjoying the calm sunshine of a peaceable quiet & easy life. Now I am 500 Miles from my Native place amongst strangers & exposed to all the hardships & fatigues of a Soldiers life, no ways Settled not knowing where I may be destined next week. Being wet & rainy (as it has been these four days past) staid at my Lodgings.

Saturday. 19. [October]. By an Express to Col. Dayton we are informed Genl. Arnold[1] our admiral on Lake Champlain has been severely handled by the British fleet & oblidged to retreat with great loss, and that our Regt. is ordered immediately to Tyconderoga & all the Militia of this & the lower Countys to Saratoga. Lt. Col. Bellinger with whom we lodge & the Militia in this place marched at 12.

[1]BENEDICT ARNOLD (1741–1801). Native of Connecticut. Merchant. Named a colonel in the Continental Army, 1775. Led one wing of the invasion of Canada, going through Maine, and linked up with Richard Montgomery's forces outside Quebec. Seriously wounded in the assault of January 31, 1775. Became brigadier general, 1776; major general, 1777. Helped to delay British invasion of upper New York in October 1776 by building a flotilla and engaging Guy Carleton's vessels at Valcour Island on Lake Champlain. Instrumental to the American victory at Saratoga, September–October 1777. Became disillusioned with the American cause and went over to the British, September 1780.

Sunday. 20. [October]. After Breakfast ferryed the Mohawk River with Capt. Potter & took our Lodgings at Fort-Harkimer in order to wait the arrival of the Batteaus.

Monday. 21. [October]. At one P.M. took passage with Lt. Col. White & Dr. Dunham in a Batteau. Crossed the Mohawk-Falls or little carrying Place at 2. At viii brought too [arrived] & took up our Lodgings 23 miles from Fort-Harkimer.

Tuesday. 22. [October]. Sett out early this Morning at viii, haveing sailed 18 Miles. Breakfasted at Major Funda's & before 4 P.M. arrived in Schenactady haveing Sailed or rather danced upwards of 30 Miles down the Mohawk-River. Spent the Eveng. at Tavern in Company with Col. White, Dr. Dunham, Capts. Ross & Paterson & Capt. Kinney from Morris-Town & other Gentn. Lodged at Private Lodgings.

Wednesday. 23. [October]. Engaged all A.M. in buying all the Cloths with Woolen Caps & Stockings in this Town for my Company. P.M. Engaged in Writeing. Capt. Ross & Paterson & Dr. Dunham sett out for Albany.

Thursday. 24. [October]. Col. Dayton & most of the Regt. came in Town. Engaged in the Evening in procuring Billets for the Men.

Friday. 25. [October]. Our Regt. was Reviewed P.M. by the Commissioners from the State of New-Jersey & the Gentn. of the Town with great Credit. Spent the Evening with all our Officers at Tavern in attending the Commissioners about engageing during the War. All our officers engaged except Capts. Potter, Reading & Sharp, Lieuts. Flanagan [Flanningham]. & Elmer & Dr. Reed Surgeon's mate. Wrote home to my Friends till after one this Night.

Saturday. 26. [October]. Marched from Schenactady at 8 recrossed the Mohawk-River. Dined at ten. Marched & Lodged at Widow Peoples on the North-River, 17 Miles from Schenact.y.

Sunday. 27. [October]. Marched to Still-Water where most of the Regt. lodged. Spent the Eveng. & Lodged with Capt. Sharp.

Monday. 28. [October]. Our Regt. Marched & lodged at Saratoga. Dined at Genl. Schuylers with the Field-officers & Capts. of our Regt. Lodged at Judge Duer's famous Mills with Lt. Hollinshead. It is common on the North-River to find the Saw-Mills go with 13 & 14 Saws at a sweep so that a log is at once divided in Boards. Genl. Schuyler's & Judge Duer's mills go in this manner.

Tuesday. 29. [October]. Marched from Saratoga. Dined at Genl. Ten Broek[1] at Fort-Edward where Our Regt. lodged except my Company which I marched & lodged at Jones's.

[1]ABRAHAM TEN BROEK [TEN BROECK] (1734–1810). Born Albany, New York. Merchant. Served in the New York Assembly, 1761–65, and New York Provincial Congress, 1775–77. Named brigadier general of New York militia. Helped to defend the Albany region in 1776 and 1777 and to defeat Burgoyne at Saratoga. Later served as mayor of Albany, 1779–83, 1796–99; state senator, 1780–83; and judge of the Albany County Court of Common Pleas, 1781–94.

Wednesday. 30. [October]. Rode back 3 Miles this Morning to see Lt. Col. Ogden on his return home from Tyca. [Ticonderoga]. Our Regt. marched all day through the Wilderness, the Minest [meanest?] worst & most Desolate road I ever travelled & Lodged at Fort-Ann. 14 M. [miles].

Thursday. 31. [October]. Sett out with Capt. Sharp in Batteaus with the Baggage down Cheshire Wood-Creek. Arrived in the Eveng. with the Regt. who marched to Skeensborough [Skenesboro] & Lodged. The Col. & all of his officers Lodged in Governor or Major Skeens[1] house. 14 M. [miles].

[1]PHILIP SKEEN [SKENE] (1725–1810). Native of England. Lengthy military career, including the French and Indian War. Married an Irish relative of Sir William Johnson and came to own 94,000 acres on Lake Champlain. Founded Skenesboro (now Whitehall), New York. Captured as a Loyalist in 1775 but eventually paroled, Skene served as the primary Loyalist adviser to John Burgoyne during the latter's invasion in 1777. All of Skene's landholdings were eventually confiscated by the Patriots. Skene returned to England, received a large settlement from the Loyalists Claims Commission, purchased a great estate, and continued his life as a landowner and gentleman.

Friday. Novr. 1. 1776. All our Regt. & Baggage embarked in Batteaus at South-Bay & proceeded through this Rocky Mountainous Country to Lake Champlain. My Batteau lead the rest & landed my Men in the Eveng. the first at Tyconderoga haveing moved 30 Miles the distance from Skeensborough. Much fatigued in the Eveng. At the Invitation of Capt. Dorsey of the 1 P[ennsylvania] B[attalion] Spent the Eveng. & lodged with him.

Saturday. 2. [November]. Busily engaged in providing quarters in Barracks for my Men & preparing for an Attack from the Enemy which is hourly expected as we frequently hear their Cannon & have already seen their advanced Guard. Spent the Eveng. & Lodged with Capt. Conway 1st. J. [Jersey] Regt.

Sunday. 3d. [November]. Breakfasted with Lieut. Bowen &c. 2d. J. [Jersey] Regt. A.M. went over Lake Champlain with Capt. Dorsey & reviewed the Forts & Citadel on Mount Independance.[1] Dined with Dr. Mc.Crea & Major Howell. Our Regt. parraded in the Evening & was much admired by all on the Ground. Lieut. Donnel spent the Evening with my Mess, now consisting of my own & Capt. Potters Officers.

[1]Mount Independence. A fortified prominence southeast of and overlooking Fort Ticonderoga from across Lake Champlain.

Monday. 4. [November]. A.M. Engaged in Writeing 17 days past of this Journal, which would be more particular, but my time & the confusion we live in wont admit of it. Spent the Eveng. with Capt. Dorsey.

Tuesday. 5. [November]. Engaged A.M. in Writeing. Major Howell Dined with me. Capt. Dorsey Spent P.M. & Evening with Capt. Conway with me.

Wednesday. 6. [November]. Mounted the Main-Guard in Montcalm's[1] fortress. Lieut. Mott & Ensn. Kinney Subalterns. Col. Roberts Field officer of the day. Nothing material. Sett up all Night.

[1]MARQUIS LOUIS JOSEPH DE MONTCALM (1712–59). Native of France. Sent to Canada in 1756 to command French forces against the British in the French and Indian War. Successfully defended Fort Ticonderoga from British attack in 1758 but abandoned it the following year. Montcalm withdrew to Quebec, where French forces were defeated in September 1759 on the Plains of Abraham and Montcalm died of wounds sustained in the battle.

Thursday. 7. [November]. Spent A.M. after being relieved by Capt. Dickerson in the Jersey Camp. Slept P.M.

Friday. Novr. 8. 1776. Spent A.M. with Capt. Dillon & Visiting Mount Independance. Capts. Conway & Dorsey spent the Eveng. with us. Nothing material.

Saturday. 9. [November]. Breakfasted with Col. White. Dined with Capt. Dillon & supped with Capt. Donnel.

Sunday. 10. [November]. Dined & spent the day with Capt. Conway, Mr. Shinn & Capt. Dorsey.

Monday. 11. Tuesday. 12. [November]. Nothing material.

Wednesday. 13. [November]. Mounted Guard Lieuts. Coxe & Paterson my Subalterns, Major Dunlap Field-officer of the day &c. Lieut. Tuttle arrived this Eveng.

Thursday. 14. [November]. Nothing material. Spent Eveng. with Capt. Dorsey. Lieut. Morrison supped with us.

Friday. 15. [November]. This morning Col. Maxwell's[1] (now Brigadier-General) Regt. decamped & marched from this place with Musick playing & Colours flying & with great Credit & honor; also the 1st. Pensila. & 1st. Jersey Regimts. in like manner. Engaged in [riseing?] my Hut to live in.

[1]WILLIAM MAXWELL (ca. 1733–96). Native of Ireland. Migrated to New Jersey with his family in 1747. Extensive service during the French and Indian War. Retired from the British army as a colonel in 1774, returned to New Jersey, and sided with the Patriots. Commissioned colonel of the 2nd New Jersey, February 1776. Went to Canada with his troops and participated in the American retreat. Named brigadier general, October 1776, which made him overall commander of the New Jersey Line. Along with William Alexander (Lord Stirling) and Elias Dayton, one of three New Jersey commanders who reached the rank of general in the Continental service before the end of the war. Retired from Continental duty in 1780 as a respected although not especially distinguished veteran.

Saturday. 16. [November]. Nothing material. Engaged in Writg. P.M.

Sunday. 17. [November]. This Morning I was Introduced to Major-Genl. Gates[1] & by his Honor appointed Deputy Judge advocate of the Northern Army. Serjt. Major Younglove (mentd. [mentioned] antea 16th. Augt.) returned on his Parole from Genl. Carleton[2] by a flag of truce. Engaged in takg. & Swearg. sundry Evidence in the Eveng.

[1]HORATIO GATES (1728–1806). Native of England. Served as officer in the British army and saw extensive action in the French and Indian War. Retired from the army and settled in Virginia during the early 1770s. Congress named him a brigadier general and adjutant general, June 1775. In May 1776 promoted to major general and assigned to the northern department under Schuyler. Replaced Schuyler as head of the northern army in the summer of 1777 and went on to gain honor through the Saratoga victory over John Burgoyne. Much of the rest of his career was unexceptional. He was the American commander of record in the disastrous defeat of the southern department army at Camden, South Carolina, August 1780.
[2]GUY CARLETON (1724–1808). Native of Ireland. Became a British army regular and fought in the French and Indian War. Named lieutenant governor of Canada, 1766; governor, 1767–70. Returned to the British Isles where he continued his military career and served in Parliament. Named governor of Quebec, 1775; commissioned to command British forces in Canada, April 1776. Responsi-

ble for driving American soldiers out of Canada during the spring of 1776. Tried to invade New York later that year but held off by Benedict Arnold's fleet on Lake Champlain and the lateness of the season. Carleton served as the last commander in chief of British forces in America, 1782–83, before the evacuation.

Monday. 18. [November]. Early this Morning Lieut. Col. White drew his sword on Capt. Varick[1] & was ordered under an arrest. At 10 Major Genl. Gates Brigadier Genl. Arnold & Brickett[2] with their attendants left this Garrison accompanied by a Regt. & sundry officers to the Landing where they Embarked in Batteaus to Fort-George on their way to Philada. &c. Went to the Landing with the General & returned & Dined with Col. Wayne the present commanding officer.

[1]RICHARD VARICK (1753–1831). Born Hackensack, New Jersey. Moved to New York in 1775 and named a captain in the 1st New York regiment. Became a military secretary to General Philip Schuyler in June 1776. Later served briefly as an aide-de-camp to Benedict Arnold, just before Arnold went over to the British. At the close of war Washington chose him to organize and classify correspondence and papers relating to his years as commander in chief. Varick went on to have an active postwar political career in New York.
[2]JAMES BRICKETT (d. 1818). Lieutenant colonel in Frye's Massachusetts Regiment, 1775. Wounded at Bunker Hill. Served thereafter as brigadier general in the Massachusetts militia.

Tuesday. 19. [November]. P.M. went to the saw-Mills with Col. Dayton. In the Evening Col. Dayton went to the Landing in order to cross Lake-George tommorrow on a Visit to the Jerseys.

Wednesday. 20. [November]. Engaged in the Duties of my office as Judge advocate. Dined at Lt. Col. Craig's. I was this day appt. [appointed] to the rank of Major by the state of New Jersey. See 12th. Jany. 1777. Spent the Eveng. with Major Barber & Capt. Varrick.

Thursday. 21. Novr. 1776. Moved with my Mess into the Room lately occupied by Genl. Brickoff [Brickett], being the Room of the brave & intrepid Genl. Montcalm lived in when He Occupied this Garrison, now called Montcalm's fortress.

Friday. 22. [November]. Engaged all day in attending the Genl. Court Martial, Swearing & giving Certificates to 69 inlisted Soldiers during the war.

Saturday. 23. [November]. Engaged A.M. on the Genl. Court-Martial. Dined with Col. Wayne. P.M. six Companies of our Regt. were reviewed by Col. Varick, D. Muster Genl. [deputy mustermaster general].

Sunday. 24. [November]. Engaged in preparing my Muster-Roll. Capt. Donnel Dined with me. Supped with Capt. Ross.

Monday. 25. [November]. Dined with Capts. Ross & Paterson at Major Barber's. Reced. [received] 1836 Dolls. the pay due my Company for the three last Months. Capt. & officer of the day for Mount-Independance.

Tuesday. 26. [November]. Engaged all day the Genl. Ct. Martial whereof Major Barber is Prest. [president].

Wednesday. 27. [November]. The Genl. Court-Martial broke up.

Thursday. 28. Novr. 1776. Engaged in paying my Men off.

Friday. 29. [November]. Busy all day in making out my Pay Rolls for the present Month. Unwell with a Head-Ack this Eveng.

Saturday. 30. [November]. Wet & Rainy all day. P.M. went with Lieut. Gifford to Mount Independance. Visted Major Dunlap & Scouted the Property of [for] a Cow taken from me.

Sunday. Dec. 1. Breakfasted with Dr. Dunham & Mr. [Norcross?]

Monday. 2. [December]. Very unwell threatened with the Jaundice. Dr. Dunham Bled me this Morning. P.M. took an Emetic which operated Very severely. This Evening red [Indian] Scouts returned from Crown-Point with intelligence of the Arrival of some of the Enemys ships, in consequence of which Col. Wayne collected the Field-officers in Council. Ordered the Cannon to be put in Readiness in Montcalm's Fort & the Army to lay on their arms.

Tuesday. 3. [December]. The Army parraded at the Revallee, Beating. Very unwell all day.

Wednesday. 4. [December]. Very poorly all day. Nothing material [illegible].

Thursday. Friday, Saturday, Sunday & Monday. Decr. 5. to 10. 1776. Very sick during this time with the Jaundice. Kept my Room & most of the days my Bed. Took Emetics & other suitable Medicines.

Tuesday. [10 December]. This day I began to grow better. Dined with my worthy Major. Mr. Gifford Very Ill this day with Camp Dysentiry.

Wednesday. 11. [December]. Visited my sick today & the officers in Barracks. Much better. Lieut. Gifford continued Very ill. Nothing material has happened several days pass [past] Cold. The lake begins to freeze.

Thursday. 12. [December]. Major Barber, Capt. Paterson, Major Hay & other officers spent the Evening with me.

Friday. 13. [December]. Breakfasted with Mr. Hay. After Breakfast walked with the Major to Tye Landing. P.M. Major Barber & Capts. of our Regimts. went over to reconitre the Barracks at Mount Independance in consequence of an order for our removal into them tomorrow.

Saturday. 14. [December]. This Morning the floating-Bridge cross the Lake to Mount Independance broke which retarded the removal of our Regts. till P.M. when the Well & hearty removed in Batteaus with the greatest difficulty as the Weather is excessive severe. Dined & drank Tea with Major Hays.

Sunday. 15. [December]. The Lake froze over last Night. Weather excessive cold & severe. Capt. of the day for Tyconderoga. Ensign Otis subaltern of the Main-Guard Dined & spent the Eveng. with me at Major Barbers. This Mr. Otis is the only son of the famous James Otis Esqr. formerly Presdt. of the Continental Congress held in 1766 [1765] at New York, & one of the greatest American Patriots in the Massachusetts Government.[1] Ointed for the Itch this Evening.

[1]JAMES OTIS. Bloomfield meant to refer to the Stamp Act Congress of 1765, in which James Otis, Jr. (1725–83), the Boston radical leader who became mentally disturbed before the rebellion, played a leading part. Otis's only son, James, was an obscure figure. He may have seen some military service, and he died aboard a British prison vessel in 1777.

Monday. 16. [December]. Very cold & uncomfortable.

Tuesday. 17. [December]. In consequence of intelligence from Genl. Schuyler that a Genl. Engagement had been between Ld. How [Howe][1] & Genl. Washington between Brunswick & Princeton & that the British Troops were entirely defeated the Regiments at Tye & Mount

Independance parraded at Tye, fired two Vollies & gave 6 cheers, after which they were served with Rum to raise their spirits & then Marched to their respective Encampments. False Intelligence [added later in margin]. This Morning I moved over to the barracks on Mount-Independance. Major Barber's & my Mess joind.

[1]WILLIAM HOW [HOWE] (1729–1814). Native of England. Attended Eton College and pursued a military career, including extensive action in the French and Indian War. Served in Parliament, 1758–80. Favored conciliatory positions toward the Americans, yet sent to Boston in early 1775 to help put down the rebels. Led the assault at Bunker Hill, June 1775, and was officially named commander in chief of the British army in America, April 1776. Having failed to extinguish Patriot resistance during the 1776 and 1777 campaigns, asked to be relieved of duties. Resignation accepted in the late winter of 1778, when Howe was holding Philadelphia.

Wednesday. 18. [December]. Ricompense Leake Junr. my first Sarjeant dyed last Night in the Hospital at Tye. Went over to Tye; Dined with Mr. Gifford. P.M. attended with my Company Serjt. Leake's funeral. In crossing the Lake on my return I broke through the Ice, by which I caught a bad cold. Unwell all the Evening.

Thursday. 19. [December]. Unwell all day. Major Ritzma, Mr. Pearce & other officers supped & spent the Evening with my Mess. Major Barber *unwell.*

Friday. 20. [December]. Visited Head-Quarters where I dined & obtained leave of absence to return home. Engaged this Evening in paying my Men November's pay.

Saturday. 21. [December]. Busy in settling my Accounts.

Sunday. 22. & Monday. [23 December]. Busy in preparing to leave Tycnderoga. Supped at Major Hays.

Xtmas. 25. [December]. Took leave of my Friends & at ix. [o'clock] Left Mount-Independance in Company with Adjt. [Adjutant] Shepperd & rode in a slay with one Mr. Everest & arrived in five Hours at Skeensborough where Dined. After Dinner rode 9 Miles up Wood-Creek & lodged at one Boyle's.

Thursday. 26. [December]. We sett out Early in the Morng. & arrived in by 12 at Fort-Ann, it snowg. Very hard all the time. Dined with

Capt. Vosburgh. After Dinner sett out again & rode to [Kinsborough?] in as Violent a Snow Storm as ever I knew. Lodged at Mr. Jones where we were Very elegantly accomodated.

Friday. 27. [December]. A Fine pleasant day. The snow being Very deep rested at Jones's to Day for the Roads to be broke.

Saturday. 28. [December]. Left Jones near Fort Edward in company with Adjutant Shepperd. Lodged at Ensigns near Still-Water.

Sunday. 29. [December]. Got to Albany. Lodged at Willetts.

Monday. 30. [December]. Sett out with Mr. Ten Ick [Ten Eyck] & much Company in Slays for Schenectaday. Lodged at Mr. Duchee's.

Tuesday. 31. Dec. 1776. This morning I reviewed the Men of our Regt. left at Schenectaday. Gave them orders to go to Albany. Returned myself.

Wednesday. Jany. 1. 1777. Dined at Genl. Schuyler's. P.M. sett out with dispatches from the Genl. to Congress. These Dispatches &c: see in Genl. Schuylers Tryal pages 17, 18 & 19 where he makes honorable mention of the Bearer [Bloomfield] to Congress.

Thursday. 2. [January]. Lodged at Esopus.

Friday. 3. [January]. Dined at Sqr. [Squire] Barbers in Hanover & lodged in Goshen.

Saturday. 4. [January]. Got to Deacon Ogden's in Sussex New-Jersey where I spent the Evening Very agreably with my Friends & lodged.

Sunday. 5. [January]. Left my chest & Valise at Mr. Ogden's & sett out on Horseback haveing rode in a Slay from Tyconderoga thus far. Lodged near Sussex-Court-House.

Monday. 6. [January]. Crossed the Delaware at Easton & lodged 11 Miles from thence.

Tuesday. Jany. 7. 1777. Got to Philada. in the Evening delivered my dispatches to the Committee of Congress, that Right Honble. Body haveing removed to Baltimore in Maryland on the irruption of the British Troops through the Jerseys. Lodged with Capt. Donnell.

Wednesday. 8. [January]. After Dinner rode to Bristol [Pennsylvania] where I lodged.

Thursday. 9. [January]. Breakfasted at Capt. Clark's & rode to Sqre. [Squire] Tate's in Trenton where I dined. Spent P.M. with Col. Dare from Amboy, & lodged.

Friday. 10. [January]. Lodged at Mr. Hills near Flemingtown, Hunterden County.

Saturday. 11. [January]. Breakfasted at Capt. Reading's & lodged at Mr[s]. White's[1] in Baskenridge, the house where Genl. Lee[2] was lately taken Prisoner by a Party of Light Horse.

[1] MRS. WHITE'S. The widow of Ebenezer White. She kept a tavern in Basking Ridge, Bernards Township, Somerset County, New Jersey.
[2] CHARLES LEE (1731–82). Native of England. Pursued studies in England and Switzerland and became a professional soldier. Resettled in Virginia during 1773. Congress named him a major general, June 1775. Lee helped to defend Charleston, South Carolina, in the spring of 1776, but he was dilatory in backing up Washington as the latter fled through New Jersey in late 1776. Captured by the British at Basking Ridge, December 13, 1776; exchanged, April 1778. Was in initial command at Monmouth, June 28, 1778, and ordered the retreat that resulted in his court martial and temporary suspension from the Continental Army. Later an insulting letter to Congress caused his dismissal from the service.

Sunday. 12. [January]. Rode to Westfield, where near 2000 Troops arrived under Genl. Sullivan in the Evening with five Field-Pieces, on an Expedition against Bonum-Town[1] and Piscataway, but a Council of War of Field-Officers advised scouting parties only to be sent out to harrass the Enemy.

I sett as a member at this Council of War being the first time I ever ranked in the Field though I was appointed to the rank of Major of the 3d. Jersey Regimt. the 20th. of November last.

Being anxious to see my Native place & Friends I offered to guide one Scout consisting of 200 Men under Col. Vosee and accordingly at viii. in the Evening we sett out. Halted and Lodged the Men at David Edgar's & his neighbourhood in the upper part of Woodbridge. Took Horse myself and rode alone to my Fathers (6 miles off) at midnight. Awakened my Parents & the Family & spent two hours with them in Mutual Joy and chearfulness at seeing each other, after near Twelve Months absence. Here I was informed particularly of the irruption and cruel Ravages of the British & forreign Troops through New-Jersey. My Father was at first taken a Prisioner and his house & farm plundered of the best moveables to the Value of £500, or more. After which my Father hearing the Enemy had got to Philadelphia & the Congress were dismissed, rather than be sent Prisoner to New-York, haveing no other alternatives, took Lord Howe's Protection, after receiving the basest Treatment & the grossest insults from the Enemy. Uncle Bloomfield & all the Wig Inhabitants in short, wherever the Enemy passed, were plundered & used in the same manner.

[1]Bonum-Town [Bonhamtown]. Now in Edison Township, New Jersey.

Monday. 13. [January]. Got to my Party by 3 O'Clock, took an hours rest or two, & Early in the Morning sett out with Col. Vosee & the Party. Marched through the lower parts of Woodbridge and returned to Connecticut Farms in the Evening without meeting any of the Enemy Except our advanced Guard under Capt. Randle took Genl. Grant's[1] Steward & a Baggage Waggon with Provisions.

I had an Opportunity of hearing the present disposition of the Enemy. Near 2,000 Garrison Amboy, 1,500 BonamTown, 300, Piscataway & the main Army uncertain perhaps 7 or 8,000 at Brunswick with Guards & Centeries planted all the way from Amboy to Brunswick.

Spent the Evening with Col. Dayton Genl. Maxwell, Parson Calldwell & other Company. Lodged at Dr. Halstead's.[2]

[1]JAMES GRANT (1720–1806). Native of Scotland. Trained as a lawyer but became a professional soldier with service in the French and Indian War. Named brigadier general and sent to America in 1776; became major general in 1777. Took over as commander of British outposts in New Jersey late in 1776 before the battles of Trenton and Princeton. Involved in the battles of Brandywine and Germantown. Sent to the West Indies in 1778. Returned to England the next year, eventually becoming a full general and serving occasionally in Parliament.
[2]DR. HALSTEAD'S. Probably Caleb Halsted (1752–1827), a physician in Connecticut Farms (now Union Township, Union County, New Jersey).

Tuesday. 14. [January]. Dined at Capt. Potter's in Turkey.[1] Lodged at Mrs. White's in Baskenridge.

[1]Turkey. Now New Providence, Union County, New Jersey.

Wednesday. 15. [January]. Spent P.M. & lodged at Col. Spencers in Mendam.

Thursday. Jany. 16. 1777. Went to Morris-Town. Spent A.M. with Genl. Heard & other Company at Capt. Kinneys.

17. [January]. Dined at Capt. Dickersons & restd. at Dr. Leddels[1] in Mendam.

[1]DR. LEDDEL. Probably William Leddell (1747–1827), a physician in Mendham, Morris County, New Jersey.

Sunday. 19. [January]. This Morning took Lodgings at Mr. Henry Wicks[1] near Mendum in order to undergo a course of Medicine for a Glandular Swelling in my throat & a Rhematic Pain in both my Shoulders.

[1]HENRY WICK'S house is preserved today as part of the Morristown National Historical Park.

Monday. Feby. 10. I continue my Lodgings at Mr. Wicks, haveing gone through a gentle Salivation. Am now getting hearty again. Went out today for the first time to Col. Spencers & Outd. [outdoors] in the Eveng.

Thursday. 13. [February]. Dined & spent P.M. at Col. Spencers. My Father, Mr. Thomas Brown & Jarvis Bloomfield[1] Visited & Lodged with me, My Father & Mr. Brown being Delegated by the distressed Inhabitants of Woodbridge to wait on Genl. Washington respecting his Excellency's late Proclamation &c.

[1]JARVIS BLOOMFIELD (d. 1794). Cousin of Joseph Bloomfield. A lieutenant until his resignation, 1781. Went to sea as a privateer; captured on his first voyage and imprisoned until exchanged because of ill health, 1782. A lumber merchant and ship captain after the war.

Feb. 19. 1777. After Visiting my Father & Friends in Woodbridge & Elizth.Town I sett out 23. Feby. on Sunday for Cumberland County & rode in a violent Snow Storm most of the way.

March 2. Got to Cohansie Bridge[1] Sunday following, where I spent several days in Visiting my Friends & providing for my Sisters sent down by my Father in order to be out of the way of the continual Alarms & skirmishing of both Armys in Woodbridge & near my Fathers at this time. Visited Miss Mc.Ilvaine at [Roadar's?] & who had fled from the Enemy.

[1]Cohansie Bridge. Now Bridgeton, Cumberland County, New Jersey.

20th. [March]. Returned to Morris-Town the 20th of March where the 3d. Jersey Regimt. had just arrived after 20 days March from Tyconderoga.

22. [March]. This day the 3d. Jersey Regimt. was discharged with honor on Morris-Town Green. Those of the Men who were engaged during the War were indulged with a Furlough for Twenty days.

Sunday the 2d. of this Month [March]. was fought the hottest Battle that has been since the Battle of Princeton, on my Uncle's & Father's Plantations. The Enemy tis said lost 52 killed in the Field, 100 Wounded & several taken Prisoners, our loss inconsiderable. During the action my Uncle's & Father's Familys were obliged to take Shelter in their Cellars on Account of the Cannon & Field-Pieces.

In consequence of this my Father & uncle moved from Woodbridge, My Father near Elizth.Town, not possessing One foot of Land he owns.

Sunday. 30. [March]. I was in an Engagement this day on Strawberry Hill in Woodbridge. Fired Eight rounds myself being the first time I ever was in an action or saw the Enemy in the Field, notwithstanding I have been in the Continental service near fifteen Months. After the Battle which was very inconsiderable more than skirmishing, I went over the Creek. Dined with Mrs. & Miss Abbe Smith, Mr. Smith[1] being gone to the Enemy. Engaged in the Evening in moving the Goods of Justice Barron[2] also gone to the Enemy or at least such as the Enemy were obliged to leave this day on our approach.

[1]MR. SMITH. Probably William Smith, a Woodbridge farmer and member of the New Jersey Provincial Congress in 1775. Went with the British army to Staten Island in 1776 and remained there for the duration of the war. His property was confiscated in 1779.

[2]JUSTICE BARRON. Ellis Barron, of Woodbridge, served on the Middlesex County Committee of Observation and became captain in the county's 1st Regiment. Became a Loyalist when British troops entered New Jersey.

April 4th. After Visiting my Father & Friends in Elizth.Town I again sett out for Cohansie, where I met my old Company the 4th of April. Payed them all their wages & back-arrearages out of my own Pocket, the Paymaster not haveing Yet drawn their Pay, treated them handsomely and dismissed them to their own Homes, haveing commanded them as their Captain near fifteen Months as they all expressed themselves, much to their satisfaction haveing proved myself their Father Friend & good Officer.

On this Jaunt I spent a Week in Philaa. with the Gentlemen of the Army of my acquaintance & had my Portrait drawn by Mr. Peale[1] now in Posession of Miss Mc.Ilvaine of Bristol.

[1] CHARLES WILLSON PEALE (1741–1827). Born in Maryland. Became one of the most distinguished portrait painters of his generation. Apprenticed to a saddler, his painting skills resulted in his being sent to England for disciplined study in 1766. Returned to Maryland in 1769 and moved to Philadelphia in 1776. Saw limited military and political service. Best known for his many portraits of George Washington and other Continental generals and officers. The portrait in question (reproduced facing p. 1) shows Bloomfield in full-dress uniform.

14. [April]. I returned to Morris-Town & joined the Regt. one third of which were the 10th. Inst. Innoculated for the small-Poxe.

28. [April]. This day my Brother joined the Regimt. being appointed Surgeon's Mate. We mess with the other officers at Capt. Kinneys.
Our Regimt. do the Duty on the Ground.

May 14. 1777. My Brother & myself being Very unwell removed from Capt. Kinney's to Mr. Wick's.

Friday. 23d. [May]. My Father being appointed Senior-Surgeon of the Hospital now at Hanover this day moved his Family & Goods to Mr. Henry Wicks near Mendam from Elizth.Town.

Monday. 26. [May]. The 3d. Jersey Regt. moved from Morris Town to the lines near Brunswick Landing. My Brother went with the Regt. Continue myself at Mr. Wicks being now afflicted with a painful abcess on my right thumb.

June 26. On Thursday Genl. Howe with all his forces marched from Amboy over the Short-Hills where Genl. Maxwells Brigade consisting of the four Jersey Regimts. engaged them for some time under command of Major Genl. Lord Stirling.[1] Fought bravely but were obliged to retire from such a Vast Army to the grand Army at Middlebrook. Our Brigade lost one Capt. & Ensign killed, One Captn. & an adjutant taken Prisoners, one Lieut. & an Ensign Wounded, & about forty Privates killed, Wounded & taken Prisoners. The Enemy acknowledged in Gaines Paper[2] the loss of One Col., one Major, sundry other officers killed & 200 Privates killed, Wounded & taken Prisoners. Immediately after this Action the Enemy returned to Amboy embarked on board their shipping & 30th. Monday left the Province of New-Jersey haveing continued in it from the Middle of last November to this time, being near Eight Months, during which time, the Enemy were guilty of the most inhuman treatment to the Wig Inhabitants wherever they fell in their power, A faithful Account of which I hope in some future day to see honestly told by an impartial Historian. Let it be handed down to Posterity, and excite in them an Indignation against the petty Island of G.B. [Great Britain] and a laudable reverence for the memory of their Patriotic Ancestors, with a view of Religiously following their Example &c. &c. &c.

[1]LORD STIRLING. WILLIAM ALEXANDER (1726–83). Born in New York City. Wealthy landowner living in Basking Ridge, New Jersey. Surveyor general and member of the governor's council before the American Revolution. Sought title as the 6th earl of Stirling but was rejected by the House of Lords, 1762. With experience in the French and Indian War, received a commission as colonel of the 1st New Jersey, 1775; named brigadier general, March 1776; major general, February, 1777. In charge of the right wing of the Continental Army at the Battle of Long Island, August 27, 1776, and saw action at the battles of Trenton, Brandywine, Germantown, and Monmouth.

[2]Gaine's Paper. A reference to the Loyalist newspaper, the *New-York Mercury*, published in New York City by Hugh Gaine (1726/27–1807).

July. 1777. The latter end of this month I joined my Regimt. at Elizth.Town which was then under marching orders for Philada. & before we reached Princeton we were countermarched at first to Peeks-Kill, soon after which we were stationed at Aqquacannac[1] Newark & Elizth.Town

[1]Aqquacannac. Variously spelled, it is now chiefly the town of Passaic, New Jersey.

Augt. 22. Friday. About day-break this Morning the 1st. & 3d. Jersey Regts. with 100 Militia went over to Staaten Island opposite the Blazing Star[1] under command of Col. Ogden. Took Col. Lawrence, Ten other officers & about 120 privates. In the small action we had with them I had my Horse Wounded. We brought off near 10,000 £ worth of [prizes?]. Genl. Sullivan with about 1,000 of his division crossed to the Island opposite Elizth.Town, took one Col. & about 40 Privates & lost his rear guard in coming off of near 127 men.

[1]Blazing Star. A tavern in Woodbridge, Middlesex County, New Jersey.

25. [August]. We marched from Elizth.Town.

30. [August]. Passed through Philadelphia & Septr. 1st. joined Genl. Washington at Wilmington.

Sept. 3. 1777. This morning our advanced party had a skirmish with the Enemy in which Capt. Dallas of Col. Spencer's Regt. was killed.

September. Camp Valley Forge. March 10th. 1778. This Book being sent off with the Baggage of the Army 6th. Sept. last, and it not being in my power to keep a particular Journal since the Army left White-Clay Creek,[1] I take this opportunity to note in general, as follows, vizt.

[1]White-Clay Creek. Near Newark, New Castle County, Delaware.

White-Clay-Creek, Monday. Sepr. 8th. [1777]. Alarm. I was sent out with Capts. Conway & Hollinshead, Gifford & Forman & 130 Men properly officered from the Jersey Brigade & 24 Cavalry, as an advanced guard two Miles in front of our lines, with directions to skirmish with the enemy till they should drive me on the Main Army which was expected would be about day break & a general engagement ensue. I was alarmed all Night with the approach of the enemy & kept my party parraded.

Sept. 9. 1777. At day-break on Tuesday I received Orders to follow our Army who had marched at two at Night for the heighths of Brandewine [Brandywine] opposite Chad's Ford, where I also arrived this evening with my party much fatigued.

Wednesday. 10. [September]. An alarm, but the Enemy did not engage.

Thursday. 11. [September]. One of the Field-Officers of the day. At 7 A.M., a true alarm. At Eight the Enemy appeared, fought & drove in our advanced parties from the heighths on the south side of Chad's Ford. Immediately a severe cannonade of Shells, Bombs &c. &c. &c. opened from each side, which exhibited the grandest scene I ever saw, a sight beyond description grand.

At 2 P.M. Our division marched towards Jones' Ford. At 3. Lord Stirling and Genl. Sullivan's divisions engaged Lord Cornwallis's light corps & the British Main Army. We broke and Rallied and Rallied & broke from heighth to heighth till we fell on our main Army, who reinforced us & about sunset we made a stand, when I was wounded, having a Ball with the Wad shot through my left forearm & the fuse set my coat and shirt on fire. Soon after this, I left the field & rode about two Miles. By the assistance of a stranger dressed my Wound with some tow from my Catorich [cartridge] box & wrapped my Arm in my handkerchief. Rode 7 miles further & lodged with in 5 Miles of Chester with Mr. Periam, my Arm swelling and being Very painful all this time.

I shall not pretend to give a description of this battle, of the loss in killed or Wounded on either side. Indeed I could not for my unfortunate situation seperated me from the Army & prevented my having an opportunity of knowing. However, be it sufficient to say, that this was an unfortunate day to our Arms, though the enemy paid doubly severe for their success, yet by leaving the heighths of Brandewine (which Our Army did in the evening & marched to Chester) we left a road for the Enemy to take possession (as they afterward did) of Philadelphia.

It is well known that after we rallied the first time & broke & were closely pursued by the British-Grenadiers that Capt. Bellard of our Regt. who was wounded in the leg & would have fallen into the hands of the Enemy had I not (though I have the Modesty to say it myself) went back upon his crying for assistance, taken him behind me & brought him from the Field of Battle: & must undoubtedly have been killed had not the Enemys fire been expended & they relyed on their Bayonetts in their pursuit as their front was within a few Yards of us when I rode off with Capt. Bellard.

Friday. Sepr. 12. 1777. Being unable through the loss of blood to follow the Army, I was carried across the Delaware in Marcus Hook to West-Jersey, my Arm being much swelled Very painful & continued bleeding till 9 O'Clock this P.M. after which I rested tolerably well.

Saturday. 13. [September]. This Evening Dr. Bodo Otto[1] dressed my Arm for the first time being Upwards of 53 hours after I was wounded 20 hours of which it bled & reduced me Very Weak & Low.

[1]DR. BODO OTTO (d. 1782). Son of Dr. Bodo Otto, Sr. (1711–87). Militia colonel and physician who resided in Swedesboro, Gloucester County, New Jersey.

Sunday. 14. [September]. I was carried from Widow Clayton's in a light covered Waggon on Beds to Dr. Otto's near 12 miles & suffered greatly by the jolting of the Waggon. Here Dr. Elmer & Col. Holmes came to see me. My wound was examined & dressed & found that the extensir Muscles of my arm were greatly lacerated, and two sinus's formed from my elbow to my wrist & being in a high fever I was Much alarmed. However by the use of medines. [medicines] & good attendance in the course of three Weeks, the inflammatory Symtoms subsided. My Fever left me & my wound began to heal.

Wednesday. Octor. 1. This evening the enemy landed 1,200 Men & five field-pieces on the Jersey shore eight miles from Dr. Otto's, and in the Night their light horses came twice to the house where I lay after the Doctor, who was a Militia Colonel & an active man agt. them but not knowing I was in the house I fortunately escaped their search, and [entry unfinished].

2. [October]. Thursday Morning they appeared near the Docters & fought the Militia under Genl. Newcomb. This old granny of a Genl. pretending with 300 undisciplined Men to make a stand, but soon retreated helter skelter with his Men, who eminently distinguished themselves by the swiftness of their heels. In the midst of the fray I was carryed off & narrowly Escaped their pursuit, takeing 10 Miles into the pines of Gloucester County where I lay this Night at a Tar kill hut, miserably Accomodated, seeing the Moon & stars all night. However, being no astronmr. I made but few observations.

3. [October]. I was carried to Salem-County.

4. Octr. Safely lodged & well attended at parson Greenman's[1] in Pittsgrove. This day was fought the Battle of Germantown, in which our brigade suffered more in loss of Officers than in any Action before. I continued at Parson Greenmans till [October] 22. when I was taken by Dr. Harris[2] to Cumberland County, where I stayed with my Friends till my Wound was healed and I was able to ride on horseback when I set out and arrived at camp [Nov. 28. 1777.] at White Marsh & continued with the Brigade till the Enemy returned from Chestnut & Edge-Hill into Philadelphia after which I returned to the Jerseys [Decr. 10.] and spent the Winter with my Fathers family & Friends, in endeavoring to restore my Arm to its former usefulness.

[1]PARSON GREENMAN'S. Nehemiah Greenman was pastor of the Pittsgrove Presbyterian Church in Salem County, New Jersey, from 1753 until his death in 1779.

[2]DR. HARRIS. Probably Isaac Harris (1741–1808), a physician in Pittsgrove Township, Salem County, and surgeon in Silas Newcomb's brigade of New Jersey Militia.

1st Jany. 1778. Went on Staaten-Island with a flag & had an opportunity to converse with my old master Genl. Skinner[1] of the Green-coated gentry and others [of] my Acquaintance in Arms agt. their Country, who I have reason to believe now wish they had taken a different part in the contest.

[1]CORTLANDT SKINNER (1728–99). Native of New Jersey. Lawyer. Last attorney general of New Jersey before the American Revolution. Raised Loyalist troops, eventually consisting of at least four battalions and known as Skinner's Brigade. Served as a brigadier general of Loyalist troops. His battalions were involved in maintaining British control of Staten Island, and also fought at the Battle of Springfield, June 1780. Retired to England after the war.

Feby. 28. Returned to camp at the Valley-Forge.

March 8. Col. Dayton resigned, & Lt. Col. Barber obtained a furlough & set out for N. Jersey.

1777. The following is a true account of the Officers killed, Wounded and taken Prisoners belonging to the Jersey-Brigades, consisting of the four Jersey Regiments, under command of Brigadier Maxwell, in Lord Stirling's division, during the last campaign.

1st Regt. Major Joseph Morris, Capts. Andrew, McMyers & Ensign Patrick Hurley, killed. Captains John Conway, Isaac Morrison & Daniel Baldwin & Lieut. Robert Robertson Wounded. Captains Elias Longstreet & John Flahaven & Lieut. John Mercer taken Prisoners.

2d. Regt. Captains Joseph Stout & Ephraim Anderson, killed. Col. Israel Shreve & Ensign James Paul, Wounded. Capt. James Lowry & Lieut Ryerson taken Prisoners. Capt. Lowry died in Prison with hard Usage.

3d. Regimt. Major Joseph Bloomfield, Captains John Ross, Jeremiah Bellard & Cornelius Henman [Hennion], Lieut. Clarke & Ensign Jarvis Bloomfield, Wounded.

4th Regt. Ensigns Sprowls & John Hays, killed. Adjutant Joseph King, Wounded & taken Prisoner, and Lieut. Jonathan Holmes, taken Prisoner.

Brigade-Major James Witherspoon killed.

Scale of the Killed etc:	Taken Prisoners	Wounded	Killed	Total		
Colonels	0	1	0	1		
Lieutenant-Colonels	0	0	0	0	21 Killed & Wounded	7 taken Prisoners
Majors	0	1	2	3		
Captains	3	6	3	12		
Subalterns	4	5	3	12		

Total of Officers disabled during the campaign, most of them in the Battles of Brandewine & Germantown — 28.

April 23d. 1778. A List of all Field-officers in the Continental Army, in the Regiments now incamped at the Valley-Forge, with the Brigades they are arranged in & the States they belong to.

Colonels

Woodfords: McClenaham; Morgan; Mason

Scott: Bowman; Wood; Grason

1 Pena.: Chambers; Becker; Ervine, Promoted; Nagle

2d. Ditto: Cadwalader; Johnston; Brodhead; Humpton

Poor: Scammel, Gilley; Hale; Cortland; Livingston

Glover: Shepherd; Wiglesworth; Vose; Bigelow

Learned: Bailey; Wesson; Jackson

Patterson: Marshall; Bradford; Tupper; Brewer

Weedons: Febiger; Green; Davis; Lewis, Steward

Mulenburgh: Hendricks; Parker, Resigned;

Matthiews; Gibson; R. Parker, Dead; Russel

Maxwell: Ogden; Shreve; Dayton; Marten, Resigned

Late Conway: Craige; Magaw; Butler, Cook; Malcomb; Spencer

Huntington: Bradley; Webb; Swift

Varnum: Green; Angell; Chandler; Durgee

McIntosh: Clark; Patten; Sumner; Polk; Buncombe; Lamb; Hogan; Armstrong; Williams

Lieut. Colonels

Woodfords: Heath; Richardson; Innis

Scott: Talifero; Nevill; Parnell; Parker

1st Pensa.: Robinson; Miller; Grier; Hubley

2nd Pensa.: Butler; Frazier; Bayard; North

Poor: Reed; Dearborn; Wisenfielt; Reignier

Glover: Sprout; Coleman; Vose; Haskell

Learned: Badlome; Miller; Brooks

Patterson: Bassett; Littlefield; Carlton

Weedons: Simms; Baford; Farmer; Parker

Mulenburghs. Dallard; Davis; Weltner; Brent; Ball

Maxwells: Dehart; Rehea, Resigned; Barber; Brearly, Ch. Justice of Jerseys

Conway: Bonner, Killed; Harmer; Smith; Gray; Burr; Lindsley

Huntington: Meade; Prentice; Sherman; Starr

Varnum: Cumstock; Olney; Dyer; Russel

Mack Intoch: Davis; Harney; Thackston; Davidson; Lyttle; Melane; Dawson; Lutthrele

Majors

Woodford: West; Cropper; Snead; Wallace

Scotts: Bell; Dark

1 Pensa.: Moore; Williams; Hay; Ryan

2 D[itt]o: Christie; Taylor; Vernum; Mentgers

Poors: Gilman; Fitcomb; Fish; Ledyard

Glover: Parks; Porter; Cogswell; Bradish

Learned: Peters; Hull

Patterson: Winslow; Tubbs; Lithgow; Farnald

Weedons: Cabble; Hopkins; Tobs; Haws; Hebbfield; Jas. Murray

Mulenburg: Campbell; Dickerson; Barkard; Ellison; Murray

Maxwell: Bloomfield, resigned; Howel, resigned; Cummins; Connay

L. Conaway: Hauling; Talbot; Nicholas; Pawling

Huntington: Johnston; Silke; Haldridge; Sedgwick

Varnums: Ward; Thare; Hait; Sumner

McIntosh: Walker; Murphey; Dixon; Armstrong; Hogge; Ash; Fenner; Eatan; Polk

General Staff of the Army Nov. 1st. 1778

General and Commander in Chief his Excellency Geo. Washington Esqr.; Virginia; 1775 June the 15th.

Major Generals.

The Honble. Charles Lee. Prisoner, Res. [resigned]; Virginia; June 17 [1775]

Phillip Schuyler, Res.; N. York; June 19 [1775]

Israel Putnam; Connecticut; [June 19, 1775]

Horatio Gates; Virginia; May 16 [1776]

Wm. Heath; Massachusetts; Augt. 9 [1776]

Joseph Spencer, Res.; Connecticut; [August 9, 1776]

John Sullivan, Res.; N. Hampshire; [August 9, 1776]

Nathaniel Green; R. Island; [August 9, 1776]

Wm. Earl of Stirling; N. Jersey; February 19th; 1777.

Thomas Mifflin, Res.; Pensilvania; [February 19, 1777]

Arthur St. Clair; Pensilva.; Feby. 19th. 1777

Adam Stephens, Broke; Virginia [February 19, 1777]

Benjamin Lincoln; Massachusetts; [February 19, 1777]

Benedict Arnold; Connecticut; May 2 [1777]

Marquis De La Fayette; France; July 31 [1777]

Robert Howe; N. Carolina; Octr. [1777]

Alexr. McDougal; N. York; [October 1777]

Baron De Calb; Germany; [October 1777]

Brigadier Generals.

The Honble Willm. Thompson; Pensilvania; March 1, 1776

John Nixon; Massachusetts; August 9th [1776]

Saml. Holden Parsons; Connecticut; [August 9, 1776]

James Clinton; N. York; [August 9, 1776]

Christr. Gadsen, Resd.; S. Carolina; Septr. 6th [1776]

WilliamMoultree; D[itt]o; [September 6, 1776]

Laughlin Mc Intosh; Georgia; [September 6, 1776]

Wm. Maxwell, Resd.; N. Jersey; October 23d [1776]

Wm. Smallwood; Maryland; [October 23, 1776]

Mathias Alexis, Res.; France; Novr. 5th.[1776]

De Roche Fermoy, Res.; D[itt]o; [November 5, 1776]

Pierre homme DeBore, Suspended & Resigned; D[itt]o [November 5, 1776]

Henry Knox, Artillery; Massachusetts; 27 [November 1776]

Francis Nash, Killed; N. Carolina; Feby. 5, 1777

Enoch Poor; N. Hampshire; Feby. 21, 1777

John Glover; Massachusets; [February 21, 1777]

John Patterson; D[itt]o; [February 21, 1777]

Anthony Wayne; Pensilva.; [February 21, 1777]

James Varnum, Res.; R. Island; [February 21, 1777]

Peter Muhlenburgh; Virginia; [February 21, 1777]

George Weedon; D[itt]o; [February 21, 1777]

Wm. Woodford; D[itt]o; [February 21, 1777]

Geo. Clinton, Governor; N. York; March 25 [1777]

Edward Hand; Penseilva.; April 1st. [1777]

Charles Scott; Virginia; [April 1, 1777]

Ebenezer Learned, Res.; Massachusets; May 2 [1777]

Jediah Huntington; Connecticut; 12th [May 1777]

Thos. Conway, Resigned; France; 13 [May 1777]

Count Pelasky, Horse, killed; Poland; Septr. [1777]

Baron Steuben, Promoted, appointed Inspector-General; Prussia; March 20, 1778

John Stark; N. Hampshire; 1777

Duportail; France [1777]

Wm. Irvin; Pensilvania; [1779]

Jas. Hogan; N. Carolina; [1778]

Jethro Sumner; D[itt]o; [1779]

Mordecai Gist; Maryland; [1779]

[Isaac] Huger; S. Carolina; [1779]

March 20th. 1778. Baron De Steuben[1] was appointed Inspector Genl. of the American Army. Sub. and Brigade-Inspectors were also this day appointed to introduce the Prussian Exercise in our Army under direction of Baron Steuben. Lt. Col. Barber was by Genl. Orders appointed one of the four Sub.-Inspectors & myself Brigade-Inspector to the Jersey-Brigade, [April] in which duty I have been & am daily engaged.

[1]Friedrich Wilhelm Augustus von Steuben (1730–94). Native of Germany. Became an officer in the Prussian army, eventually serving on the staff of Frederick the Great, king of Prussia. Fell from favor and was discharged in 1763. Through intervention of American commissioners in France, came to America late in 1777. Presented himself to Congress, asking to serve as a volunteer. Put in charge of troop training at Valley Forge. Eminently successful and commissioned as major general and inspector general, May 5, 1778, based on Washington's enthusiastic support. Was essential to molding an effective Continental fighting force, and his training program was used until the War of 1812.

May 5. Extract from general Orders.

It having pleased the Almighty Ruler of the Universe propitiously to defend the cause of the United American States, & finally by raising us up a powerful friend among the princes of the earth, to establish our liberty and Independance upon a lasting foundation: It becomes us to set apart a day for gratefully Acknowledging the Divine goodness & celebrating the important event which we owe to his benign interposition.

The several Brigades are to be assembled for this purpose at Nine O'Clock tomorrow Morning, when their chaplains will communicate the intelligence contained in the postcript of the Pensilvania Gazette of the 2d. inst. & offer up a Thanksgiving, & deliver a discourse suitable to the occasion.

At half past ten O'Clock a cannon will be fired, which is to be a signal for the Men to be under Arms. The Brigade-Inspectors will then inspect their dress & arms, form the Battalions according to the instructs. given them, & announce to the commanding officers that the Batts. are formed. The Brigadiers & Commandants will then appoint the Field-Officers to command the Battalions, after which each Battn. will be ordered to load & ground their arms. At half past eleven O'Clock another Cannon will be fired as a signal for the March; upon which the several Brigades will begin their March by wheeling to the right by Platoons & proceed by the nearest way to the left of their Ground in the new position that will be pointed out by the Brigade Inspectors. A third signal will be given upon which there will be a discharge of thirteen Cannon. When the thirteenth has fired, a running fire of the infantry will begin on the right of Woodford's, & continue throughout the whole front line; it will be then taken up on the left of the second line, & continue to the right. Upon a signal given, the whole Army will huzza, *Long live the King of France*!

The Artillery then begins again & fires thirteen rounds. This will be succeeded by a second general discharge of the Musketry in a running fire, *Huzza! Long live the friendly European powers*! Then the last discharge of thirteen pieces of Artillery will be given, followed by a general running fire, *Huzza for the American States*!

This acct. I drew up, sent & was published in the Jersey Gazette.[1]

[1]Jersey Gazette. *New-Jersey Gazette* (Trenton), a weekly newspaper commencing publication in 1778.

Wednesday. 6. [May]. Agreably to the above Orders, his Excellency Genl. Washington, his amiable lady & suite, Lord Stirling, the Countess of Stirling, with other general officers & ladys, attended at Nine O'Clock at the Jersey Brigade, when the Postscript mentioned above was read, & after Prayer a suitable discourse delivered to Lord Stirling's division by the Revd. *Mr. Hunter.*

Upon the signal at half past eleven the whole army repaired to their Alarm posts; upon which Genl. Washington & the Genl. Officers reviewed the whole Army at their respective posts; & after the firing of the Cannon & Musketry & the huzza's were given agreably to the orders, the Army returned to their respective brigade-parrades, & were dismissed.

All the officers of the Army then assembled, & partook of a collation provided by the Genl., at which several patriotic toasts were given, accompanied with three cheers. His Excellency took leave of the officers at five O'Clock, upon which there was a universal huzzaing, *Long live Genl. Washington*! & clapping of hands until the Genl. rode some distance.

The non-commissd. officers & Privates followed the example of their officers as the Genl. passed their Brigades.

Approbation indeed was conspicuous in every countenance, & universal joy reigned throughout the Camp.

Monday. 18. [May]. Three thousand Men properly officered under command of the Marquis De la Fayette & Brigadier Poor[1] left the camp at Ten this Morning with four Field-officers in order to proceed to the lines near Philadelphia.

I forgot to mention that some time past Col. Shreve's[2] (2d. Jersey) Regt. marched to West Jersey & last week Col. Ogden's (the 1st.) Regt. marched from camp to West-Jersey also.

[1]ENOCH POOR (1736–80). Native of Massachusetts. Early military experience in the French and Indian War. Named delegate to two provincial congresses in New Hampshire; commissioned colonel of the 2nd New Hampshire regiment, 1775. Rose to rank of brigadier general, 1777, after having taken part in such battles as Trenton and Princeton. Later fought at Saratoga and Monmouth; also involved in Sullivan's expedition.

[2]ISRAEL SHREVE (1739–99). Native of New Jersey. Farmer in Gloucester County. Commissioned lieutenant colonel 2nd New Jersey, November 1775; promoted to colonel, November 1776. Served at Brandywine, Germantown, and on Sullivan's expedition. Migrated west after the war and once again became a farmer.

May. The latter part of this month the 3d. & 4th. Jersey Regts. with Genl. Maxwell marched to Mount-Holly in West-Jersey where we were joined by the 1st. & 2d. Jersey Regts. & Forman's Corps.

June. We kept large commands on the lines below Haddenfield, Moores-Town &c. which were relieved weekly. Engaged myself in Exercising the Brigade & introducing the Baron de Steubens Instructions.

18. [June]. On the 18th. of June (whilst the officers of the Brigade & Gentn. of the Town were feasting on Turtle & Punch &c. &c.) Information was brought that the Enemy were advancing from Haddenfield and Moores-Town to Mount-Holly.

19. [June]. At break of day our alarm Guns were fired. The Brigade immediately marched to the Black-Horse (six miles) & Halted. Genl. Clinton[1] at 12 entered Mount Holly, where he continued with the whole Army till [June 22].

[1]HENRY CLINTON (ca. 1738–95). Born at a time when his father was governor of Newfoundland. Well connected with leading British families and held a number of military commissions. Also became a member of Parliament, 1772, the same year he received a major generalship. Sent to the American theater, 1775, and saw extensive campaigning. Named to replace William Howe as commander in chief of British forces in America, 1778. Retreated from Philadelphia to New York, June 1778. Left his post in 1782 in favor of Guy Carleton and returned to England.

22. [June]. Monday morning when they occupied our quarters at the Black-Horse & we moved by way of Borden Town to Crosswicks.

23. [June]. The Enemy advanced, their front overtook our rear at Crosswicks-Bridge where a smart skirmish ensued, the 3d. Jersey Regt. covering the retreat of the Brigade & militia.

24. [June]. The Brigade lay this night at Maidenhead, Wednesday near & Thursday night at Hydes-Town.

25. June. 1778. This night I lay with Capt. Voorhees Lieuts. Wm. Pyatt & Bloomfield with 50 Contl. Soldiers & 40 Militia on Taylor's heights within a quarter of a Mile of Clinton's Main-Army. Fired upon & alarmed them several times in the night, and in the morning followed their rear. Capt. Voorhees party took 15 Prisoners & had several skirmishes with the Jagars.[1] Took three Jagars myself Prisoners when I was reconnitreing within sight of the Enemys Rear. The Jersey Brigade with the Marquis D. la Feayette, Genl. Wayne & Scott's[2] chosen corps lay together this Night in Upper-Freehold.

[1]Jägers. German light infantrymen.
[2]CHARLES SCOTT (ca. 1739–1813). Native of Virginia. Associated with George Washington in the French and Indian War. Named lieutenant colonel, Virginia Continental Line, February 1776; colonel, May 1776; brigadier general, April 1777. Commanded capably at Brandywine, but criticized for his performance at Germantown. Heavily involved at Monmouth, Scott spoke out against Charles Lee after the battle. Later moved west and served as governor of Kentucky, 1808–12.

Friday. 26. [June]. Marched & Lodged with the above Troops to English Town where we were reinforced by Genl. Lee's Division.

Saturday. 27. June. 1778. Lay on our Arms at English-Town, waiting the motions of the Enemy.

Sunday. 28. [June]. Genl. Lee's Division the Marquis's corps & the Jersey Brigade advanced within full view of the Enemy near Monmouth-Court-House but were ordered to retreat, and form, and form & retreat in sight of the British Grenadiers who continued advancing till we fell in with Genl. Washington's Main-Army, when we were ordered to form the second line whilst the Front line commanded by our illustrious Genl. in person engaged the flower of the British army on the highths near Freehold Court-House in the County of Monmouth. Drove the proud

King's-Guards & haughty British-Grenadiers, & gained Immortal-honor, to the Shame & infamy of Genl. Lee who acted the part of the base [word omitted] in not engaging the Enemy when he had received positive orders to attack them. But History I expect will give a full account of this memorable action, justly censure Lee for his scandalous behaviour & give due credit (if possible for the pen of a writer) to Genl. Washington's bravery & merit.

The Front Line of the Army lodged on the Field of battle. The Rear line at EnglishTown.

29. [June]. The whole Army lay at & near English-Town.

Tuesday. 30. June. 1778. Genl. Washington & the Main Army marched to Brunswick. The Jersey Brigade to the lines near Middletown where we continued till 7th. July as the Enemy had all embarked & left this State (*thank God*) the 5th. of July, after which we marched to Elizth.Town & relieved the Militia from Monmouth to Aqucanong by Weekly Commands sent from the Brigade which (*now 25th. Augt.*) continues, & is like to continue in Elizth.Town where we want for Nothing to make our time Pass Very agreably.

June. 1778. I forgot to mention that Lt. Col. Barber was wounded (a Ball passing through his right side) in the action 28 ulto. and that a day of *feu de joy* in commemoration of the late Battle was kept by the Main-Army in Brunswick the 4th. of July which far exceeded the *feu de joy* of the 6th. of May last at the Valley Forge.

September 12th. General Reed[1] by Direction of Congress waited on the Officers of the Jersey Brigade, &c. &c. &c.

See, postea &c.

[1]JOSEPH REED (1741–85). Born Trenton, New Jersey. Established law practice in Philadelphia during 1770. Appointed lieutenant colonel of Pennsylvania militia, 1775; adjutant general of the Continental Army, 1776. Highly critical of Washington's defense of Manhattan. Resigned army commission, January 1777, but assisted Washington as a volunteer at Brandywine, Germantown, and Monmouth. Served in the Continental Congress during 1778 and became president of the Supreme Executive Council of Pennsylvania, 1778–81, making him the nominal head of Pennsylvania's government.

Salem Augt. 25th. 1779. Continuation of my Diary. It is now a Year since I have taken any Notice in this my Diary, how and where I have passed my time, and this has been owing to the Multiplicity and Variety of Business I have been engaged in. I therefore now propose to give a short Account of my Life for the last Year.

But first it will be necessary for me to observe, that *at the time* the Provincial Congress issued a Warrant appointing me a Captain in the 3d. New-Jersey Regimt. and *Before* I received the said Warrant or recruited a Man, I was on a Jaunt with Mr. Alexander Moore Junr. of Cumberland in order to attend his Nuptials at Newton, Bucks-County, Pensilvania where, on the 14th. February being Valentine's day, 1776, I first saw Miss *Polly Mc.Ilvaine,* who, on the Marriage of my Friend Mr. Moore (to whom I was Grooms-Man) was Miss Sally Tate's now Mrs. Moore, her Brides-Maid. This Lady Miss Mc.Ilvaine, at this Celebration fairly and in short Inlisted me for Life; from this Time and not before, I began to think seriously of a Partner for Life and wished I was discharged from my new appointment of a Captain, which by this Time I found was sent to the County of Cumberland for me. I accordingly came to the Resolution of returning to Cumberland and Recruit my Company, but was determined at the same time to Engage Miss Mc.Ilvaine's affections, by every opportunity that lay in my power; that I fulfilled my engagement to the Publick, appears before by my Diary in February and March 1776 and the continuation thereof to 25. Augt. 1778 [1779]. And also that my Resolution with respect to Miss Mc.Ilvaine succeeded to my best wishes will appear by what follows:

My Friend Moore on bringing his Bride home to Cumberland was attended by her Brother and Sisters, and, amongst others by her Bride's-Maid, the amiable Miss Mc.Ilvaine. I immediately waited on them and Devoted every moment of my Time I could spare from my other Avocations in paying my Respects to the Lady who engrossed all my thoughts, and, I had the agreable satisfaction to find that my addresses met with the desired effect, for on Thursday the 27th. April 1776, *we engaged* to write to each other, and, as soon as the Campaign was over with the Consent of Friends we were to be qualifyed to our Inlistment agreable to Law and Gosple. We accordingly corresponded by Letter whilst I was in the Northern Army. But on my return from Tyeconderoga in January 1777, the distressed situation of the Jerseys and especially of my Fathers Family and Miss Mc.Ilvaine having fled for fear of the Enemy (at the Time they were at Trenton & Burlington) to Reading prevented the accomplishment of our Wishes. See my Diary for Jany. Feby. & March 1777. I visited her at Reading (See March 2d. 1777.) and here we agreed I should serve another Campaign. In September following I was badly wounded (See Sepr. 11. 1777.), and did not get well of my wound till the Spring of 1778, when the Campaign opened and not having any promiseing prospects in Civil-Life I was determined to serve this Campaign also; which I did till the 12th. of September, when General (now Governor) Reed, one of the Commissioners of Congress called on the Officers of the Jersey Brigade, and give (by Direction of Congress) Leave to all those Officers who chose to retire from the army an Opportunity of doing it; as all the Regiments in the army of the United States were to be reduced, The four Jersey Regiments to three and the promise of a Years pay advance. I well knew that this was the Time (if ever) for me to retire from the Army to fulfill my *Best* wishes, especially as the Enemy had evacuated the State of New-Jersey, and the Courts of Law were now opened and Invited all of my *Profession* (the *Law*) to enter into Civil Life; the strong solicitations of all my Friends, and the still stronger *Tye*, I was about entering into, (which would never answer whilst I continued in the Army) Induced me to accept of this good opportunity of retireing from the Army.

Accordingly, on Monday the 14th. Septr. 1778, I gave a handsome and elegant Entertainment to the Officers of the Third Jersey Regt. and those Officers who were nearly Connected to me in the Brigade, in consequence of my determination of Retireing from the Army, which I immediately did, having Leave of absence from General Maxwell 'till my Resignation was Accepted of, and, which was not till the 1st. of February 1779, till which Time, I was mustered and continued on the Pay-Rolls as Major of the 3d. New-Jersey Regimt. and received pay as such, and from the said first day of February 1779, had a Year's pay in advance; though as it will appear in the sequel, I was engaged from the 14. September and enjoyed the most of the Time several offices in Civil Government and, Notwithstanding my thus leaving the Army, Yet, when a party of the Enemy advanced into the Jerseys by Newark-Bay towards Hackinsack, the latter end of September I again joined my Regimt. and felt my inclination so strongly attached to a Military Life that I verely believe, if I had not attended Mr. Moores Wedding or seen the Lady so often above mentioned, I should have continued in the Army till the war or my Life had been ended; for, having a Natural turn for the Military Profession, and, as I can say with Truth and Confidence was honored and esteemed by my Superior Officers, and repected & beloved by my Inferior Officers and the Soldiery, and having always had My Rank, and being in a fair Way of Promotion, it is not to be wondered at, especially from my Youth and the Gaiety & Variety attending a Soldiers-Life.

I was a Captain in the 3d. New-Jersey Regiment from the 8th. Feby. to 20th. November 1776, and a Major from 20th. Novr. 1776, to the first of February 1779, being three Years a Soldier wanting Eight days.

The Person that succeeded me as Major of the third New-Jersey Regimt. is now a Lieutenant Colonel.

The following Certificate, unsolicited, was sent to me In April last, attended with a polite Letter from Col. Brearley, now Chief-Justice of New-Jersey. (To wit)

> WHEREAS Major Joseph Bloomfield, having been wounded in the Battle of Brandywine, and thereby disabled in one of his Arms, made application to the Committee of Arrangement for Leave to retire from the service; they accordingly at his request put him on the Supernumerary list, with the following honourable Note, "That He was a deserving officer, and worthy the Honorable Notice of Congress."
>
> But as no formal discharge has been given by Congress, it is therefore a duty the General and Field-Officers of the Brigade owe Major Bloomfield, to Certify, from their own knowledge and personal Acquaintance, that He was a Brave, vigilant Officer attentive to Duty and Discipline and is a real loss to the Service.

Elizabeth-Town
April 19th. 1779
(Signed)
Wm. Maxwell, B. Genl.
Elias Dayton, Col. 3d. Jersey Regt.
M. Ogden, Col. 1st. J. Regt.
Israel Shrieve [Shreve], Col. 2d. Jersey Regt.
David Brearley, Lt. Col. 1st. J. Regt.

Francis Barber, Lt. Col. 3d. Jersey Regt.
Wm. De Hart, Lt. Col. 2d. Jersey Rgt.
Danl. Piatt, Major 1st. J. Rgt.
Jno. Ross, Major 2d. Jersey Regt.
Jno. Conway, Major 3d. Jersey Regt.

So much for my Life whilst a Soldier.

After my leave of absence from the Army in September I attended the Courts of Essex, Morris, Somerset, Middlesex, Monmouth and Hunterden, and, on the 29th. October 1778 I was chosen Clerk of the House of Assembly of New-Jersey, and officiated as such accordingly. (See their Votes at this Time Jr. [January?] 7.)

On the 9th. of November 1778, I received a Licence as Counceller & Advocate at Law and was commissioned by the Governor accordingly.

On the 12th. December I was unanimously chosen by the Joint-Meeting of the Council & Assembly, Register of the Court of Admiralty in this State and received a Commission as such &c.

On Thursday Evening the 17th. December. 1778. Agreable to the aforementioned Engagement, made the 27th. April 1776 and the continued correspondence, by Letter as well as by my Visits from that Time to this day, Miss Polly Mc.Ilvaine honored me with her hand, and we were *Marryed* by the Revd. Mr. Boydd, at Fairview near Bristol, the late elegant seat of Mrs. Bloomfield's Father & now in Possession of John Clark, Esqr. (who Marryed Mr. Mc.Ilvaines Widow).

So that this Lady, now Mrs. Bloomfield is the Partner of my good and ill-fortune for and during Life.

She is the Daughter of William Mc.Ilvaine, Deceased, formerly an eminent Merchant in the City of Philadelphia, and a Native of Scotland. Her Mothers maiden-Name, was Ann Emerson, a native of Ireland.

In February & March 1779, I was appointed to Prosecute the Pleas of the State for the Counties of Cumberland & Salem.

On the 15th. May 1779, I was appointed One the Surrogates of the Ordinarys Court in this State and commissioned by the Governer accordingly.

On the 18th. May, I arrived with Mrs. Bloomfield, accompanied by my Brother Dr. Bloomfield & Sister Nancy Bloomfield at Salem, in the County of Salem, where I am settled, and have been and am now engaged in attending the Business incident to my Profession and the offices I hold in the State. On the 15th. June I was appointed to prosecute the Pleas of the State for the County of Gloucester.

Augt. 22d. This week received a Commission from the Governor & Privy-Council as Commissioner of Loans for the County of Salem.

Those singular marks of favor as well from the State, as the Counties, lays me under the strongest obligations to exert myself to fulfill the respective Trusts reposed in me, with care and attention & fidelity, so as to meet with the approbation of the Publick, and thereby secure to myself their Friendship and Esteem. JOS. BLOOMFIELD.

Sept. & October (Salem) Novmbr. 1779. Mrs. Bloomfield was taken about the middle of September, with an Ague followed by a remitting and continual Fever (the seasoning as they call it of Strangers to this Fever & Ague-Country.)

This Fever was attended with the most alarming symtoms, which her Physicians prognosticated would be fatal, but the Supreme Physician, in his benevolent and most merciful Goodness, restored her, after near three months Illness, to her usual health.

Finding my situation at Salem no ways central to my business, as I ride abt. 20 Miles below Salem to Cumberland Court, and near 100 Miles to the Eastward in attendance on Middlesex & Monmouth Courts, and entirely out of the way of the Courts of Admiralty which are generally held at Allen Town or Burlington, and Being Register of this Court, requires my constant attendance, and withal, Salem being a very unhealthy & sickly place, & Mrs. Bloomfield dreading the consequence and risque attending another seasoning to this unwholesome *fever* and *Ague*

Country, determined us to remove to a place more healthy & more central to my business, and thereby prevent (if possible) Sickness, so much absence from home and Waste of Time in travelling &c. &c. &c.

March 13th. 1780. Urged by those strong Inducements, we therefore, on Monday the 13th. of March, removed with our two servants to Haddonfield, in the County of Gloucester; This pleasant little village, being esteemed one of the most healthy situations in all the Country, but six Miles from the City of Philadelphia, the Metropolis of America, 45 Miles from Cumberland (the lowest Courts I attend) & between 50 & 60 Miles from Middlesex & Monmouth, (the farthest Courts I attend to the Eastward), and in the direct road from Egg-Harbour & the Seashore to Philadelphia so that I am now central to my business. In a most agreable situation pursuing my Profession & the business incident to the offices I hold in the State.

Oct. 11th. 1781. Mrs. Bloomfield's Brothers & Friends living at Bristol, directly opposite Burlington, and She being Very desirous to live as near them as my business would permit; also inclining to purchase & settle myself for Life, and Burlington being near central to my business, and promising as fair as any place for my Profession, induced me to purchase a House Lot & some Meadow in Burlington. And on the 11. Octr. 1781, I removed from Haddonfield with my Family & Goods to my House on Greenbank in Burlington, where I now reside, and hope to abide during my Natural-Life.

Dec. 25th. I was re-appointed Register of the Court of Admiralty of New-Jersey.

Febry. 12. 1782. I was this day appointed to prosecute the Pleas of the State for the County of Burlington; so that I now prosecute the Pleas of the State in the countys of Cumberland, Salem, Gloucester & Burlington, being all the Counties I attend steadily, except Monmouth, where the Atty. General of the State attends himself.

My Business therefore arises in those five Counties, the Courts held in which several Counties I always attend, together with the Supreme Courts & Courts of Chancery held at Trenton and the Courts of Admiralty generally held in Burlington & Allen-Town.

Appendixes

1. Farewell Address to Bloomfield's Company, March 1776 (from the "Plain Dealer" [Bridgeton, New Jersey], RUL)

A Short Valedictory Address to Capt. Bloomfield's Company of Continental Forces Delivered the Evening before they march'd, March 26th, 1776.

To Joseph Bloomfield, Esqr., Capt. And To the other Officers of the first Company of Continental Forces belonging to the third New Jersey Battalion, raised in Cumberland County.

This short and imperfect address as a small token of his Zeal for the cause of Liberty, and respect for you & the Company under your command, is humbly inscribed By The Author.

Friends, Countrymen, and Soldiers,

As most of you were born and brought up in this place with me, I feel myself greatly interested in your welfare & success. Permit me then, my dear friends, to take my Serious *farewell* of you, with a Short address.

Words cannot express the Satisfaction I feell, on seeing such a number of respectable persons, voluntarily sacrificing their Ease and present Interest, for the sake of serving their country; & generously offering, at this critical juncture, to hazard their lives on the high places of the field, in order to defend those rights & priviledges, which our cruel and unnatural enemies, are endeavouring to wrest from us, with the points of their Bayonets. The Sun, my friends, never shone on a contest more just, nor does the History of mankind afford a single instance of a people engaged in a cause more important, than that in which you are now engaged. Greece, Italy, Holland, Switzerland, & even Great Britain herself, (now our bloody foe) have faught & bled in the cause of Liberty. But what are any, or what are all those countries united? They are little more in comparison with these American Colonies, than this County of Cumberland is, to the whole province of New Jersey. In short, the fate of millions, of a whole Continent of people, depends on the event of the present unhappy dispute. And since the irrevocable blow is struck, and our adversaries have left the merits of their cause to the Decision of the Sword, nothing but a resolute and manly resistance, can save our devoted Land from inevitable ruin. Go on then my brave friends, in the glorious cause you have undertaken; let no difficulties however great: let no obsticles however discouraging, hinder you from persisting in what you have begun. As the military life you are now entering upon is new to most of you, give me leave to recommend it to you, as my parting advice, to live sober, temperate, & regular, & carefully guard against all those vices & irregularities, that are too common in Camps & Armies, particularly profane Swearing and the excessive use of spiritous liquor. These will injure your health, blast your reputation, & unfit you for the service of your country. Should you be called into the field of Action, it is more than probable, that some of you will lose your lives in Battle. For your comfort & encouragement I would remind you that, should it be the fate of any of you to fall there, you will die gloriously; you will expire in the defence of your country, and suffer martyrdom in the cause of Liberty. Remember the illustrious *Hampdon*[1] who fell in the cause of Liberty in the cruel & arbitrary reign of Charles the 1st. Remember *Docr. Warren,*[2] the *Hampdon* of America, who fell at the Battle on Bunkers Hill, in the still more cruel, & arbitrary reign of George the 3d. Remember the brave General *Montgomery,* the spirited McPhearson,[3] the gallant Capt. Cheeseman[4] & many other of our brave countrymen (as well Soldiers as Officers) who have boldly Sacrificed their lives, in the glorious cause of Liberty, in which you are now engaged. Imitate their noble example. Let the same patriotic Spirit that glowed in their breasts, animate yours also. Asscend the Summit of military honour, by acts of bravery & heroism like theirs. Let not the faithful pages of some future historian, be sullied with the recital of a single cowardly or inglorious action which any of you may be guilty of; but may you conduct so, as to gain immortal honour to yourselves, & be a credit to the place to which you belong.

May you all serve your Country with courage & fidelity. May you go forth, to oppose your cruel Enemy, in the name of "The Lord of Hosts, the God of Armies." Trusting in him, may you always prove victorious. May he preserve you in safety, in the midst of the greatest danger. And, having by your valour and activity, procured peace and tranquility to your oppressed & bleeding country, may you all return home to your friends, loaded with trophies of victory, & crowned with wreaths of unfading *Laurels.* May you then all prove victorious & useful citizens, untill you have compleated the measure of your days. And having faithfully served your Country in your day & generation; according to the will of Heaven, may you all die like *Christians.*

With these my Sincere wishes, & ardent prayers, for your success, welfare, & safe return home, I now take my leave of you, and with the feelings of humanity, & affection of a friend, I bid you one and all Farewell!

[1]JOHN HAMPDEN (ca. 1595–1643). English Parliamentary leader of the opposition to King Charles I. Raised troops against the Crown in the English Civil War and was killed at Chalgrove Field while holding out against Royalist forces.

[2]JOSEPH WARREN (1741–75). Major general of Massachusetts rebel troops. Killed at the Battle of Bunker Hill, June 17, 1775.

[3]JOHN MACPHERSON. Captain from Delaware. Aide-de-camp to Major General Richard Montgomery. Killed at the Siege of Quebec, December 31, 1775.

[4]JACOB CHEESMAN. Captain, 1st New York. Aide-de-camp to Major General Richard Montgomery. Killed at the Siege of Quebec, December 31, 1775.

2. Orders to Colonel Elias Dayton, May 1776 (Elias Dayton Papers, NJHS)

FROM PHILIP SCHUYLER

Saratoga, May 14th, 1776.

Sir,

General Sullivan will order you to proceed to Johnstown with a Detachment of the Regiment under your Command: On your Arrival there you will take up your Quarters at the House of Gilbert Tree, Innholder, and give Notice to the Highlanders who live in the vicinity of the Town to repair to it; and when any Number are collected there, you will send off their Baggage, Infirm, Women and Children in Waggons, for which you will apply to the Committee of Tryon County, or [for] some of them.

You will make an exact List of the Men, Women, and Children, distinguishing those under five years old, and those from five and under Twelve from those beyond that age. Copy of which you will transmit to me.

You will give the strictest Order that no abuse be given to the Persons of these People, and that all their Effects be secur'd in such a manner that the most trifling Part of their Property may not be destroy'd.

After having secur'd the Highlanders you will let Sir John Johnson know that you have a Letter from me which you are order'd to deliver in Person, and beg his attendance to receive it. If he comes, as soon as you have deliver'd the Letter, and he has read it, you are immediately to make him *close* Prisoner, and carefully guard him that he may not have the least opportunity of Escape. When you have done this you are to repair to his House, taking him with you, and after having plac'd proper Sentinels to prevent any Person belonging to the Family from carrying out Papers, you are to examine his Papers in his own Presence, and in the Presence of William Duer, Esquire who accompanies you; and with whom I wish you to consult when any Difficulty arises.

If you find any Papers relative to any intended Operations against the Cause of America, or any Letters from British Governors of Officers or Agents of the Ministry, you will make a List of such Papers and Letters, Copy whereof you will deliver to Sir John Johnson, and another, together with such Papers and Letters, you will transmit to me.

You and Mr. Duer will both give your Words of Honor that you will discover to no Persons whatever the Contents of any Papers or Letters which are of a private Nature, and which do not effect the Cause of America.

Although Sir John Johnson is to be closely guarded he is by no means to experience the least ill treatment in his own Person, or those of his Family: and you are to be particularly careful that none of the Men under your Command, or any Persons whatever, destroy, or take away the most trifling Part of his Property, except Arms, and Ammunition, which you are to secure and bring down with you and deliver to Mr. Philip V. Renslaer, Store-Keeper, with a Charge to keep them safe 'till further Orders from me.

In securing Sir John Johnson, and in searching his House, I wish the least Tumult possible, and to that End, you are not to suffer a private soldier to enter, unless by your immediate Order.

You will constantly keep strong Guards, and a good Lookout that you may not experience a Surprise both in marching up, whilst you remain there, and on your Return. Having secur'd Sir John Johnson, and brought him to Albany, you are there to cause him to be guarded with the same Attention, and to send me Notice of his Arrival.

> I am Sir your most Hum. Servant,
> PH: SCHUYLER, M. General.

PHILIP SCHUYLER TO SIR JOHN JOHNSON[1]

Saratoga, May 14th, 1776.

Sir,

After candidly scanning, cooly considering and Comparing the variety of Information which Imputes to you the most Hostile Intentions against the Country, I could have wished for the sake of human nature to have them groundless, unhappily they are so well Supported by the testimony even of those who were Intrusted with the Secret of your Intended operations and whose Remorse has Induced them to a full discovery, as not to leave a doubt upon my mind that you have acted Contrary to the Sacred Engagements you lay under to me, and thro' me to the public. It is therefore necessary for the Safety of the Inhabitants and the weal of the Country that I should put it out of Your power to Embroil it in domestic Confusion, and have therefore ordered you to be made *close* prisoner, hereby discharging you from your parole, and sent down to Albany to be thence conveyed to his Excellency General Washington: but Influenced by, and acting upon principles which will never Occasion a remorse of Conscience, I have at the same time ordered that no Insult should be offered to Your *person* or *family* and that Your *property* should be guarded and secured with a Scrupulous attention, for Sir, American Commanders Engaged in the Cause of Liberty remain uninfluenced by the savage and Brutal Example which has been given by the british Officers, In wantonly *setting on fire the buildings of Individuals* and otherwise destroying their property.

> I am Sir, Your Humble Servant,
> PH: SCHUYLER.

To Sir John Johnson, Bar[one]t.

¹Letter enclosed in Schuyler's order to Dayton, May 14, 1776.

FROM JOHN SULLIVAN

Albany, May 17th, 1776.

Sir,

In your march from this to Tryon County, and at that place, every method must be used to prevent The Soldiers from Firing their pieces, Insulting the Inhabitants or doing any act of Rudeness whatever. A Strict Silence must be observed by the men at all Times. When you are arrived and have Seized Sir John Johnson, you are to Seize the following persons or either of them which you may find at his House, namely: James Grey, John Munroe, Thomas Swords, Capt. McAlpine, Hugh Munro, Mr. Clyde of Stillwater, Isaac Mann of Stillwater, or either of his Sons, Joseph Anderson or Samuel Anderson.

Your men are frequently to be Cautioned against offering any Insult or abuse to the Indians, as one act of Rudeness in a Soldier might Involve America in a Dangerous war with a Savage Enemy.

> Sir I am your Humble Servt,
> JNO. SULLIVAN, B. Genl.

Colo. Dayton.

3. Colonel Elias Dayton's Account of the Battle of Brandywine, September 11, 1777 (Elias Dayton Papers, NJHS)

September 11 [1777] was fought the battle of Brandywine, near Chad's Ford and Birmingham meeting house. The Cannonadeing begun about eight O'clock in the morning. At the same time a party of light troops under General Maxwell attacked a party of the Enemy on the opposite side of the river. The action was warm for some time, & who should keep the field doubtfull, but upon the Enemy advancing a Brigade in the rear of those allready engaged, our people gave way, though not untill they had killed a considerable number of Howe's men, with little loss on their [Maxwell's] part.

About 1 O'clock we received Intelligence of the main body of the Enemy haveing croossed the creek about six miles above us, which was westward in the Country. Why this pass was not attended to is truly astonishing, but so it was; & after the Enemy was properly formed on our Side, G[eneral] Sullivan's, Ld. Stirling's, & G[eneral] Stephen's[1] Devissions was ordered to march & attack them   Accordingly they all marched immediately, & between 3 & 4 O'clock in the afternoon, formed the largest part of the three Divisions upon a hill near B[irmingham] meeting house. The Enemy very soon advanced to attack. I believe before G[eneral] S[ullivan's] D[ivision] was formed, as they changed their ground on which they first drew up. A number of them was marching past my Regiment when the first fire began, consequently I believe never fired a gun. In half an hour at furtherst, the whole of our men gave way. The Enemy pursued briskly, by which means a number of our wounded, as allso some well men fell into their hands, in the whole about 400, and six or eight peices of brass Cannon six-pounders. The pursuit continued untill after sun set, when the Night approching, and allso a check they got from a part of General Greene's Devision, caused the Enemy to give over the pursuit.

[1]ADAM STEPHEN (d. 1791). Native of Virginia. Appointed colonel, 4th Virginia, February 13, 1776. Commissioned major general, February 19, 1777. Court-martialed for his behavior at the Battle of Germantown; convicted and dismissed, November 20, 1777.

Bibliographical Note

Joseph Bloomfield's name appears often in the primary sources and secondary accounts of New Jersey in the revolutionary and early national periods. Given his prominence as a Continental officer and Jeffersonian party leader, this is not remarkable. What is somewhat surprising is that he has never been the subject of a major biography—the available accounts of his life are only sketches. Yet enough is known about Bloomfield to prepare the preliminary biographical sketch entitled "Gentleman-Republican," which should serve as a basis for any future biographical study. In preparing the Bloomfield journal for publication, a large number of books and manuscripts were consulted. While space limitations prevent any detailed listing, what follows presents the most important titles and collections.

There are a few brief but helpful Bloomfield biographical sketches. Family genealogical information is found in William Nelson, *New Jersey Biographical and Genealogical Notes . . .* , Collections of the New Jersey Historical Society, vol. 9 (Newark, N.J., 1916), pp. 32–38. Nelson dealt not only with Joseph Bloomfield but his father Moses, including excerpts from original documents. A highly personal treatment is in Lucius Q. C. Elmer, *The Constitution and Government of the Province and State of New Jersey . . .* , Collections of the New Jersey Historical Society, vol. 7 (Newark, N.J., 1872), pp. 114–37. A balanced, sympathetic view is in Carl E. Prince, "Joseph Bloomfield," in Paul A. Stellhorn and Michael J. Birkner, eds., *The Governors of New Jersey, 1664–1974: Biographical Essays* (Trenton, N.J., 1982), pp. 85–88. There is a short sketch in the *Dictionary of American Biography*, 20 vols. (New York, 1928–37), 2:385–86.

A variety of primary sources dealing with Bloomfield's political and military activities are available in printed form. Among the most important is the 1775–76 campaign account of Ebenezer Elmer, Bloomfield's friend and junior officer. Elmer's "Journal Kept during an Expedition to Canada in 1776," *Proceedings of the New Jersey Historical Society*, 2 (1846): 95–146; 2 (1847): 150–94; 3 (1848):21–56, 90–102, complements Bloomfield's journal and provides an interesting view of army life at the company level. At various points, Elmer copied major portions of Bloomfield's account into his own. See also "The Lost Pages of Elmer's Revolutionary Journal," again in the Society *Proceedings*, new series, 10 (1925):410–24. The orders and correspondence that sent the Third New Jersey Regiment into the Mohawk Valley, with related correspondence between Philip Schuyler, John Sullivan, and Elias Dayton, are also reprinted in the *Proceedings*, 5 (1850–51):34–37, and, along with Dayton's account of the battles of Brandywine and Germantown, in 9 (1860–64): 180–87. William Nelson privately printed the Bridgeton "Plain Dealer" as *The First Newspaper in New Jersey* (n.p., 1894), along with some not always accurate explanatory notes. Copies of the volume, which are scarce, are held in Special Collections, Alexander Library, Rutgers University, New Brunswick, New Jersey, and in the library of the New Jersey Historical Society, in Newark. Material on Bloomfield's regiment is also in John C. Fitzpatrick, ed., *The Writings of George Washington from the Original Manuscript Sources, 1745–1799*, 39 vols. (Washington, D.C., [1931–44]), especially for the years 1776–78.

A number of monographs, primarily studies of New Jersey in the revolutionary and early republican periods, also shed light on aspects of Bloomfield's career. Larry Gerlach's fine study, *Prologue to Independence: New Jersey in the Coming of the American Revolution* (New Brunswick, N.J., [1976]), offers considerable detail on the early Whig activities of Bloomfield and his fellow young South Jersey radicals (especially the Elmers). For information on the New Jersey military effort, including the raising and deployment of the Third New Jersey and the rest of the New Jersey Brigade, readers should see Mark E. Lender, *The New Jersey Soldier*, New Jersey's Revolutionary Experience, no. 5 (Trenton, N.J., 1975), and "The Enlisted Line: The Continental Soldiers of New Jersey" (Ph.D. dissertation, Rutgers University, 1975). Richard P. McCormick's *Experiment in Independence: New Jersey in the Critical Period, 1781–1789* (New Brunswick, N.J., 1950) has some pertinent material on Bloomfield's early political career, while Carl E. Prince offers considerable detail on his activities as governor and Republican Party leader in *New Jersey's Jeffersonian Republicans: The Genesis of an Early Party Machine, 1789–1817* (Chapel Hill, N.C., [1967]). Bloomfield is seen from the Federalist perspective in Rudolph J. Pasler and Margaret C. Pasler, *The New Jersey Federalists* (Rutherford, N.J., [1975]). Interesting glimpses of the soldier-politician's personal nature are in Joseph F. Folsom, ed., *Bloomfield Old and New* . . . (Bloomfield, N.J., 1912). Bloomfield's role in the framing of revolutionary veteran's legislation is found in William H. Glasson, *Federal Military Pensions in the United States* (New York, 1918). There are no accounts of his command experiences during either the Whiskey Rebellion or the War of 1812.

Other secondary works provided background information on the events and individuals mentioned in Bloomfield's account of the war years. The Continental occupation of the Mohawk Valley has a fairly extensive literature, and we relied mostly on William W. Campbell, *Annals of Tryon County; or, The Border Warfare of New-York, during the Revolution* (New York, 1831); Martin H. Bush, *Revolutionary Enigma: A Reappraisal of General Schuyler of New York* (Port Washington, N.Y., 1969); Barbara Graymont, *The Iroquois in the American Revolution* (Syracuse, N.Y., 1972); and Don R. Gerlach, *Philip Schuyler and the American Revolution in New York, 1733–1777* (Lincoln, Nebr., 1964). For the fighting in 1777 and 1778, see John S. Pancake, *1777: The Year of the Hangman* (University, Ala., 1977); Ira D. Gruber, *The Howe Brothers and the American Revolution* (Chapel Hill, N.C., 1972); Willard M. Wallace, *Appeal to Arms: A Military History of the American Revolution* (New York, 1951); and Christopher Ward, *The War of the Revolution*, 2 vols. (New York, 1952). Useful interpretive histories of the Continental Army and the war itself are Don Higginbotham's *The War of American Independence: Military Attitudes, Policies, and Practice, 1763–1789* (New York, 1971) and James Kirby Martin and Mark E. Lender, *A Respectable Army: The Military Origins of the Republic, 1763–1789* (Arlington Heights, Ill., 1982).

General reference volumes also provided essential information. Names and service records of Bloomfield's fellow officers were listed in William S. Stryker, *Official Register of the Officers and Men of New Jersey in the Revolution* (Trenton, N.J., 1872) and Francis Bernard Heitman, *Historical Register of the Revolution, April, 1775, to December, 1783* (Washington, D.C., 1893). A good biographical sketch of Elias Dayton is in Mark Mayo Boatner, *Encyclopedia of the American Revolution* (New York, 1966), while overviews of Jonathan and Ebenezer Elmer are found in the *Dictionary of American Biography*, 6:116–17. John Warner Barber and Henry Howe, *Historical Collections of the State of New Jersey* (New York, 1844), contained considerable data useful in annotation.

Bloomfield papers are scattered throughout a number of collections and focus mostly on his military and political activities and his private real-estate investments. The Joseph Bloomfield Papers, Elias Dayton Papers, Jonathan Dayton Papers, and Ely Collection, all at the New Jersey Historical Society, were especially rewarding. Several Bloomfield letters are in the Gratz Collection, Governors of States, of the Historical Society of Pennsylvania, Philadelphia. There are also some Joseph Bloomfield papers in Special Collections, Rutgers University. Political matters are represented in the Thomas Jefferson Papers, Library of Congress, Manuscript Division, Washington, D.C. Interesting documents are also in the Emmet Collection, New York Public Library, New York City; the John W. Taylor Papers, New-York Historical Society, New York City; the Lloyd W. Smith Collection, Morristown National Historical Park, Morristown, New Jersey; the Samuel L. Southard Papers, Special Collections, Firestone Library, Princeton University, Princeton, New Jersey, and the Oliver Wolcott Papers, Connecticut Historical Society, Hartford, Connecticut. The Papers of the Continental Congress, National Archives, Washington, D.C., have a number of Moses and Joseph Bloomfield letters and documents. These are conveniently referenced by John P. Butler, comp., *Index: The Papers of the Continental Congress, 1774–1789,* 5 vols. (Washington, D.C., 1978).

Index